Bike Rides around West Gwent and the Borderlands

Alwyn Thomas

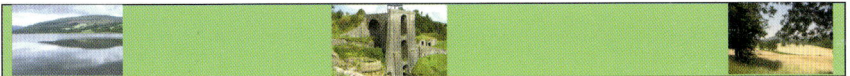

Published by Odyn Books
Ty'r Odyn, Blaenavon Road, Govilon, Abergavenny, www.odynbooks.co.uk

Printed by MWL Print Group, New Inn, Pontypool. www.mwl.co.uk

Distributor: Old Bakehouse Publications, Abertillery www.oldbakehousepublications.co.uk

Copyright   Alwyn Thomas   2006

First published   June 2006

Photographs by the author

Redrawn Mapping by ArtMatters 2 Belle Vue, Maesgwartha Road, Gilwern www.artmattersstudio.co.uk

ISBN 0-9553192-0-X
ISBN 978-0-9553192-0-4

Forward

I was delighted to be given the opportunity to write a Forward for this Guide on Bike Rides around the West Gwent and Border region.

Having lived in Monmouthshire most of my life I am well aware of the breathtaking places of natural beauty that make the area one of the most desirable locations to visit and settle down in the entire United Kingdom. I am therefore extremely pleased that this book will be available to guide cyclists through some of the most unspoiled and picturesque routes in the country and allow people to experience the wonders of this great region.

Cycling is a clean, healthy and enjoyable way of experiencing the wonders of the natural world and it is no wonder that in today's environmentally aware society interest in cycling is undergoing a massive renaissance. There are few better ways of experiencing the myriad of heritage sites, areas of natural beauty and stunning towns and villages in the area than on a bicycle, as not only do you have the freedom of the roads but you may also shed a few pounds into the bargain!

Tourism is a thriving industry in South Wales and this book will do much to reveal historically and culturally significant sites to the interested. For example, the Blaenafon World Heritage Site and the surrounding valleys of Gwent played a major role in the Industrial Revolution in Britain and many early industrial icons still survive today as monuments of the past. The bike rides described around the sites of the old coal mines and iron works that once dominated the valleys are poignant and fascinating reminders of Gwent's early industrial heritage. You only have to glance at the many stunning photos in this book to be reminded of the sheer breadth of visual wonders on offer to the adventurous.

I believe that anyone who picks up this book is going to find something of interest, from the most dedicated of cyclists to the casual history buff. It's a fascinating read and a great reminder of the beauty and variety of this most stunning of regions.

David Davies MP
House of Commons
June 2006

CONTENTS

Table of Rides

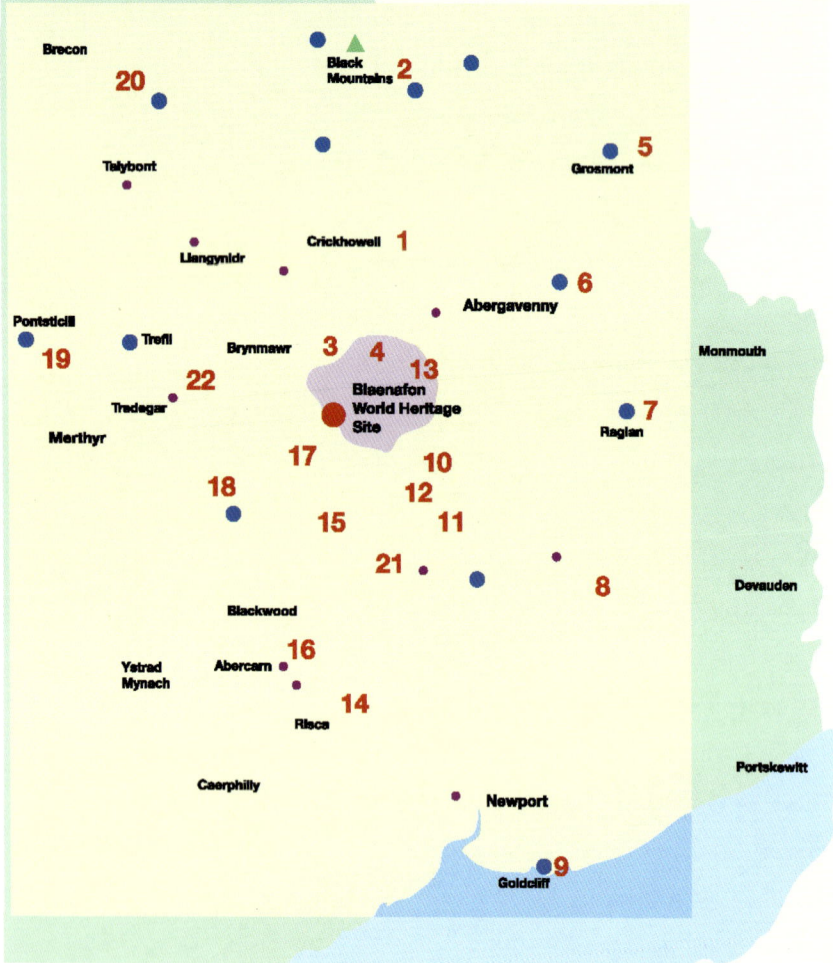

RIDE LOCATION MAP
West Gwent and the Borderlands

Brecon

20

Black
Mountains **2**

Talybont

5

Grosmont

Crickhowell **1**

Llangynidr

6

Abergavenny

Pontsticill

19

Trefil

Brynmawr **3** **4**

13

22

Blaenafon
World Heritage
Site

Monmouth

Tredegar

7

Raglan

Merthyr

17

10

18

12

15

11

21

8

Devauden

Blackwood

16

Ystrad
Mynach

Abercarn

14

Risca

Caerphilly

Portskewitt

Newport

9

Goldcliff

Legend

Energy Level Indicator

These indicators should be used as a guide only in judging how much energy is needed to complete the ride. Indicator depends on a combination of the following:
- Hills encountered on ride - how many are there, how long and steep are they.
- Overall distance of ride – is it short (eg 10 miles) or long (eg 50 mile plus)
- Type of terrain - how much is on-road and how much is off-road

*	Minimum:	demands very basic levels of fitness; fairly easy
**	Low to moderate	demands a little more than basic level of fitness; still reasonably easy
***	Moderate to high	demands a reasonable level of fitness; moderate but not difficult
****	High	demands a reasonably high level of fitness; but you don't need to be superman

Gearing

Mid gear climb – refers to selection of the front middle chain ring for climbing up hills with gentle to moderate gradients. Usually non strenuous
Low gear climb – refers to selection of the front little chain ring for climbing up hills with moderate to steep gradients. A low-low selection 3-4 mph climb is going to be strenuous

Off-Road Grade Indicator

These give an idea of how easy or challenging a particular off-road section might be. They are included as a guide only, since all challenging off-road descents can be bike-wheeled and therefore a high indicator should not be a key factor in deciding whether or not to try the ride. Energy levels are far better indicators of the overall ride challenge.

G1	Little to no experience of off-road riding: tracks are typically hard compacted gravel, dirt or grass: G1 sections are typically over towpaths, disused railway bed or something similar
G2	Some experience preferable: G2 includes flat, ascending and descending mountain tracks with some loose stones and ruts; Inclines may need to be walked in parts;
G3	More experience preferable: G3 can include some steep descents over very stony (loose) tracks with considerable rutting; Inclines need to be walked; Descents are challenging.

Maps

Based on Ord Survey Landrover (1:50,000) Series 161, 171, and 160. The route maps for each Ride are included at end of each ride section. The west/north access route maps (used when leaving and returning to Blaenafon Ironworks) are included at end of "Bike Access Route" section.

Introduction

Bike riding today

There is little doubt that bike riding activity throughout Britain seems to have experienced something of a revival in the past ten years or so. It is not uncommon these days particularly during the warm summer months to see many riders up and down canal towpaths or perhaps meandering leisurely through the parks.

The new breed of mountain bikes has undoubtedly widened the appeal of cycling. Their lightweight construction and versatile design enable bikers to access and reach the most far flung places in the land. It is now possible to ride a bike over the tops of mountains and down through remote valleys, crossing terrain that would normally be the preserve of the most adventurous walkers and experienced pony trekers
.

Some cyclists however may choose to simply disappear into the midst of the countryside along tarmac lanes well off the beaten track and far from the madding crowd. They may have a desire to experience what travel might have been like a century ago when cars were a rarity and life in general moved at a much slower pace. Others may prefer the more exhilarating experience and challenge of descending steep stony tracks down the sides of mountains. Whether the preference is for lazy summer-time cycling along canal towpaths and country lanes or the more adventurous energy-demanding mountain crossings there's plenty to choose from.

Although the number and choice of mountain bikes seem to be expanding each year, so too are the number of cycling routes that are being made available up and down the country. The organisation who are pushing forward the development of the national cycling network within the UK are Sustrans, who regularly announce each year the addition of new traffic free routes to their network. These new routes provide more opportunity for local people to commute to their work place, explore a different mode of travel and at the same time help us all expend a little more energy. Many of the rides featured in this book are over parts of the Sustran network.

The Gwent area

The series of rides described later are within the central and western parts of Gwent extending out just beyond its borders (see Ride Location map). Gwent is effectively the old county of Monmouthshire covering approximately 600 square miles and bordering on Breconshire (now Powys), Glamorganshire, Herefordshire, Gloucestershire and the Severn Estuary. In 1996 the county of Gwent was split up into three unitary council authorities – Torfaen in the south, Blaena-Gwent in the west and "new" Monmouthshire in the north-east. Newport is now a city with its own authority. The Brecon Beacons National Park also extends over a large part of Monmouthshire.

A county with a rich history

Gwent's strategic borderland location with England has made it a focus of conflict for thousands of years. The Celts, Saxons, Romans and Normans have all played their part in shaping Gwent's turbulent history and many monuments survive as testimony to their presence. In the past two to three hundred years the iron and coal working *valleys* of Gwent were at centre stage in shaping Britain's Industrial revolution leaving behind not only some ugly landscape scars but also some remarkable and unique remnants of the early industrial period.

World Heritage Site (WHS)

At the end of the year 2000, the area surrounding Blaenafon in north-west Gwent was designated a World Heritage Site by the United Nations body UNESCO, who considered the industrial landscape to be an outstanding example of the dominant role played by South Wales in the production of iron and steel throughout the World during the 19C

Blaenafon WHS as a central point for all the Rides

The Blaenafon WHS is now a major tourist attraction within the UK. A brief history and description of the area and sites is provided after this section. Whilst many people walk or drive to the various sites within the WHS another option is to use a mountain bike. This is an easy and convenient way of visiting the surrounding landscape within the World Heritage zone.

The Ride Location Map shows that the Blaenafon WHS is more or less at the geographical centre of a large part of Gwent including the border regions in the north. It also happens to be in the midst of some of the region's most diverse and spectacular landscape that bears testimony to 2000 years of bloody history. This includes monuments such as iron-age campsites, Saxon dykes, Roman forts, Norman castles, medieval manors and industrial icons such as old tramways, Victorian railways, 18C Ironworks and 19C coal pits.

Virtually all the landscape within a twenty five mile radius around the WHS is easily accessible with a mountain bike, and even the longest rides of around fifty miles that start and finish at Blaenafon can be completed comfortably within a day. All the featured rides are through highly scenic landscape with easy access to the heritage sites along the route. The WHS is therefore an ideal location from which to launch a series of bike rides to the outer reaches of Gwent and its borders.

For those who may not be able to start the ride from the WHS there is the option to access the ride at other convenient locations along the circular route.

The area covered by the Rides

All twenty two rides are within the central and west area of Gwent including the area around the Herefordshire and Powys borders and the Brecon Beacons National Park, but do not extend out to the lower Wye valley and Cobblers Plain between Monmouth and Chepstow. See the Ride Location Map.

Type of Rides

The featured rides are devised to suit a broad range of biker interests - some easy, some challenging but most falling somewhere in the middle. Several rides will appeal to those who enjoy an element of "cross-country" riding that involves a little bike-wheeling along parts of the route. Some rides will appeal to those who prefer riding along remote country lanes whilst others will suit those who enjoy exhilarating descents down the sides of mountains.

Virtually all the rides are over routes that are either traffic free or almost traffic-free where you may see the odd car or farm vehicle. There are one or two exceptions where perhaps a half mile of the route is over a road which can occasionally be busy. Most of the rides will involve some hill climbs, or in a few cases gently ascending inclines.

The short rides are typically less than 20 miles, the longer ones stretch into the 50 mile category and the rest are in the middle The time to complete the ride is highly dependent on the number of hills, type of terrain and overall length of ride and this figure is provided in the route information box of each ride. A star rated system is used throughout the book as a guide to how easy or hard the ride (see Legend).

Type of terrain

Most of the rides are over a mix of on-road and off-road routes that will require the use of a mountain bike. There are however a few rides that are virtually on-road all the way - where it would be possible to use a road bike (Rides 2, 5, 6, 7 and 9).

The on-road sections are typically single access tarmac lanes that are well off the beaten-track where a vehicle is indeed a rare sight, or sometimes they are over sections of quiet B-roads where the traffic is virtually non-existent or very light.

The off-road sections are over a mix of terrain sometimes easy sometimes challenging. The easy sections include disused railway tracks, canal towpaths and flat grassy mountain trails. The more challenging sections can include steep stony tracks down the side of a hill or mountain. All types of off-road terrain are clearly graded in terms of degree of challenge (see legend)

Off road tracks and footpaths with Public Right of Way

With the exception of a few cases the off-road tracks included in the rides are for the most part tracks that have been designated in Ordinance Survey maps as public rights of way *Bridleway* or *Road used as a public path* or sometimes *Byway open to all traffic*. It is legal to ride a pedal bike over these types of tracks. The Forestry Commission in general (maybe exceptions) allow pedal bikes to access their forest tracks. British Waterways in most cases allow pedal bikes over their canal towpaths but there maybe some exceptions.

There are just a few small unavoidable cases where the featured ride is routed a short distance over designated *public right of way footpaths*. Usually they are the only connecting track between two bridleways on top of a mountain or sometimes an ascending track where the bike in any case needs to be wheeled (identified in the Ride). It is not legal to ride a pedal bike over a public footpath but it is legal to wheel the bike.

There is a useful Sustrans publication which provides general safety guidelines to cyclists when cycling over their routes that are sometimes shared with walkers and others. The information sheet "Cycling Code for Cyclists" is available on the Sustrans website.

Access Routes from and to Blaenafon Ironworks

All rides emanate north, east, south and west around Blaenafon and use a combination of on-road and off-road routes when leaving the Ironworks at the beginning of a ride as well as returning to the Ironworks towards the end of a ride. Because these access routes are common to a number of rides, they are described in a separate section called "Bike Access Routes". The route description for all the Rides will indicate which combination of access route segments to use when leaving and returning to Blaenafon. The maps of the West Access and North Access routes show all the access route segments A B C etc.

Using the Ride Maps

To make it easier to follow the route of each ride, the overall route is parcelled into numbered segments eg 1 2 3 etc, and each of these segments is described under the section heading "The Route" and shown on the Ride map at the end of each section.
On some of the longer rides it will be necessary to refer to both the Ride map for the main segments and the Access Route map (west-north) for the segments at the start and end of ride from/to the Ironworks.

The maps are based on the Ordinance Survey Landrover series but are scaled to enable the best presentation of the route. The distance of each segment is given under the heading "The Route" included in all the featured ride sections.

Try out parts of the Ride

There may be some who are not yet quite ready to tackle a complete three or four star circular ride, but may nevertheless like to try out some of the less demanding but spectacular sections of the route. There are plenty of opportunities to try out part of a route on many of the rides where the entry point can be reached by a car. For example the Ride 19 reservoir valley ride includes a magical 7 mile off-road descent from Torpantau mountain-pass down the Caerfannel valley to Talybont canal wharf. In this case drive to the top of the mountain-pass and enjoy this superb descent that demands less than one star of energy. A car will be needed to pick you up at Talybont (or ride back to Torpantau).

Towns and Canal in the Gwent and border region

Many of the rides are either routed through or around a number of towns within an approximate twenty-five mile radius of the WHS. Some of the rides are also routed over towpath sections of the Mon & Brecon canal. A brief history of the towns and canal as well as general information on the heritage sites are included in the section "Towns and Canal".

Authors Notes

1 *Books Reference*: many of the local books included in the "Book Reference List" section were used as the prime source in developing the sections on the "Blaenafon World Heritage Site", "Towns & Canals" and the box sections included in each the rides entitled "Heritage Interest along the Route"

2 *Upgrading Clydach Gorge railway track route:* at the time of writing (06) the disused railway track between Llanfoist and Brynmawr (along Clydach Gorge) is not accessible along the Gilwern section of the route. All other parts of the railway track route are however already rideable and the section between Llanfoist and just beyond Govilon is currently a designated Sustrans route (46). Sustrans have now begun work upgrading a 5 ½ mile section of the track (which includes the Gilwern segment) and it is anticipated that the work will be complete by around 07.

Rides 1, 2, 5, 6 and 7 described in later sections of this book utilise the Gilwern Hill – Pwlldu route (which includes a 3 mile climb) when returning to Blaenafon Ironworks from Llanfoist. Once the Gilwern disused railway track segment is open there will be an alternative (but longer) route that avoids the Gilwern Hill climb when returning to Blaenafon from Llanfoist.

Referring to the North Access Route Map the above Rides currently utilise segments R, Q, S and W when returning to Blaenafon from Llanfoist. As soon as the Gilwern railway track section is open to bikes there will be an alternative cycleway route from Llanfoist to Clydach Halt returning to Blaenafon Ironworks along Segments K, D, B and A (see West Access Route Map).

Blaenafon World Heritage Site

Blaenafon

The town of Blaenafon is located just over a 1000feet above sea level at the top of the Afon Lwyd valley in the north-west corner of Gwent in the midst of some of the most extraordinary diverse landscape in Britain. It sits on the border between the rural north and the old industrial valleys of the south and in this sense it has the feel of a border town. To the north lie the spectacular Black mountains and unspoilt borderlands (the Marches) that stretch up through Hereford and Shropshire. To the south are the narrow, steep and winding valleys whose urban and industrial development is intrinsically linked with iron and coal industries over the past two centuries.

The town is located on south facing slope of Garn-fawr ▼

Although the name Blaenafon is mentioned in the Llanover records of the 16C, the town itself came into existence just over 200 years ago at the start of the industrial iron-making period. It was created largely to house the workers of the new multi-furnace Ironworks as well as those who worked in the nearby coal mines and quarries. During the early 19C Blaenafon was one of several major Ironworks that were located along the heads of the valley between Nantyglo and Hirwaun at a time when South Wales dominated the market in iron production and trade.

Towards the end of the 19C the new works at Forgeside Blaenafon provided the venue for the budding entrepreneur-chemist Sydney Gilchrist Thomas and his cousin Percy to develop and patent the process that eliminated phosphorous during the conversion of wrought iron into steel, and this technology ultimately paved the way to the wide spread production of steel throughout the world. It is ironic however that Blaenafon having played such a key role in opening the door to one of the worlds most prosperous industries did not participate in this prosperity.

With steel in demand and iron in decline the then Blaenafon Company along with others began to focus their efforts towards the extraction and production of coal needed to fuel Victorian Britain and the rest of the world's rapidly expanding railway, locomotive and steam ship industries.

13

For more than 100 years Blaenafon along with other Monmouthshire and South Wales towns were dominated by the coal mining industries, and most people living in the town either worked down the mines or at least had some association with the industry. Coal mines provided the work whilst chapels, churches and pubs provided most of everything else. At the start of the 20C the Blaenafon collieries were employing thousands of men who were producing half a million tons of coal a year but by the 1950's only three collieries were working and the era finally came to an end in 1979 when the last pit (Big Pit) was closed for ever.

The World Heritage Site

Although the Iron and coal industries had left numerous scars on the landscape surrounding Blaenafon, many remnants from the past still survived as testimony to the contribution made by Blaenafon as well as other South Wales towns to Britain's industrial revolution. Impressive remains of an 18C Ironworks, an almost intact working pit (Big Pit) from the 19C, primitive water courses and ponds used for scouring ironstone and coal, reservoirs to supply expanding demands, limestone quarries, workers houses and miles of tramroads, railroads, tunnels, canals, and old packhorse trails that served as early transport networks.

Landscape of World Heritage Site around (north-west) Blaenafon ▼

14

This unique preservation of early industrial landscape around Blaenafon was recognised by UNESCO at the turn of the millennium when the area was designated a World Heritage Site ensuring that this important window into Britain's industrial past is kept alive for future generations.

Blaenafon World Heritage Site is now a major tourist attraction in the UK, with venues like Big Pit Museum attracting each year over a hundred thousand visitors who are drawn to the unique underground tour at pit bottom. It was the 2005 winner of the prestigious Gulbenkian prize for museum of the year. The World Heritage Site has also been the subject of a Channel Four Time Team documentary that searched for and discovered the lost Viaduct that was linked to the Ironworks but has been buried for many years. The World Heritage Site extends well into the Brecon Beacons National Park covering an area of just under 13 square miles (33 square Kilometres).

World Heritage Site: Blaenavon.Ironworks@BTopenworld.com
                                               www.world-heritage-blaenavon.org.uk
Brecon Beacons National Park: www.breconbeacons.org

Places of Interest – Brief Outline

The Ironworks; established in 1796 by Ironmasters Hill, Hopkins and Pratt; five coke fired furnaces with sixth added later; air blast for furnaces was generated by steam blowing engine that was connected to a massive chimney stack located at Stack Square; Balance Arch is a massive stone arch used to lift a loaded tram by balancing it against an empty tram filled with water; coking ovens were used to refine the coke and calcinating kilns to burn off the impurities from iron ore; molten iron was tapped from the furnace and fed into the sanded moulds inside the Casting House.
Impressive remains of Ironworks and worker housing; museum inside old company shop

Casting Houses Blaenafon Ironworks ▼

Big Pit: sunk by Thomas Price in 1860; seams worked in late 19C using longwall and pillar and stall methods employing horses underground; it had four steam operated haulage engines for hauling the trams and a Fowler winding engine that could raise two trams in each cage; a Waddle fan was used for ventilation in the upcast shaft. Today it is major heritage museum with tours underground

Big Pit Museum: good example of an early Water BalancePit ▼

Workmans Hall: opened by RW Kennard in 1895 - a stunning architectural icon from this period; constructed of pennant stone it has three massive arched doorways with impressive ornamental spandrel over central arch; attractive gable pediments on three sides; it was built to house upper hall for seating 1500, and on ground floor a Library, recreation room, newspaper room and billiard room; financed by the workers contributing a halfpenny a week from their wages plus a contribution from the Blaenafon Company

St Peters Church: erected in 1805 and built of local ironstone; financed by Ironmasters Thomas Hill and Samual Hopkins; galleries around three sides of the nave supported by iron pillars; font inside is also made of cast iron; many other parts of church are constructed in iron.
Impressive early 19C building of the ironworking period

St Peters School: built in 1816 and closed 1982; financed by Sarah Hopkins sister of the Ironmaster Samual Hopkins; the earliest known Ironworks school in Wales; it is currently being restored and intended to be used as a Visitor Centre for the World Heritage Site ; expected to be opened in 2006/07.

Big Steam Hammer near the Ironworks is start and end point of all bike rides ▼

Towns and Canal

Towns

Many of the bike rides included in this book are along routes that pass through or circle close to some of the major towns in the area. All these towns have a rich and fascinating history and many fragments from the past still survive. A bike is one of the easiest ways of moving around the town and highly versatile in accessing those heritage sites that can sometimes be found on the top of a mountain or along remote valleys near the town. The Heritage Boxes included in each of the Ride descriptions refers back to this section. The following is a brief outline of the town's history including sites of interest.

Pontypool

Brief History

Pontypool has been associated with the iron industry since the 16C, and it was here that the Hanbury family set up the first tinplate works in Britain at the beginning of the 18C. During this period the Allgood family established the technique of "Japanning" – the oriental lacquering of metal ware, and many of these early products are now much sought after by collectors. Some fine examples can be seen at Pontypool museum and also at the Museum of Wales in Cardiff. During the first part of the 19C Pontypool was a focal point for the transportation of iron and coal from the Eastern valley along the Mon & Brecon canal. The town has always had strong associations with the coal mining industry and during the 19/20C there were numerous coal mines operating close by along the Eastern and Glyn valleys. In Victorian times Pontypool was an important railway town boasting no less than four stations. The Park formerly part of the Hanbury estate is now one of the major assets of the town, covering a vast area of some 64 acres and undoubtedly the finest in Gwent. Roy Jenkins the distinguished politician and son of Arthur Jenkins MP hails from Pontypool. Ray Milland the famous Hollywood actor of the 1950's was raised in Pontypool and Anthony Oliver another talented old British actor hails from nearby Abersychan.

Mosaic depicting industrial heritage: cycleway is through tunnel▼

Places of Interest

Museum: provides social history of the Torfaen valley and excellent display of Pontypool Japan-ware artefacts; located in the former stable block of Pontypool Park House, the one-time home of the Hanbury family.

Park: originally part of the Hanbury estate but now under the Council; includes Italian Gardens, Folly Tower, Shell Grotto, Gorsedd Stone Circle, Nant-y-gollen ponds, Ice houses, Pontymoile Iron Gates

Tourist Information: www.visittorfaen.co.uk; Pontypool Museum 44 (0) 1495 752036

Newport

Brief history

Norman town, flourished as Port during medieval period but few architectural remains. A 15C boat found recently in the Usk is being restored as a heritage monument. The castle gates have long disappeared but the West Gate was still being used as town gaol as late as 1790. Newport grew in stature as a major port and docks during 19/20C and became known as the commercial capital of Monmouthshire. Iron and coal from the industrial valleys were transported on the Mon & Brecon canal to the town wharfs for onward shipment around the world. The Town and Alexander docks could handle the largest ships in the world. Newport still retains many fine and handsome Victorian buildings particularly those along the top end of Commercial Street near the Westgate Hotel. The town was upgraded to city status some years ago and there has been a number of recent prestigious projects including the attractive Riverside development as well as the beautifully designed bridge over the Usk.

Newport castle: cycleway goes through castle ▼

Places of Interest

Newport Transporter Bridge : Recently refurbished steel Arial Ferry built in 1906 over an exceptionally high tidal river; up to six cars, bicycles and pedestrians transported on a suspended platform (gondola) that is hauled along by an electrically operated cable and drum; designed by Ferdinand Arnodin is 75m high and spans 210m; enabled early high-masted sail ships and tall steamers to pass under bridge during early 20C;

Newport Castle: built by Normans in 14C to protect river and surrounding settlements

Newport Town Bridge: stone arched bridge early 19C; original timber bridge dates from 12C

St Woolos Cathedral: large parts Norman but was an earlier Saxon foundation.

Newport Docks: Alexandra, and South docks Pillgwenlly, built during 19C; town docks built in the 1840's and filled in during the 1930's; there are major plans to redevelop the docks area; passenger steamers bound for Cardiff, Penarth and Weston were a common sight in Newport even during the 50's.

Mon & Brecon canal wharves: location of the various wharves that served the Ironworks and coalmines of the valleys; Wharf names can be seen along the attractive riverside front starting near the castle.

Museum: includes displays of archaeology and local history including Chartist Uprising

Tredegar House & Park: magnificent house dating from Restoration period and former residence of the Morgan family; set in parkland now owned by council and open to public

Tourist Information: John Frost Square; Tel 44 (0) 1633 223327; e-mail newport.tic@newport.gov.uk

Monmouth

Brief history

13C Town Gate and Tower ▲

There was an early Roman fort at Monmouth but the origins of the town stem largely from the Norman period. A Norman castle was built on a high point overlooking the Monnow river. The market at Agincourt square occupies the outer bailey of the castle. Town walls were built in 13C and the fortified bridge over the Monnow still survives. The town depended largely on agricultural trade during medieval period and by the

17C Monmouth was a wealthy town and the seat of the County's legislature. Monmouth was also a busy river port during the 18C with many quays and warehouses dotted along the river Wye. Many handsome town buildings still survive including Haberdashers school near Wye Bridge and Shire Hall in Agincourt square. The old market hall now houses the Nelson Museum. Henry V was born in Monmouth and Charles Rolls lived just outside.

Places of Interest

Norman Castle: dates from 12C; Henry V born in the castle 1387; Great Tower and Hall survive.

Great Castle House: built 1672 - Marquis of Worcester; used as Court room in 18C; Monmouthshire regiment dates back to early Militia;

Nelson Museum: has one of the world's best collections of Nelson material commemorating the life of Britain's most famous Admiral; includes history of Monmouth; Nelson sailed down the Wye to Monmouth early 19C.

Bridge and Town Gate: only survivor of its kind in Britain; 13C gate tower on bridge over Monnow providing entrance to town.

St Mary Church: former Benedictene priory of St Mary founded in 1075.

Tourist Information: Agincourt Square; tel 44 (0) 1600 713899; monmouth.tic@monmouthshire.co.uk

Merthyr

Brief History

Ironmaster's home Cyfarthfa castle ▲

Merthyr's rich and turbulent history is intrinsically linked with the 18/19C ironworking period. In 1794 there were four large Ironworks in the area – Dowlais, Cyfarthfa, Plymouth, and Pendarren. Merthyr was a world leader in iron production for most of the 19C and was visited by Nelson, Lord and Lady Hamilton in 1802. At the turn of the 19C there were 8000 people living in Merthyr making it the largest town in Wales and known at that time as the unofficial capital of Wales. The Taff Vale railway which was completed in the first half of the 19C was the most important transport link in the valley enabling goods to be transported to Cardiff in less than an hour. The roots of the labour movement stem from the Merthyr uprising of 1831 and the distinguished MP Kier Hardie was the first Labour MP to represent Merthyr and Britain. Wales best known composer Joseph Parry of Myfanwy fame was born in the Ironworkers cottages at Chapel Row Merthyr. As with other towns in the 21st century Merthyr is now moving forward with new challenges in a new age but it has not forgotten its former industrial roots as one of the greatest iron towns in south Wales.

Entering Merthyr along the cycleway over the Cefn Viaduct ▼

Places of Interest

Cyfarthfa Castle: a very impressive castle like mansion in parkland surroundings overlooking the Taff; home of the Ironmaster William Crawshay in 1824; now a heritage museum

No 4 Chapel Row: Joseph Parry the well known composer born here in 1841; Chapel row was originally built for Cyfarthfa ironworkers in 1820's; monument outside marks start of Glamorgan canal.

Ynsfach Engine house: opened 1801; housed the beam engine which blew air into the adjacent furnaces

Site of Cyfarthfa Ironworks: remains can be seen from cucleway not far from Cefn Viaduct

Tourist Information: tel 01685 379884; e-mail tic@merthyr.gov.uk

Crickhowell

Brief History

Historic town with Norman origins located on the north side of the river Usk beneath Table mountain where the welsh prince Howell Dda is reputed to have camped out in the 10C. The town is named after Crug Howell or Howell's Rock. [Howell Dda codified the laws that were administered throughout Wales up to the Act of Union in 16C.] The 13C Norman castle was unable to withstand the ferocity of Owain Glyndwr and the present day ruins are but a small reminder of the former stronghold. Crickhowell developed from a manorial estate to a thriving market town during the medieval period. In the early 19C it was an important stopover for the Brecon and Milford stagecoach that passed through the town twice a week. Today as in the Victorian period it still attracts many tourists who come to enjoy the splendour of the surrounding Black mountains and the seclusion of the Usk.

River Usk at Crickhowell ▼

Places of Interest

Porthmawr Gateway an impressive stone gatehouse that was once the entrance to Stag Court (Cwrt-y-Carw) owned by the Herbert family

Alisby castle ruins: built in 13C by Sir Grimbald de Pauncefote

Town Bridge: Seventeenth century fourteen arch stone bridge spanning the Usk; Bridgend Inn a former Tollhouse at end of bridge; famous Bear Inn in town centre

Glanusk Park: in 19C was owned by Joseph Bailey former Lord Glanusk and relation to the well known Ironmaster Crawshaw Bailey

Gwernvale Manor (private hotel): birthplace of George Everest who gave his name to Mount Everest

St Edmonds Church: very attractive exterior whose tall tower and steeple dominate the landscape above the river for miles around

Iron Age Fort: on top of Table mountain above Crickhowell

Tourist Information: Beaufort Chambers tel 44 (0) 1873 812105 open Easter-October

Abergavenny

Brief History

A small market town surrounded by seven hills in an enviable location on the north bank of the Usk. . A Roman fort known as Gobbanium was located here in the first century AD as part of the strategic chain of forts running north-west from Caerleon. The Norman motte and bailey castle and St Marys Benedictene priory were built by Hamelyn de Baladon in the 11/12C. The walled and gated town was ruled for several centuries by the Marcher Lords who were forever staving off attacks from the local Welsh chieftans. The marcher Lordships disappeared in the 16C under the rule of Henry VIII and the Benedictine priory became the new St Mary's priory church. The town was granted a royal charter and King Henry VIII grammar school was established in the parish church of St John whose functions were transferred to St Mary's. The administration of borough affairs was run by town bailiffs, recorders and burgesses and during the medieval period Abergavenny grew and prospered as a busy market town. In the 19C it was an important railway town and had strong links with the nearby iron and coal industry through the Mon & Brecon canal. The town still boasts many fine buildings including the attractive Georgian facades in Neville street and the medieval raised pavement and colonnades along market street (Traitors Lane). Abergavenny still attracts many tourists throughout the summer months but its "market" status may soon disappear in a new commercial redevelopment plan.

Town Hall tower beyond castle wall ▼

Places of Interest

Castle: Norman 11C castle overlooking river largely destroyed by the raids of Owain Glyndwr but dealt a final blow in the 17C by Parliament troops who wrecked its defences; still impressive ruins plus museum

St Marys Church: evolved from the former Benedictene priory; includes many medieval effigies as well as the famous Jesse tree; opposite is the medieval Tithe Barn that is currently being restored

Town Hall: early French gothic style built in 19C replacing former Market house; its green copper pyramid roof is a distinctive landmark from miles around; town hall clock denoted by Ironmaster Crawshay Bailey.

Bailey Park: fine park at north end of town and created on land given by the Crawshay Bailey Jnr; superbly decorated ornamental iron gates

Linda Vista Gardens: beautiful gardens located just above the Usk.

Angel Hotel: fine Georgian building in centre of town; former Coaching Inn stopover on route to Milford Haven

Llanfoist Bridge: handsome stone arch bridge spanning the Usk at Llanfoist; structure dates from both 15C and 19C.

Pen-y-Fal Hospital: former Victorian lunatic asylum now converted into modern housing but façade of old hospital retained

Tourist Information: tel 44 (0) 1873 850 217; e-mail abergavenny.tic@monmouthshire.gov.uk

Usk

Brief History

The first Roman legionary fortress (20th Valeria Victrix) was established in Usk during the first century AD to control the southern coastal lowlands and the northern Usk valley towards Abergavenny. The timber and earthworks fortress covered a large area on the south side of the town but no remains are visible today. The Norman castle was built during the 12C and stands on high ground overlooking the river and Twyn Square. The castle ruins would normally have a dominating and powerful presence on the town but is unfortunately largely obscured by trees etc. Just near Twyn Square which is thought to be the site of the first medieval market, is St Mary's Priory church that that grew out of the Benedictine nunnery established by the Normans in the 12C. During the 16/17C the technique of oriental "Japanning" established at Pontypool by the Algood family was also set up at Usk and some of these early pieces of decorative artwork are held at Cardiff Museum. Today the architecture of Usk is largely 19C but there are still a few handsome buildings dating back to the medieval period such as those along New and Old Market street. The country town still retains much charm and character and places like Twyn square attracts many artists during the summer months.

Twyn Square with castle in background ▼

Castle: believed to be established by the de Clares in the 12C; still some impressive remains including the Garrison Tower; under private ownership but opened on set days to general public.

St Marys Priory: medieval church founded as Benedictine nunnery by Richard "Strongbow" de Clare

Sessions House: a stylish 19C "Italianate" building on Maryport street not far from the Victorian Gaol.

Town Hall: handsome medieval building dating from 16C along New Market street

Twyn Square: picturesque square with attractive Inns and clock tower; overlooked by castle

Bridge over Usk: attractive looking 18C stone bridge with five segmental arches

Rural Life Museum: houses many early agricultural and farming implements from a bygone age

Tourist Information: www.visitwyevalley.com/townguide

Brecon

Brief History

Brecon Castle ▲

A Roman fort was established a few miles to the north west of Brecon and this formed part of the Roman's strategic control of the Usk valley stretching from Caerleon through Usk, Abergavenny and Pen-y-gaer. In the 11C the Normans built a Motte and Bailey wooden fortress that was later replaced by a stone castle whose ruins can be seen today overlooking the river. Although the castle withstood the incursions of the Welsh Princes in the middle ages it was slighted by the Parliamentary troops in the 17C and during this period the town walls were also destroyed by the citizens of Brecon; the town gates were later demolished in the 18C. The Cathedral Church is a splendid piece of medieval architecture standing outside the castle bailey on high ground above the river. Brecon evolved as the principal town in the county with many fine 19C buildings including the museum that was formerly Shire Hall - seat of the Quarter Sessions and Assize Court. Not far from the attractive stone arched bridge over the Usk river are the imposing buildings that comprise Christ College - a public school since the 19C, an endowed grammar school in the 16C and a Dominican Friary in the 13C. During the 19C Brecon was a busy market town closely associated with the industrial valleys through the canal and later the railways; at one time there were three railway stations in the town. Today it still retains the charm of a Welsh county town that has more recently become renowned for its annual staging of the Brecon Jazz Festival

Places of Interest

Castle: established by Bernard de Newmarch as Motte & Bailey in the 11C; impressive stone remains overlooking the river.

St John's Cathedral Church: former Benedictene priory established by Bernard de Newmarch in the 11C; at one time the second richest Benedictine house in Wales; its architecture is largely Gothic style dating from the 13C

Gaol: Original gaol was in the castle until 17C but later transferred to prison near Struet Gate; the county gaol (now a Bank) was erected in the Watton in late 17C; a new replacement gaol was erected on east bank of the Tarell (Newgate St) in 18C replaced again in the 19C together with adjacent Governers house; Newgate converted to private premises in the 1970's;

Canal: major industrial and agricultural transport link during 19C; wharf area is completely refurbished and today it is a very picturesque setting with the new theatre overlooking the canal

Christ College: very impressive looking public school close to the river and bridge; much of architecture is late19C but there are some medieval survivals including the chapel and dining halls
.

Shire Hall: imposing 19C building used originally for the Courts of Assize but now houses Brecon Museum;

Tourist Information: tel 44 (0) 1874 622485; brectic@powys.gov.uk; www.Brecon.co.uk

Christ College Brecon ▼

Tredegar

Brief History

Tredegar grew out of the need to house workers for the Sirhowy and Tredegar ironworks at the end of the 18C. The town was named after Tredegar House in Newport. It was an important ironworking district and formed part of the string of Ironworks along the heads of the valleys that dominated the iron trade in Britain and the rest of the world during the early 19C. It was Samual Homfray, son-in-law of Charles Morgan of Tredegar House Newport who founded the works at Tredegar not long after Sirhowy Ironworks had been established. Tredegar did convert to steel during the latter half of the 19C but it was not able to drive this successfully forward and the ironworks finally closed down in 1895. Ebbw Vale Ironworks (not far away) was also successful in converting to steel production that lasted up until the thirties when Richard Thomas and Baldwin replaced the old works with a completely new plant and the rest is history. Tredegar as with other valley towns expanded and developed during the 19C and 20C as a result of the coal mining industry. Bedwelty House a regency style mansion standing in beautiful parkland was the home of Samual Homfray the Ironmaster and is a sharp reminder of the contrasting style of living at that time. It is now used by the council, and the grounds are open to the public. The massive iron clock in front of the old market house is an impressive icon from the ironworking age standing 72 feet high in a central space called The Circle. Life in the valleys during the 19Cand 20C was harsh and unforgiving for most people and the workers soon adopted a radical and feisty style of politics that undoubtedly spurned great political leaders like Aneuran Bevan who was MP for Tredegar for many years. Another well known MP Neil Kinnock the former leader of the Labour Party and now in the House of Lords also hails from Tredegar

The Iron Clock Tower ▼

Places of Interest

Tredegar Ironworks: there are no remains and therefore nothing to see: works was established by Samual Homfray and others; production started in 1801 although an earlier single furnace had been started around 1760 by Kettle; towards end of 19C Tredegar Ironworks had successfully converted to steel production with Bessimer converters; works however closed in 1895

Sirhowy Ironworks: remains of 18C coke fired furnaces; site under CADW located about half mile from Tredegar Ironworks on east bank of Sirhowy river; see Ride 22 for heritage information

Sirhowy Tramroad: opened in 1805 ran for 25 miles connecting Tredegar Ironworks and Sirhowy Ironworks with Pilgwenlly wharves in Newport; horse drawn tramroad also carried passengers and in 1828 a steam locomotive started to operate along the track; later converted to railway line.

Harfords Tunnel: over one mile long it connected Sirhowy Ironworks with Ebbw Vale Ironworks

Bedwelty House: elegant 18C home of Samual Homfray in 26 acres of parkland; gift to town from Lord Tredegar;

Iron Clock: impressive looking mid 19C town clock on site of old market place; 72 feet cast iron Tuscan like column commemorating Duke of Wellington.

Cefn Golau: cemetery on hillside above Tredegar; grim reminder of those who died in the cholera outbreak of 1832

Tourist Information; www.blaenau-gwent.gov.uk/tourism

Bandstand Bedwelty park ▼

Mon & Brecon Canal

A number of bike rides included in this book are routed over various sections of the towpath along the Mon & Brecon canal. Much of the canal's architecture including locks, bridges, aquaducts, wharfs etc is still intact and all highly visible when cycling along the towpath. Some of the Govilon-Llanfoist section is within the boundary of the World Heriitage Site. The following provides brief information about the canal including an outline of what can be seen from the towpath (see book reference list for more comprehensive information):

Llanfoist Wharf on border of World Heritage Site ▼

Brief Outline of canal

The 33 mile course of the six-lock Abergavenny – Brecon Canal between Brecon and Pontymoile is largely along the Usk valley within the Brecon Beacons National Park. It is considered to be one of the most scenic and unspoilt canals in Britain.

The 9 mile course of the thirty-lock Monmouthshire Canal is along the Afon Llwyd valley between Pontymoile and Newport (Malpas) but included in addition a short two mile spur from Pontymoile to Pontnewenydd as well as an eleven mile branch from Newport along the Ebbw valley to the Navigation Inn (viaduct) Crumlin.

In 1812 both canals were amalgamated and joined at Pontymoile and it became known as the Mon & Brecon Canal.

The original eleven mile thirty two lock spur between Newport (M4 Malpas) and Crumlin now stops at Pontywaun. The section between Crumlin to Pontwaun was dismantled some years ago to make way for the new road. The former two mile eleven-lock section between Pontymoile and Pontnewenydd was dismantled around 1850 to make way for a railway line.

The canal in Newport originally terminated at Potter street which is quite a long way down almost at the bottom of Commercial road. From here the iron and coal from the barges would have been taken to the Wharves along the river and loaded on to the ships. Before 1879 the canal termination point was moved further up to Canal Parade and then afterwards to Llanarth street. After 1931 it was terminated at Mill street bridge but today the final termination point is Barrack Hill. From here it extends a short way to the canal junction under the M4 bridge.

Interest along Towpath Sections

Talybont – Llangynydr section:

Talybont: historic Brynoer wharf and tramroad, Limekilns, railway bridge Brecon-Merthyr railway (now part of Taffs trail), Drawbridge.
Just outside Talybont is the 375 yard Ashford tunnel,
Buckland house, and Llandetty Hall not far from canal; suspension bridge over the Usk (visible around bridge 141/140);
Approaching Llangynydr there is a five Lock section for about three-quarters of a mile; aquaduct over the Crawnon river,

Llangynydr-Llangattock section:

Llangynydr road bridge (early 17C six arch stone bridge with narrow crossing) over the Usk not far from canal bridge 131; Gliffaes Country Estate (now Hotel); Glan Usk park; Ty Croeso Hotel - was Crickhowell Union Workhouse

Canal near Llangynydr ▼

Llangattock – Gilwern Section:

Llangattock wharf and Limekilns; old tramroad route from Darren Cilau quarries (Llangattock mountain to the south); aquaduct over stream between bridges 114 and 113;

Gilwern – Govilon section

Gilwern: 18C Clydach and Llanelli wharfs: Terminal for 18C Clydach railroad; Limekilns Llanelli Wharf; Dadfords enormous embankment and aquaduct - a massive 90 feet high embankment constructed in 1797 effectively bridging the bottom end of the Clydach Gorge and providing tunnelling for the river Clydach as well as a tramway that used to connect with Glangrwynney Forge .
Overflow weir near bridge 103; Llanwenerth House off bridge 99; aqueduct over Llanwenerth stream; access to Govilon church near Bridge 98; 17C Llanwenerth Baptist chapel near bridge 98.

Govilon- Llanfoist section

Govilon Wharf: 19C terminal for both Crawshay's Tramroad between Nantyglo Ironworks and Govilon as well as the important Llanvihangel – Govilon tramroad.

Frozen canal at Govilon Wharf ▼

Llanfoist Wharf (photo page 30): terminal for Hills 19C tramroad from Garnderris Forge that connected with Blaenafon Ironworks via the Pwlldu tramroad tunnel.

Llanfoist – Goitre section

Llanellen village and church near bridge 92; overflow weir between bridges 94 and 93;

Llanover village (very attractive) accessed from Bridge 79; aqueduct over Nant Ochram and overflow weir between bridges 86 and 85; aqueduct over the Nant Rhyd-y-meirch near bridge 78;
Goitre Wharf – limekilns, Heritage centre, restaurant, aqueduct; lengthmans cottage near bridge 65

Approaching Goitre Wharf ▼

Goitre – Mamhilad - Pontymoile

Impressive aquaduct over Avon Lwyd river near Pontymoile wharf (Pontypool) and nearby tunnels underneath canal to control floodwater; tram-road tunnels under canal near bridge 52;

Pontymoile Wharf – nearby original toll cottage used as a guaging point to check tolls for boats

Pointymoile-Newport (Sustrans route 46)

This 9 mile section through the urbanised and densely populated lower eastern valley is still surprisingly attractive and rural. It is an easy and leisurely bike ride along the largely tarmac towpath.

The first section of canal from Pontymoile is via Griffaithstown and Sebastopol up to Five-Locks on the outskirts of Pontnewydd. This section has been recently upgraded to allow boats (not easy) to navigate to the Marina. This is the end point for boats but not for bikers and walkers who can still continue along the towpath.

Between here and the Forgehammer there were originally 15 locks some are still visible whilst others have been attractively landscaped as a series of waterfalls. The section of towpath and canal through Cwmbran is interrupted for about half mile but the connecting cycleway is well signed and the canal continues through a further two locks to the start of the flight of Ty Coch Locks at Llantarnum. From here it descends through Malpas via another three locks to the junction of the Newport town spur and Crumlin branch under the M4 bridge.

The Crumlin Branch to Pontywaun Bridge (Sustrans route 47)

Top of 14 Locks Rogerstone ▼

This section is again rural and very attractive and includes the Cefn fight of locks between Allt-yr-yn and Rogerstone. Superb towpath ride but the many culverted bridges means it is not navigable by boat.

From the M4 junction the canal passes through the seven Allt-yr-yn locks before turning west to ascend the fight of fourteen-locks emerging in Rogerstone area in the Ebbw valley. From here it weaves its way through Pontymister, Risca and Crosskeys to Pontywaun bridge near Cwmcarn.

The Newport town spur

There is a short section of canal and towpath between the M4 junction and Barrack Hill. The cycleway however continues over the road bridge and along the side of the river to the castle in the centre of Newport (see Ride 9).

34

Bike Access-Routes

All the Bike Rides described in the later sections of this book utilise one or more of the following access-routes when leaving from or returning to Blaenafon Ironworks. The routes emanate roughly north, south, east and west from the Blaenafon and are typically over a mix of mountain bridleways, disused railway tracks, designated cycleways, tarmac lanes and B-roads. Several of the access routes are common to more than one ride. The on-road segments are all virtually traffic-free with the exception of bike access-routes C and W (B-roads used in downhill direction only) where traffic can occasionally be busy.

The route directions included in each of the twenty two Rides indicate which access-route segments to take at the beginning and end of the ride. The North/West access route maps are included at the end of this section.

Access West & North

Route A: From Blaenafon Ironworks to Whistle

An easy bike ride from the Ironworks through the attractively landscaped Garn lakes to the end of the cycleway near the Whistle Inn. Used also in direction from Whistle to the Ironworks.

Route (just over 1 ½ miles): At the Blaenafon Iron Works car park fork left towards Forgeside on the Industrial Estate Road, continue for half a mile and turn right just in front of an Iron Bridge. Look out for the cycleway sign at the the turn-off. Follow the Sustrans Route 46 cycleway tarmac path which terminates at a road junction after about half a mile (Blaenafon Heritage Railway on left). Turn right on this road and left again at the cycleway signpost. Follow the cycleway which sweeps around the two wildlife lakes. After about a mile the cycleway leads to the tarmac road near the Whistle Inn.

Route B: From Whistle to Waunafon

From the Whistle the route to Waunafon is along a disused railway bed that was once part of an important Blaenafon Brynmawr branch line run by the LNWR (London & North West Railway). It is earmarked as a continuation of Sustrans cycleway from the Whistle. Used also in other direction from Waunafon to the Whistle.

Route (just under 1 mile): From the cycleway access near the Whistle simply follow the grass-stone track bed of the old railway line towards the west as far as the junction of the B4248 road at Waunafon.

Route C: From Waunafon to Brynmawr Market Square

From Waunavon it is an easy descent along the B road into Brynmawr. Used in this direction (go) only.

Route (2 miles) : From the old railway crossing at Waunafon on the Blaenafon road (near the cattle grid) continue west on the B road, descend the hill into Brynmawr, straight ahead at the first roundabout, first turning right by St Marys church. Go through the bus stop area and cross over into market square (War Memorial).

Route D: From Waunafon to Lower Cwm Nant-gam

An easy bike route over mainly flat and descending minor roads and tarmac tracks. From Waunafon the route descends down through Llanmarch and connects with the disused Abergavenny railway track above the Clydach Gorge at Lower Cwm Nant-gam. Used also in other direction from Lower Cwm Nant-gam to Waunafon.

Route (just under 1 ½ miles): From the old railway crossing at Waunafon on the Blaenafon road (near the cattle grid) turn right and then turn left on to the Llanelly Hill road. Descend the hill (pass Cold Water ponds) for about half a mile, turn left (watch for it) on to a single track tarmac road.
Follow this road through Llanmarch for just under a mile going straight over the cross roads and down the hill to the road-crossing junction of the old Abergavenny- Brynmawr railway track at Lower Cwm Nant-gam.

Route E: From Lower Cwm Nant-gam to Brynmawr roundabout

From Lower Cwm Nant-gam it is an easy ride along the disused Abergavenny-Brynmawr railway track above the spectactular Clydach Gorge to Brynmawr. Used also in other direction from Brynmawr to Lower Cwm Nant-gam.

Route (¾ mile): From the road-crossing junction (Crossing Cottage) of the old Abergavenny-Brynmawr railway track at Lower Cwm Nant-gam pass through the gate and follow the tarmac track over old railway heading south west towards Brynmawr. After about ¾ of a mile the track terminates above the roundabout at the Heads of Valley road in Brynmawr.

Routes F G H: From Brynmawr via Llangattock Escarpment to Llangattock or Gilwern

It is a superb flat ride along the top of Llangattock escarpment where there are stunning views over the Gorge and Black mountains; the route is popular with local cyclists. A steep descent down to the canal bridges at Llangattock or Gilwern. Used in this direction (go) only.

Route F: From Brynmawr to Llanelli turn-off (2 ¾ miles): At the EMS factory junction Brynmawr head west on the Llangattock mountain road (single track tarmac minor road) crossing a cattle grid and passing a small heritage plaque depicting a tram-wheel and rail.

The minor road skirts above Blackrock following an approximate route of an early tram-road between Brynmawr and Llanagttock wharf and connecting with Daren Cilau limestone quarries.

Stunning views over the Heads of Valley road and Clydach gorge; able to see the old Abergavenny-Brynmawr railway track, Gellifelen tunnels, Clydach viaduct, Llanelli Sidings, and quarries on west side of Gilwern Hill.

After a mile or so the road begins to bend around towards the west skirting around the side of Pen-cyrn mountain and overlooking a vast expanse of the Usk valley and distant Black mountains.

After a while the turn off to Llanelli church will be seen on right (the access to the "Lonely Shepherd" is on the left).

Route G From Llanelli turn-off to Llangattock (2 ¾ miles): Continue along the mountain road, passing some sheep pens on right and car park sign on left up to the start of the steep descent to Llangattock.

From here descend with care down the tarmac road which is quite steep in parts passing over a cattle grid and overlooking Crickhowell in the distant valley below. Old Daren Cilau quarries

can be seen in mountains above towards left. At the bottom of the hill turn left at the tee-junction and continue to the canal bridge 114 (Lower Yard Bridge) Llangattock.

Route H From Llanelli Turn-off to Gilwern: (1 ½ miles): At the Llanelli turn-off descend the hill to the hamlet of Llanelli. Turn right past the church descend the hill to the canal bridge in Gilwern.

Route I: Llangattock Canal Bridge to Gilwern Wharf

From Llangattock moorings it is an easy ride along the canal towpath to Gilwern Wharf

Route (3 miles): Follow the towpath of the Mon & Brecon canal all the way from Llangattock to Gilwern; grass path for about half distance and good hard dirt path for the remainder; easy riding.

Route J: From Brynmawr via Blackrock to Gilwern Wharf

From top of Black Rock road Brynmawr it is a fast and exhilarating long descent down Black Rock road through Mysgwartha to Gilwern wharf on the Mon & Brecon canal. Used also in other direction from Gilwern to Brynmawr

Route (just over 4 miles): From the junction with the Llangattock mountain road in front of the EMS factory continue straight ahead descending Black Rock road (very little traffic). This is a long fast descent down through Black Rock and Clydach passing the Drum & Monkey Inn on right and Rock & Fountain Inn on left.

After passing through Clydach about two and a half miles down, turn left on to an unsigned road (watch for it – it is just after the old commercial shop signs on the wall of house). Follow this road down eventually passing Bethlehem Baptist Chapel on left and then passing through Maesygwartha village as far as the canal bridge 104 near Gilwern Wharf.

Route K: From Clydach Station (Halt) to Lower Cwm Nant-gam

From Clydach Station follow the disused railway track bed through Gellifelon to the road-crossing near Crossing Cottage at Lower Cwm Nant-gam. Used also in other direction from Crossing Cottage to Clydach Station.

Route (just under 2 miles): From Clydach Halt (top of viaduct) there a short section bypassing the Clydach railway tunnels.

Cross over the minor tarmac road near Nazareth Baptist chapel and after passing some cottages and traversing a small gate, the west facing mouths of the Clydach tunnels and large brick embankment can be seen on the left.

Rejoin the railway line and move on up the track passing over a three arch viaduct; the old Llanelly sidings and quarries can be seen on left. At this point the Rock and Fountain pub can easily be seen in the distance on the Blackrock side. Traversing another minor road-crossing and passing through more black iron gates, the first set of Gellifelon tunnel mouths appears directly ahead with breathtaking views towards the Drum and Monkey Pub in the distance on the Black Rock side.

Continue along a short section of track that bypasses the Gellifelon railway tunnel section until it rejoins the old railway line on the Brynmawr side of the tunnels. At this point it is best to keep to the right passing by an old railway house and then join the track bed just before the old Gellifelon Halt. From here continue up the track passing through a broken gate until the next minor road crossing at Crossing Cottage in Lower Cwm Nant..

Route L: From Clydach Ironworks to Clydach Halt

An off-road track that links the Ironworks with Clydach Halt on the old Abergavenny-Merthyr railway track. The top half is a bike wheel up a fairly steep footpath.

Route (½ mile): From Clydach Ironworks ascend a dirt track (on the south side) for a couple of hundred yards joining a road just near the new highly stylistic Clydach Community centre building. The track continues on the other side of road and is signposted to Clydach Station.

The track emerges just outside Bath Row near a telephone kiosk. Bear around to the right and after about hundred yards or so look out for a sign on left to Clydach Station (towards Troedyrhiw cottages).

Wheel bike along the dirt path which crosses a brook and then makes a steep ascent up the hillside to the old Clydach Halt on the disused Abergavenny Merthyr railway bed. The track joins the old railway line just at the end of Clydach viaduct near the old Railway Inn which is now a private house.

[There is an alternative on-road route to the railway track from the Clydach Community centre. Near the Centre bear left and ascend the hill southwards for about half a mile as far as the old road-railway crossing just near Llanelly sidings and Quarry. This is about half mile up from Clydach Halt]

Route M: From Gilwern Wharf to Clydach Ironworks

A largely off-road ride through a wooded section of the Gorge alongside the Clydach river to the nearby Clydach Ironworks. Used also in other direction from the Ironworks to Gilwern wharf.

Route (1 ¼ miles): At Gilwern Wharf a short distance from bridge 104, descend the steps just opposite Castle Narrow Boats premises, go under the aqueduct tunnel and follow the path of the old tramroad as far as the signpost to Clydach.

Turn left on to dirt path, follow it up to the bridge over the Clydach river and continue straight ahead (alongside river) as per signpost direction to Forge Row [can be a little overgrown in summer]. The path eventually exits near Forge house on to a tarmac lane.

Follow the lane up to junction of Mysgwartha road with Clydach House (four storey period stone house) on right. Continue to junction of Black rock road; follow road for less than a quarter mile and look out for signpost on left to Clydach Ironworks. Take this track under the Heads of Valley road, through a gate and the Ironworks is along a sign-posted path on the right.

[There is an alternative on-road route from canal to Clydach house. From canal bridge 104 just before Gilwern wharf turn right on to the road and then left towards Maesygwartha. At the end of the village turn left down the hill past Clydach house to the junction just near Forge House. The route to Clydach Ironworks is then the same as above]

Route N: From Ty-Cerrig to Clydach Station

The next easy access to the Abergavenny-Merthyr railway track after Govilon is a road crossing between Gilwern and Clydach Halts. From this access there is an easy ride over the trackbed above the lower half of the Gorge to the impressive stone viaduct at Clydach Halt. Used in this direction (go) only.

Route (just over a mile) Turn left at the 3-way junction near Ty Cerrig, head down the hill a short distance and look out for the old railway crossing which is near a stone cottage with shutters. Turn left on to what was the original Abergavenny Merthyr railway but is now a disused track bed earmarked as a cycleway by Sustrans.

The track is already easily rideable all the way to Brynmawr. Follow the grass stony track bed in a south westerly direction and after passing some cottages on the left and crossing over a small iron bridge the track reaches the very impressive eight arch Clydach viaduct which spans a steep and narrow valley that stretches up from the main Clydach gorge.

Old Limestone workings, kilns and quarries reaching up to Blain-dyar can be seen on the east side of the Viaduct. Continue over the viaduct, pass near the old Clydach Halt the remains of which can be seen on the left just before the road crossing.

Also near the Viaduct is a private house named "Old Railway Inn" which marks the location of a long gone railway pub. The east side of Clydach railway tunnels are difficult to see but are just a short distance from the old Halt.

Route O: From the Whistle over Garn-yr-erw mountain to Pwlldu

From the Whistle Inn to the moorlands and moonscape of Garn-yr-erw mountain descending the northern side down a stony and bumpy incline (Dyne Steel) to join Pwlldu road just near the Lamb & Fox Inn. Used in this direction (go) only.

Section From Whistle to top of Garn-yr-erw mountain (just over ¾ mile): From the Whistle Inn follow the tarmac road a short distance down to the junction of Blaenafon-Brynmawr Road. Cross over this busy road with care and pass through the gate on opposite side which joins the start of an old tarmac road leading up to Garn-yr-erw mountain. A quarter mile moderate-to-steep climb up an old tarmac road; towards the top bear right and continue on this track for a short distance until the top of mountain plateau is reached.

At the top of mountain bear right and head northwards following the stony-grass-dirt track where there are several muddy ruts to negotiate.. After a short distance the track eventually loops around and meets an old disused concrete track heading east.

Section From top of Garn-yr-erw mountain to Pwlldu (1 ¼ mile): Follow the broken concrete track in an easterly direction. The Coity mountain can be seen on the right and Sugar loaf is on the left. The track is fairly level with dips here and there. After a little under half a mile, look out for an old boundary stone (Carreg Main Caro) on the right side.

Take the right fork towards the boundary stone and follow for a short distance until the track forks left and right. Take the left fork and carry on over the fairly wide stony track passing a moon like desolate hollow landscape on the left. As the track moves gently downwards keep to the right and continue on the stony track heading east.

The two Radio masts on the Blorenge are directly ahead, the TV transmitter on Gilwern Hill is on the left (North), and an old brick building can be seen on the right. After a short distance the track joins a wider and very stony track (Steels Incline) that continues downwards in a northerly direction to meet the Pwlldu minor road with the Lamb & Fox pub directly in front.

Route P: From Pwlldu to Ty-Cerrig via the Tyla

A superb off-road route around the east side of Gilwern Hill (Tyla) above Cwm Llanwenarth opening up to some amazing panoramic views over the Usk valley. Used in this direction (go) only.

Route (1 ¾ miles): From the Lamb & Fox Inn Pwlldu proceed west on the Pwlldu minor road; pass by Hills tram-road tunnel entrance and after a short distance (couple of hundred yards) two tracks can be seen on the right hand side. The upper track leads to the TV transmitter via a gate and the lower track (bridleway) skirts around the East and North sides of Gilwern Hill.

Take the lower grass/stone track and follow it northwards passing through some large rocks laid out on track and then passing a disused limestone quarry (Tyler quarry) on the left. Just past this quarry another track will be seen veering off to the right to join a tarmac lane at the bottom of the hill. However don't take this track but continue on the top track that begins to curve around to the west.

Continue for about quarter mile past another quarry on left, then look out for a track on the right (easily missed) just about where the mountain heather on right side ends. Follow this path downwards towards the north and after short distance at a four way track intersection take the right path still moving downwards and towards the right.

This grass track eventually leads on to a tarmac mountain lane. Fork left on this road following it down over the cattle grid for about quarter mile until a three way junction near a cottage called Ty Cerrig is reached (just above the Wenault).

Route R-Q: From Llanfoist ascending Gilwern Hill to Pwlldu

A key return route to Blaenafon from the northern side but don't be put off by the long climb. There are steep bits at the bottom but the overwhelming ascent is easy-moderate.

From Llanfoist Crossing car park the cycleway route follows the old railway track through Govilon and then along a minor tarmac road that eventually climbs up around the west side of Gilwern Hill with spectacular views over the Clydach gorge. Used also in direction Q-R.

Route Q Section from Ty-Cerrig to Pwlldu (2 miles):

From Ty-Cerrig continue up the hill turning right after about 100 yards. There follows a short strenuous low gear climb over the cattle grid winding up along the side of Gilwern Hill towards Blaendyar.

Just after the cattle grid there is a moderate half mile mid-gear ascent flattening out over the rise. Stunning views overlooking Clydach Gorge and the distant Llangattock ridge. Once over the rise it becomes a relatively easy and gentle mid-gear climb for just over a mile up to the Lamb & Fox Inn at Pwlldu.

Route R Section from Llanfoist to Ty Cerrig (3 miles):

From Llanfoist Crossing car-park continue westwards climbing gently along the old railway track (Sustrans route 46) for about 1 ½ miles. Pass over a road-crossing at Govilon Station House through the site of the old Govilon railway station (the wall on the the right is site of the passenger platform) as far as the Forge car-park on right.

Exit the cycle track at this car park turning left on to a minor tarmac road; go past a small three arch railway viaduct and the site of the old Wildon furnace (on left). Take right hand fork at top of short section of hill near a white house with black iron entrance gates.

After a short distance turn left at the next tee - junction and follow the minor road up a hilly section for about a mile. There are several flat bits and two short steepish low gear climbs. Continue past the Wenault as far as a three-way island opposite a cottage called Ty Cerrig. This is the start of the Gilwern Hill climb (Route Q)

Route S-T-U-V: From Pwlldu via Llanellen Valley to Llanfoist

The route from Pwlldu is along a tarmac lane around the top of the Blorenge descending the steep remote and wooded Llanellen valley to Llanfoist. Used in this direction (go) only.

Route S (¾ mile):

At the Lamb and Fox Inn Pwlldu follow the road up towards the east as far as the junction of Blaenafon road opposite the Keepers pond (Pen-fford-goch pond). Turn right and then immediate left on to Llanellen road.

Route T (1 mile): From the Llanellen road junction just above the Keepers pond continue along the tarmac lane to Foxhunters car-park opposite the radio masts on top of the mountain.

Wide stretching panoramic views almost 360 degrees. Continue down Llanellen road to the small lay-by on the right which is the start of a bridleway around the mountain (used in Ride 13).

Route U (½ mile): From the lay-by continue to descend Llanellen road a short way to the cattle grid just at the junction of the bridleway to the Punchbowl (used in Ride 4).

Route V (2 ½ miles): From the cattle grid continue down Llanellen road heading north east passing through a wooded steep section as far as a tee-junction. Turn left and proceed down another quite steep section until it crosses the Mon & Brecon canal at Bridge 95.

Pass over the bridge and continue down until the tarmac lane joins the B4269. Turn left and then after a couple of hundred yards turn left again and follow the road through Llanfoist residential area (you will need to go through a short section of one-way].

After a short distance the road joins the B4246 just past St Faiths Church Llanfoist. Cross over the road to the Llanfoist Crossing car park opposite.

Route W: From Keepers Pond to Blaenafon Ironworks

A one mile fast descent from just above the Keepers pond down the B road to Blaenafon Ironworks. Used in this (return) direction only.

Route (1 miles): From the Keepers pond descend the hill towards Blaenafon (take care with cars) passing the Riflemans Arms on the left towards the bottom.

Follow this road down, pass two petrol stations on either side and bear right on to North street. Stack Square and the Ironworks can be seen on right. Turn right on to Estate road and then immediate left to the Ironworks car-park.

Route X-Y-Z: From Blaenafon Ironworks via Llanover road to Canal Towpath

A gentle climb through the attractive Llanover road district to join the mountain road on the moorland slopes of Garn Fawr. From this road there are three different access routes; one continues east along an old mule track on the slopes of Garn Clochdy; the second heads north-east descending the Llanover valley on a tarmac lane to Pencroesuped joining the canal near Goitre; the third heads north descending the Llanover valley on a tarmac lane to join up with canal several miles from Llanfoist. All used in this direction (go) only.

Route X From Blaenafon Ironworks to Llanover Cross (2 miles): From the Blaenafon Ironworks car park turn right on to estate road and then right again at the junction of North street which bends around in an easterly direction joining up with Church Street.

Continue on down passing Ty Mawr (Nursing

Home) on left, St Peters School on right until the traffic light junction near Workmans Hall with St Peters church just opposite. Pass through traffic lights, forking left at the old co-operative building on Ivor Street crossing over to Market street heading east. Bear right past the bus shelter taking immediate left along James St turning left at junction with Ton Mawr St.

Towards the top bear right just in front of St Paul's church gently ascending Llanover road; after about half mile pass by the the Pottery Inn and follow road up to the first cattle grid which marks the start of the mountain route.

Continue on this mountain road in a north-east direction; the stony ridge of Mynydd Garn-fawr dominates the northern skyline and a forested area stretches down towards the Avon Lwyd valley in the south-west.

As the road bends around left look out for a cross on right side marking the site of an early chapel (Capel Newydd) dating back to the 16th century.

The east route used by Ride 12 is a pack horse trail just around the bend on the right

Route Y From Llanover Cross to 2nd Cattle grid (¼ mile): Continue a short distance to the second cattle grid.

From here there are two access routes descending down to the canal: the grass track towards the right (used in Ride7, 8, 9 10) leads to a tarmac lane past the Goose & Cuckoo to Pencroesoped not far from the canal. The tarmac lane straight ahead (used as alternative access routes in Ride 5 and 6) is a steep descent down to the canal in Llanover as per Route Z below..

Route Z From 2nd Cattle Grid north to Canal Bridge 95 (4 ¾ miles): From the cattle grid descend the tarmac lane which can be steep in parts but flattens out at several points. Approaching the lower part of the descent, the Sugar loaf and Skirrid mountains begin to come into view directly ahead in the distance.

Very shortly the tarmac lane crosses Bridge 89 over the Mon & Brecon Canal at Llanover; continue along the canal towpath for a further 2 ¾ miles to Bridge 95 near Llanfoist. From here follow the latter part of Route V (¾ mile) to Llanfoist Crossing car park.

Routes through Llanfoist and Brynmawr

Route Through Llanfoist

Via the Cutting (just over ½ mile : From Llanfoist Crossing car park turn left on the B4246 road towards Abergavenny and turn left again on to The Cutting just opposite the Llanfoist Inn (now a resteurent).

Continue along the Cutting (tarmac road), pass under the Heads of Valley road and proceed up to the junction of the roundabout near Waitrose supermarket and the Llanfoist road bridge over the Usk.

Via the Nursery (just over ½ mile): From Llanfoist Crossing car park head north on a recently constructed tarmac lane a short distance to Llanfoist Nursery.

Follow tarmac lane under Heads of Valley road, go past the cemetery and chapel on the hill and proceed to the junction of the road at Llanfoist Bridge.

Routes Through Brynmawr

Route from cycleway above Heads of Valley roundabout to junction of Llangattock and Black Rock road (½ mile):

Follow the short track leading down to roundabout just outside Brynmawr; take the second turning left off the roundabout heading south west on to King Street (A4047); follow this a short distance and then take the third road on right called Intermediate road.

Cross over bridge above the Heads of the valley road; Bynmawr school is up on the left. Continue on the road a short distance as far as the turn-off to the the Llangattock mountain road (on the left) just in front of the EMS factory.

Route from Market Square to cycleway above Heads of Valley roundabout (½ mile):

Starting at Market Square, head down Alma street passing by the Library and Brynmawr museum. Just before the junction with Beaufort street take the lane on the right that leads to the

walkway under the roundabout. Ascend a short section of steps up to the road, cross over to the east side and ascend the path that leads to the start of cycleway above the roundabout.

Route from Market Square to junction of Llangattock and Black Rock roads (½ mile):

From Market Square Brynmawr turn right by the Griffin Hotel on to Bailey street and continue to the junction of the A4047. Cross over on to Intermediate road pass over Heads of Valley road bridge and proceed up to junction of Black Rock road and Llangattock mountain road just in front of the EMS building..

Access South East

From Blaenafon to Pontypool along the Cycleway (shown on Ride 10 Map)

An easy 9 mile cycleway route. Near the Ironworks the Sustrans cycleway is along the track of the old Blaenafon Pontypool railway winding its way along the steep wooded slopes of the Avon Lwyd valley.

It passes through the old Varteg Station and over a magnificent nine arch stone viaduct bridging the steep narrow Frwyd valley. The cycle-way cuts through uncluttered countryside well away from the built up urban settlements that pepper the lower eastern valley, passing through old but almost unrecognisable railway Halts.

45

The ride continues unhindered through Pontypool over a recently constructed superb cycleway whose many elevated bridge sections gives one the feel of gliding high up in a gondola well away from the urban sprawl of traffic below, cutting through busy roads and junctions with ease allowing the rider complete freedom and safety. Used in both directions

Route from Blaenafon to Pontnewenydd (7 ¾ miles):

From Blaenafon ironworks car-park proceed along the Industrial Estate road for half a mile and just before the iron Bridge turn left on to the Sustrans (route 46) cycleway track which used to be the old top railway line from Blaenafon to Pontypool; LNWR above Talywaun and GWR below.

The trackbed is now tarmaced all the way to Pontypool. Leaving Forgeside there are superb views overlooking Blaenafon towards Garnfawr and down through the trees into Cwmavon below. The railway track makes a very gentle descent along the side of the mountain directly above the Avon Lwyd valley and after about 2 ½ miles Cwmavon reservoir can be seen below on the left.

The track passes under old iron and stone railway bridges near what used to be Varteg Station where there are some wooden sculptures of old travelling trunks reminding us of past times. Snail Creep lane passes over one of the iron bridges linking Varteg with Cwmavon. Down below in the valley are Forge Row, Forge House, and the old Westlake Brewary.

The cycleway continues its gentle descent through Garndiffaith and Talywain passing over a magnificent nine-arched stone viaduct that spans and curves around a deep narrow gorge at Cwmffrwd. Views begin to open up down the eastern valley and towards the British.

Pass through old Talywaun station, over the Big Arch, over a road crossing at Pen-twyn and continue down the cycleway above Abersychan and Snatchwood passing under a road bridge near Pentre-piod .

The old railway track then makes a wide horshoe loop around Cwm Ffrwd-oer and Cwmnantddu away from the Avon Lwyd valley and then swoops back down and over a road crossing near Pontnewenydd. (The original Halts along this railway line stood at Garndiffaith, Talywaun, Pentwyn, Pentre-piod, Cwm Ffrwd-oer and Cwmnantddu).

Route through Pontypool (1 ½ miles):

Near Pontnewenydd the old railway disappears and the cycleway follows a purpose built route. Continue along the Sustrans route 46 track passing over another road-crossing in the Pontnewenydd area and follow through skirting along the top side of Pontypool towards the east.

Cross over the next major road junction with traffic lights and bollards and follow the cycleway keeping right (don't go left under the tunnel). Proceed another half mile on the cycleway up to the roundabout then go right on the grass verge for 100 yards cross over the road and head towards the Transport and General Workers Union building with the new Tesco's in front and towards the left.

Follow the cycleway down under the tunnel

then turn right picking up the cycleway which routes past Tescos. Cross over another two Bridges passing West Mon School, over the cycleway and pedestrian road crossing dropping down on the other side to Cwmynscoy roundabout

Access route A: riding past Garn Lake Blaenafon ▼

Access route G: riding along mountain lane Llangattock escarpment ▼

47

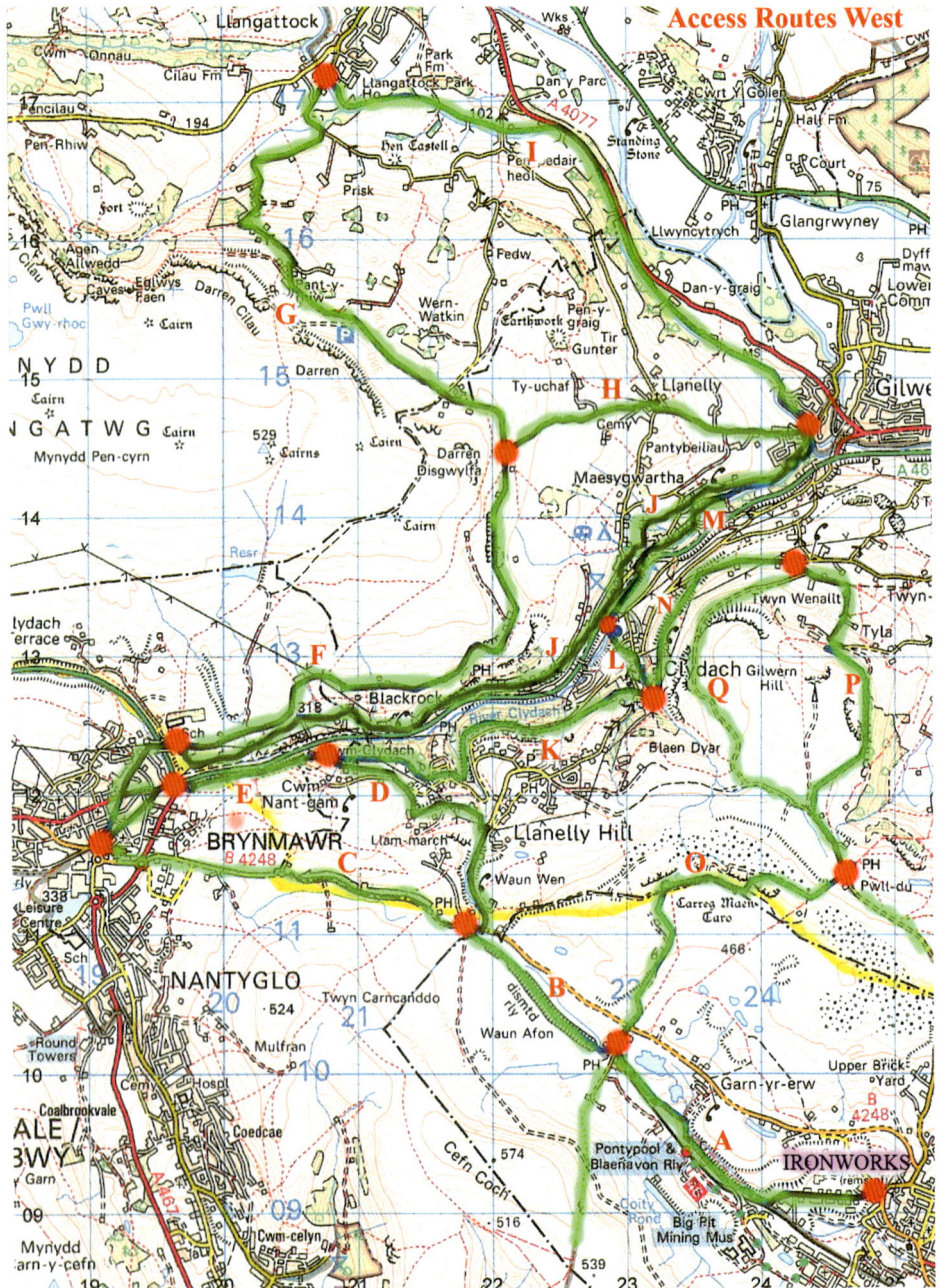

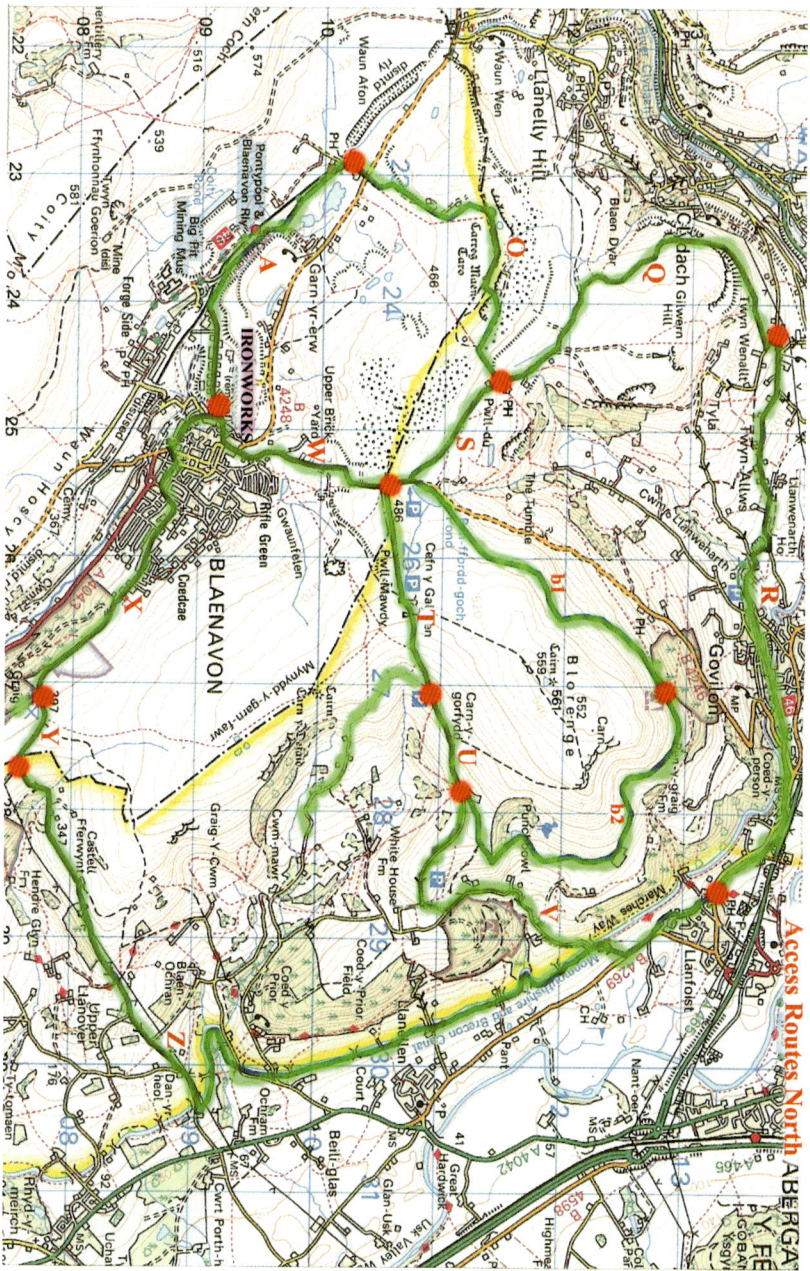

Ride 1: Loops around Llanwenarth, Rholben and Sugarloaf Mountains

The Ride

Four superb loops around the Sugarloaf, Rholben and Llanwenarth mountains that dominate the skyline above Abergavenny. The ride will appeal to those who like riding over remote mountain bike trails away from it all. Try out all Loops on a different day.

From Blaenafon Ironworks the ride follows the west access route around the rugged Llangattock escarpment descending a tarmac lane through the secluded hamlet of Llanelly to Gilwern Wharf on the Mon & Brecon canal.

Route Information	
Start and Finish	**How easy is the Ride**
Blaenafon Ironworks car park	Moderate. Almost 10 miles of flat and descending lanes to Gilwern; Loops A/B begins with a long steep climb up a tarmac lane; involves a little bit of bike wheeling on some parts of the mountain tracks. Long flat and descending mountain stretches; Loops C/D begins with a short section of steep climb up tarmac lane followed by long descents; Ride ends with a 3 mile ascent around Gilwern Hill - some steep bits at bottom but overwhelming ascent easy-moderate
Distance/ Ride Time	
Ride - Loop A: Distance 26 miles: Ride Time 5 hrs	
Ride - Loop B: Distance 26 miles: Ride Time 5 hrs	
Ride - Loop C: Distance 24 ½ miles: Ride Time 4 ½ hrs	
Ride - Loop D: Distance 24 ¼ miles Ride Time 4 ½ hrs	
Energy Level	**What sort of terrain**
*** Loops A or B	Mix of on-road tarmac lanes and grass stoney bridle-way tracks.
** Loops C or D	
Off-road Grade	
G1/G2	

50

From here the route is along the old Glangrwyney tram-road (now a tarmac lane) crossing over an Iron bridge and heading north along the Grwyne Fawr valley towards the small tucked away village of Llangenny.

The Llangenny minor road is the starting point for all four loops.

Start of Loops A & B alongside Grwyne Fawr river Llangenny ▼

The Sugarloaf Rholben and Upper Llanwenarth mountain rides (Loops A and B) begin with a steep climb up a tarmac lane through pastures and woodland along the lower slopes of the Sugarloaf. It joins up with a bridleway towards the top near Pentwyn and then skirts around the west side of the mountain overlooking a stretch of Cwm Gwenffrwd towards the south. The track weaves its way through ferns and grassland crossing over the Gwenfrwd stream almost 300 metres below the summit of the Sugarloaf.

This is the point to choose either the Loop A or B route down to Abergavenny.

Loop A begins with a bike-wheel up a steep section of track before making a wide eastward sweep around the breast of the Sugarloaf almost 200 metre beneath the peak. The route soon joins a long but exhilarating descent down an excellent track along Rholben ridge. There are stunning views over Abergavenny as well as the Vales of Cibbi and St Marys as you drop down the side of the mountain to join a tarmac lane below.

Loop B skirts around the top of a large wooded area to join a wide grass track along the lower slopes of Sugarloaf and the top of Llanwenarth before gently descending southwards towards a small car park overlooking the vast panorama of Usk valley. From here there is a steep descent along a tarmac lane down Llanwenarth hill to the attractive rural outskirts of Abergavenny.

Riding above Cwm Gwenffrwd to begin Loops A & B ▼

The Lower Llanwenarth Loops (Loops C and D) begin about half a mile below Llangenny bridge climbing up a short steep section of tarmac lane above Cwm Gwenffrwd joining an off-road track at the top. The ride then traverses open grassland above a large wooded area overlooking the Usk valley and southern ridges, crossing the Gwenfrwd brook and looping around towards the south.

From just near the Brook there is also an option to take an alternate short route northwards following Cwm Gwenffrwd to the edge of the forest where you can access Loop A and B rides

The Loop C and D rides however continue south climbing up through a short section of woodland and emerging on the lower slopes of Llanwenarth mountain.

The Llanwenarth Breast (Loop C) route begins along a grass track that heads east around the breast of Llanwenarth mountain eventually joining up with Sugarloaf road (tarmac lane) almost 200 metres above the Usk valley. There follows another steep descent down this narrow road sweeping around the Sugarloaf Vineyards at the bottom of the hill not far from the top of Chapel road on the rural outskirts of Abergavenny.

The Lower Llanwenarth route (Loop D) descends directly towards the south along a well defined woodland track that soon joins up with a tarmac lane more than 200 metres above the valley floor. There is an exhilarating long descent down the steep hill to the bottom of the valley followed by an easy relaxing ride through the flat lanes of rural Llanwenarth passing the church and following the river almost into Abergavenny.

The return ride from Abergavenny is partly along Sustrans cycleway route 46 through Llanfoist on the border of the World Heritage site, ascending the west side of Gilwern hill above the Clydach Gorge to Pwlldu. From the near-by Keepers pond there is a fast descent back to Blaenafon Ironworks.

Heritage Interest Along Route

Llangattock mountain road: path of old tramroad route from Brynmawr to Llangattock quarries and Llangattock canal wharf

Llanelli church: St Elli - parish church of Llanelli; stunning position overlooking Gilwern and Usk valley; medieval origins with imposing octagonal tower; gravestones indicate association with Clydach Gorge industrial past

Canal Wharfs at Gilwern: see section "Towns and Canal".

Gilwern-Glangrwney road: path of old tramroad from Gilwern wharf (tramway tunnel) to site of Glangrwney Forge; crosses the Usk over the iron girder bridge

Abergavenny see section "Towns and Canal"

Abergavenny Merthyr railway; built in 1862 and opened by Ironmaster Crawshay Bailey; closed 1958; Govilon station still recognisable.

Pwlldu: a one time bustling village built for iron and coal workers but demolished in sixties; there were two terraced rows of houses, two pubs, a shop and chapel; now all that remains is the welfare hall (outdoor centre) and Lamb & Fox Inn.

Pwlldu Tunnels: the tramroad route between Blaenafon Ironworks and Pwlldu went through a tunnel almost one and a half miles long under Garn mountain; tunnel portal can be seen on side of road just below former Welfare Hall

Keepers pond (Pen-fford-goch pond): named after Keepers cottage now a popular sightseeing spot on top of Blorenge; originally used as a feeder during 19C for Garnderys Forge

The Route

Inns Along Route

Whistle	Garn-y-erw
Racehorse	Waunafon
Corn Exchange	Gilwern
Bluebell	Glangrwyney
Dragons Head	Llangenny
Bridge Inn	Llanfoist
Riflemans Arms	Blaenafon

See section "Bike Access Routes" for description and maps of access routes from and to Blaenafon, reference the route segments at beginning and end of ride.

Segment 1 (1 ½ miles): From Blaenafon Ironworks follow the west access route around Garn lakes to the Whistle Inn as per *Access route A*

Segment 2 (just over ¾ miles): From the Whistle continue along the old railway track bed to Waunafon as per *Access route B*

Segment 3 (1 ½ miles): From Waunafon continue through Llanmarch to Lower Cwm Nant-gam as per *Access route D*

Segment 4 (just under ¾ mile) : From Lower Cwm Nant-gam continue along the railway track bed to its termination at Brynmawr just above the A465 roundabout as per *Access route E*

Segment 5 (¾ mile): From the A465 roundabout follow the route via Intermediate road to junction of Black Rock road and Llangattock mountain road just in front of the Brynmawr EMS building as per *Route through Brynmawr*

Segment 6 (2 ¾ miles): From the junction near

the Brynmawr EMS factory continue along the west access route around Llangattock escarpment as far as the Llanelli turn-off as per *Access route F*

Segment 7 (1 ½ miles): From this junction continue through Llanelli village (pass by church) to Gilwern Wharf canal bridge 104 as per *Access route H.*

Segment 8 (just under 2 miles): From Gilwern canal bridge 104 descend the hill to the junction with the B road in front of the Corn Exchange Inn. Cross over the B road and follow the minor road (path of old tramroad to Glangrwney Forge) for about a mile crossing over the old Iron Bridge at Glangrwney (near Forge House) leading to the junction of the busy A40 near the Bluebell Inn.

Turn right and after about 100 yards turn left on to the Llangenny minor road. Follow this minor road up the Grwyne valley and after just under half a mile watch out for a turn-off on the right. A bench seat on the side marks the turn off point.

From here choose either the slightly more energetic Sugarloaf-Rholben and Llanwenarth-Upper mountain rides (Loops A and B) or the Llanwenarth Breast and Llanwenarth-Lower rides (Loops C and D).

To try out the Loop A/B rides go to Segment 9a. To try out the Loop C/D rides or alternate route to Loops A/B go to Segment 9b.

Loops A/B

Segment 9A (just under 2 ½ miles): From the turn-off point near the bench seat on Llangenny road continue along the minor road heading north for just over half a mile as far as the bridge over the Grwyne fawr just opposite the Red Dragon Inn in Llangenny. Take the turn-off to the right just off the bridge and make a steep low-low gear climb (strenuous) for about quarter mile to the crossroads near Glan Frwd house.

Go straight ahead and continue the ascent which is steep in parts; it is about three-quarters of a mile to Pentwyn farm. This is the end of the tarmac lane and the start of the off-road section.

Go through the gate and follow the bridle-way grass track that ascends a short way to another gate just above Pentwyn. Continue on this well defined bridleway track which bends around into an open area fairly high up on the mountain. There are wide panoramic views in all directions. The wooded Cwm Gwen Ffrwd is on the right towards south.

Go through the next gate near a stone wall and just at the start of the open field watch out for the bridle-way track (easily missed) directly on the left heading north. At the top of field there is another gate near a derelict stone cottage and one more gate a short distance away leading to the open mountain.

At this final mountain gate near the sheep pen, bear right (east) towards the Sugar loaf and after

a short distance a well defined grass track soon emerges.

Follow this track that descends down to the dip (almost top of Cwm Gwen Ffrwd) just on the edge of the Forest. This is the same end-point as Segment 9c.

From here choose either the Sugarloaf - Rholben ride (Loop A) or the Llanwenarth-Upper ride (Loop B)

Loop A: Sugarloaf Breast-Rholben (3 ¼ miles)

From this dip near the edge of the forest cross over the Gwen-frwd stream and wheel the bike up a short section of steep mountain slope. It is steep but its not far.

At the top bear left on the wide well defined track which heads towards the east across the lower slope of the sugar loaf. This west-east track crosses several north going tracks that ascend to the top of the Sugarloaf.

55

Continue on this flat east-going track well above the top of St Marys Vale and just below the peak of the Sugarloaf. Superb views to south.

After just over a mile the track turns around to the south just at the sign for Park Lodge. This is the start of the ride along Rholben ridge.

Descend all the way down Rholben on this excellent track. At the bottom it gets a little steep but only for a short distance down to a gate. Go through gate and path joins a narrow rough tarmac lane.

Follow this down a short way past the house turning left on to another lane. Follow this lane past a farmhouse to the junction of another lane. Descend this lane for about half a mile down to the junction of Pentre lane and Chapel road just near Chain House. This is the same end-point as Segment 11. Continue the ride at Segment 12.

Loop B: Llanwenarth-Upper (1 ¼ miles)

Following on from Segment 9a. From this dip near the edge of the forest cross over the Gwen-frwd stream and ascend the track a short way as far as the end of the tree line and then take the track that bears around to the right heading south. The track follows the stone wall on the boundary of the tree line a short way before emerging on to the open mountain near a field joining up with another track coming down from the left.

Continue on the track that descends gently towards the south. After a short way the track splits but rejoins further down. It is easier to stay on the right hand track. However at the next split of tracks keep to the left track (heading south) that very soon emerges at the small car park overlooking the valley.

From the car park there is short descent down to a point where it merges with another lane on the right. The other lane is the termination of Loop C (Llanwenarth Breast). Continue the Ride at Segment 11.

Loops C/D and Alternate Route to Loops A/B

Segment 9b (just over a mile): At the junction near the bench seat on Llangenny road turn right (towards east) and ascend the tarmac lane which is a fairly easy climb at the beginning but a low gear steep climb (strenuous) for the final quarter mile.

At the top of the tarmac lane there are two gates. Pass through the gate on the right and follow the wide track past the house and through the fields where there are wide sweeping panoramic views towards the south overlooking Cwm Gwenffrwd.

Continue north-east along the grass track which leads down through a wooded area splitting left-right near a signpost (says to the mountain).

From here choose either to continue on the Loops C/D route (segment 10) or take the alternate route (via segment 9c) to access the Loop A/B rides.

Segment 9c (just over ½ mile): Turn left and gently ascend the woodland path above the Gwenffrwd stream. Very shortly the path emerges on to the open mountain.

Follow the track above Cwm Gwenffrwd and after a short while it soon emerges at the dip near the Gwen frwd stream on the edge of the forest. This is the same end-point as Segment 9a. Go to Loop A or B section to continue the ride.

Segment 10 (just over ¾ mile): Following on from Segment 9b. At the track junction near the "to the mountain" signpost go straight ahead, cross over the brook (Gwenffrwd) where the track swings around and heads south. Pass by Cwm-cegyr farmhouse, track begins to ascend the hill; keep straight ahead at the four-way track junction still heading south.

There follows a short wheel-up to the top and then a flat stretch to another four-way track junction not far from Pen-y-graig farmhouse. Sugarloaf car-park can be seen towards the

north east. Pass through the gate still heading south, begin to descend the grass track. After a short distance and just at the point where the fence on the left ends, watch out for a dirt path heading east through the woods.

From here choose either the Llanwenarth Breast (Loop C) ride or the Llanwenarth-Lower (Loop D) ride. If you prefer a long tarmac lane descent choose Loop D.

Loop C Llanwenarth Breast (just under 1 ½ miles)

Following on from Segment 10 take the track on the left through the wood heading east. Follow this down a short way through the wood, pass through a gate; cross over a stony section and on to a grass track.

Continue along this track around the breast of Llanwenarth still heading east passing by the ruins of an old stone cottage. The track begins to descend down the mountain through more open fern and gorse landscape.

Views over the Usk towards Govilon. Pass through a gate and continue descending the wide track that eventually joins a tarmac lane near several cottages where there is a grass island with a bench seat in the middle.

Continue east along the tarmac lane until it merges with Sugarloaf lane after about half a mile. This is the same end-point as Loop B. Continue the Ride at Segment 11.

Segment 11 (1 mile): From the junction of these two lanes continue the steep descent down Sugarloaf Lane.

A40 (past the hospital) as far as the mini-roundabout opposite the Cantref Arms. This is the point at which Loop D joins the same route as the other Loops. Continue the Ride at Segment 13.

From the Sugarloaf Vineyard at the bottom of the hill bear east on to Pentre Lane and follow this to the junction with Chapel road just opposite Chain House. This is the same end-point as Loop A.

Segment 12 (¾ mile): From the junction of Pentre Lane and Chapel road descend Chapel road to the junction with the A 40. Turn right and proceed to the mini-roundabout opposite the Cantref Inn. This is the same end point as Loop D. Continue the ride at Segment 13

Loop D Llanwenarth-Lower (just over 2 ¾ miles)

Following on from Segment 10 descend the leafy-dirt track (steep) heading south through a heavily wooded area. Pass through a gate at the bottom of slope and follow through to a tarmac lane via another two gates near a farm on right. Blorenge is directly ahead.

It is a very steep descent down a single track tarmac lane for about ½ mile joining the A40 at the bottom. Cross over the busy A40 with care and continue on the tarmac lane through the quiet Usk river valley, passing St Peters church Llanwenarth on left.

After about one and half miles the lane joins the A40 near Nevil Hall Hospital. Continue on the

Segment 13 (just over a mile): From the Cantref mini roundabout head south towards Llanfoist. At the next mini–roundabout keep straight ahead, cross over the River Usk road bridge and proceed to the Waitrose roundabout. From here follow the route back through The Cutting (or Nursery) to Llanfoist Crossing car park as per *Access Route through Llanfoist*.

Segment 14 (3 miles): From Llanfoist Crossing car park continue through Govilon as far as the three way junction just at bottom of Gilwern Hill near Ty Cerrig cottage above the Wenault as per *Access Route R*

Segment 15 (2 miles): From Ty Cerrig ascend Gilwern Hill to the Lamb and Fox at Pwlldu as per *Access Route Q*

Segment 16 (2 miles): From the Lamb & Fox follow the road to the Keepers pond and descend the B 4246 road to the Ironworks as per *Access Route S-W.*

Descending Rholben from Sugarloaf▼

58

Ride 1: Loops around Llanwenarth and Sugarloaf Mountains

Loop A/B Riding towards top of Cwm Gwenffrwd ▼

Loop A Riding down Rholben towards snow capped Blorenge ▼

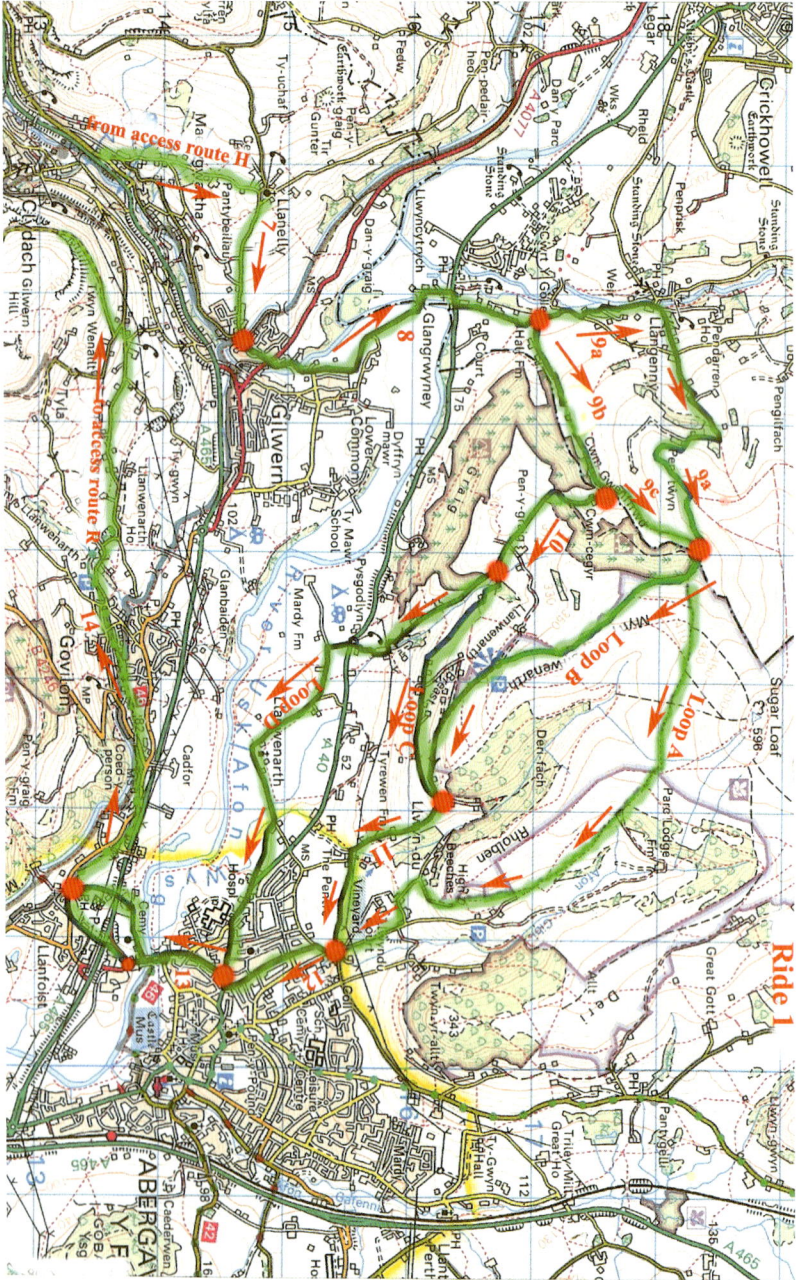

Ride 2: Loops around the Grwyne and Hondu Valleys in the Black Mountains

The Ride

A highly scenic ride around the rugged slopes of Llangattock escarpment to the border of the Black mountains on the northern side of the Sugarloaf.

An opportunity to try out detours to some well known historic sites along three of the remote Black mountain valleys - the old Hermitage at the top of the Grwyne Fechan, the Reservoir dam at the head of the Grwyne Fawr and Llanthony Abbey in the vale of Ewyas.

Route Information

Start and Finish Blaenafon Ironworks

Distance/ Ride Time

Ride + Detour A Grwyne Fechan Valley & Hermitage: 37 ½ miles: Ride Time: 4 ½ hours
Ride + Detour B Grwyne Fawr Valley & Reservoir: 46 ½ miles: Ride Time: 5 ½ hours
Ride + Detour C Hondu Valley & Llanthony Abbey: 44 ½ miles: Ride Time: 4 ½ hours

Energy Level   ***

Off-road Grade   G1

How easy is the Ride

Moderate: Some long mid gear climbs, but lots of flat sections and gentle inclines. The final 3 mile climb around west side of Gilwern Hill to the Keepers pond includes some short steep sections but most of it is a fairly easy mid-gear climb.

What sort of terrain

Mostly tarmac with a few grass stoney sections over mountains and disused track beds. Virtually all rideable

From Blaenafon Ironworks it is an easy ride along the old railway track bed to Waunafon descending the B road into Brynmawr. The route then follows the path of an old tramroad (now

61

a tarmac lane) around Llangattock escarpment before making a steep descent down to Llangattock village in the Usk Valley below. From here the route is over the old stone arched bridge into Crickhowell and then along a minor road around the base of Table mountain to the picturesque village of Llanbedr just above the Grwyne Fechan river.

The first optional ride along the Grwyne Fechan valley starts from Llanbedr. The route to the old Hermitage is along a flat and gently ascending tarmac lane through a wooded valley between the Gadair and Allt Mawr ridges. The bridge near the Hermitage marks the turn-around point of the detour although there are bridle-way tracks still continuing up through the valley. The ruins of the Hermitage can be seen through a wooded vale lying peacefully and undisturbed on the bank of the river near the bridge.

Detour A: Hermitage Grwyne Fechan Valley ▼

The ride back down the valley follows a tarmac lane this time on the opposite side, crossing the Grwyn Fechan river over the bridge at Pontyfelin, eventually rising up to a high point where there are spectacular views towards the high ridge of Pen Alt mawr and Table mountain. The lane sweeps around to the east eventually joining the main circular route along the back of the Sugarloaf

The second optional detour is a ride up the long and gradually ascending Grwyne Fawr valley between the Ffwddog and Gadair ridges following the route of the old railway track which is now a minor tarmac road. The ride up this remote and wooded valley is a mid gear but not difficult climb that tracks the nearby river all the way up to the carpark at Blaen-y-cwm which is where the old village once stood. From here the reservoir route is along another old railway track (stone dirt track) that gently climbs up to the top of the mountain where there are spectacular views over the top of the reservoir and the massive stone constructed dam that spans both sides of the valley.

Detour B: Grwyne Fawr Reservoir ▼

The return leg of this detour is a fast eight mile descent down the valley along the same minor road joining the main circular route near Forest Coal Pit..

The third optional detour is a flat easy ride through the beautiful Vale of Ewyas along Sustrans route 42 close to the river Honddu between the Hatterall and Ffwddog ridges as far as Llanthony. The ruins of Llanthony Abbey stand defiantly in splendid isolation in a remote part of the valley on the Welsh side of Offa's Dyke path that runs along the border on top of Hatterall Hill ridge above the ruins. The return part of the detour is along the same minor road joining the main circular route near Forest Coal Pit.

From Forest Coal Pit the ride continues eastwards along a minor tarmac road sandwiched between the Sugar Loaf and Bryn Arw mountains passing through the quiet hamlet of Bettws and joining Sustrans route 42 at Pantygelli village. It then heads south along the Gavenny valley skirting around the top of Abergavenny dropping down through an attractive residential district to the village of Llanfoist on the border of the Blaenafon World Heritage site.

The final section of the ride is a moderate climb with just a couple of short steep bits around the west side of Gilwern Hill above the spectacular Clydach Gorge to Pwlldu. From the Keepers pond there is a fast exhilarating descent down the other side of the hill to the Ironworks.

Heritage Interest Along Route

Llangattock mountain road: path of old tramroad route from Brynmawr to Llangattock quarries and Llangattock canal wharf

Early limestone quarry: Llangattock Daren Cilau quarries

Llangattock canal wharf: old Lime Kilns and termination of quarry tramroad

Grwyne Fechan Hermitage: remains of house once owned by Lord Glan Usk in remote location on banks of river

Partrishow Church: ancient beautiful church dating from around 11C located on hillside amidst magnificent panorama of Black mountains; known as the Church of Merthyr Issui and Patricio.

Twyn-y-Gaer Fort: remains of low banks and ditches of Iron-age fort on top of hill; one of three forts guarding the southern extent of the Black mountains; turn on to lane from Queens Head Inn car park – steep climb (part bike-wheel) for almost a mile go through gate turn left on to track which leads to the remains of fort at the top of Twyn-y-gaer.

Grwyne Fawr Reservoir: built in the early 20th century to feed Abertillary district; pipeline crosses Usk valley and passes through a tunnel under Coity mountain near the Whistle Inn; tarmac road to reservoir was originally the route of railway used during construction of reservoir; old reservoir village of Blaen-y-Cwm vanished many years ago.

Llanthony Abbey: impressive remains of 13C Augustian Priory located in Vale of Ewyas amidst Black mountains.

Crickhowell/ Abergavenny: see Towns & Canal section.

Pwlldu: a one time bustling village built for iron and coal workers but demolished in sixties; there were two terraced rows of houses, two pubs, a shop and, chapel; now all that remains is welfare hall (outdoor centre) and Lamb Inn.

Pwlldu Tunnels: the tramroad route between Blaenafon Ironworks and Pwlldu went through a tunnel almost one and a half miles long under Garn mountain; tunnel portal can be seen on side of road just below former Welfare Hall

Keepers pond (*Pen-fford-goch*): named after Keepers cottage now a popular sightseeing spot on top of Blorenge; originally used as a feeder during 19C for Garnderys Forge

The Route

See section **"Bike Access Routes"** for description and maps of access routes from and to Blaenafon reference the segments at beginning and end of route

Inns Along Route

Whistle Inn	Garn-yr-erw
Racehorse	Waunafon
Lamb and Fox	Pwlldu
Bridge/ Bear Inns	Crickhowell
Red Lyon	Llanbedr
Queens Head	Cwmyoy
Abbey/Half Moon	Llanthony
Old Crown Inn	Pantygelli
Cantref Inn	Abergavenny
Bridge Inn	Llanfoist

Segment 1 (1 ½ miles): Follow the west access route from Blaenafon Ironworks around Garn lakes to the Whistle as per *Access route A*

Segment 2 (just over ¾ miles): Continue along the West access route from The Whistle along the old railway track bed to Waunafon as per *Access route B*

Segment 3 (just over 2 ½ miles) : Continue along the West access route from Waunafon descending hill to Brynmawr market square as per *Access route C* [you can optionally take access route D and E via Lower Cwm Nant-gam to Brynmawr but this is a little longer]

Segment 4 (½ mile): From Brynmawr Market Square proceed via Bailey and Intermediate road to junction of Black Rock road and Llangattock mountain road just in front of the EMS building as per *Route through Brynmawr*

Segment 5 (5 ½ miles): From this junction near the EMS factory continue along the west access route around Llangattock escarpment (superb bike route) descending the road to the canal

bridge in Llangattock village as per *Access routes F-G*

Segment 6 (just over 3 miles): From the canal bridge descend road through Llangattock village passing the Horseshoe Inn up to the traffic lights at the junction of road near Crickhowell bridge. Cross over the bridge, pass the Bridge-End Inn on other side and continue up to junction of Brecon road. Turn right passing the well known Bear Inn on left and then take the first turning left. Go up Standard street passing over small round-about at Greenhill-Way, turning left at the next road junction which is sign posted to Grwyne Fechan.

Gentle to moderate climb for half mile up to point where it joins another road from Crickhowell. The road continues to climb for another half mile before eventually flattening out. Table mountain is on the left (west) and Grwyne valley stretches out to the east. At the junction with Llanbedr road turn right and head towards Llanbedr village. The church and Red Lion Inn are are centrally located within the village.

For those choosing the Grwyn Fechan *valley Hermitage Ride follow the route described in Detour A option below.*

For those choosing the Grwyne Fawr *Valley/Reservoir Ride or* Honddu *Valley/Llanthony Abbey Ride continue at segment 7*

DetourA: Grwyne Fechan Valley and Hermitage Ride (8 miles)

From the Red Lyon Llanbedr follow the tarmac lane heading north. A gentle and then moderate climb for just over half mile up to the junction of another road. Bear right heading north up the Grwyne Fechan valley. Good views on either side but particularly to the south where the two radio masts on Blorenge mountain above Blaenafon can be seen in distance. Continue along this fairly flat road, passing a sign post to Table mountain until the junction with Bont (towards right) is reached just under a mile.

Continue straight ahead, pass over a bridge and then a telephone kiosk a little further on, eventually meeting a three way intersection near Cwm farm. Keep heading north for another mile following the Grwyne Fechan river passing through a gate and finally terminating at the Bridge near the remains of old Hermitage. This is a fairly remote point at the top of the valley and in the midst of the Black mountains.

On the return leg follow the same minor single track lane but this time forking left at the intersection near Cwm farm. Pass by the Old Chapel, cross over the bridge at Pont-y-felin and bear left at the intersection with Bont road. A short steepish climb followed by a flat and gentle descent along the side of the valley. Superb views over the Grwyne Fechan and towards the Black mountains.

After about one and a half miles from the Bont intersection, Llanbedr church can be seen in the distance towards the west.

From here continue for another three quarters of a mile up to the junction of the Llanbedr-Forest Coal Pit minor road. Continue as per segment 8.

Segment 7 (1 mile): From the Red Lyon Inn Llanbedr follow the minor road going south, forking left after about half a mile in direction towards Partrishow/Forest Coal Pit . Stay on this minor road for another half mile up to the intersection of the Llanbedr-Forest Coal Pit road with the Grwyne Fechan valley road..

Segment 8 (2 ½ miles): At the junction with the Llanbedr-Forest Coal Pit minor road continue north east towards Forest Coal Pit forking right after about one and half miles at the sign-posted junction. Pass over the bridge at Pont Newydd and continue on this minor road which parallels the Grwyne Fawr river for a further mile up to another junction at Forest Coal Pit.

Go to Segment 9 if you are continuing the return route back to Blaenafon Ironworks

For those choosing the Grwyne Fawr Reservoir Ride follow the route described in Detour B below.

For those choosing the Honddu Valley Llanthony Abbey ride follow the route described in Detour C below.

Detour B: Grwyne Fawr Valley & Reservoir Ride (16 miles loop)
Continuing from Segment 8:
Turn left at the Forest Coal Pit junction and follow the minor road for about quarter mile up to a four way intersection. Take the

minor road heading north west (left) which is sign-posted to Grwyne Fawr reservoir and cross over the bridge at Pont Escob.

[For those feeling really energetic take a one and half mile detour (steep strenuous climb) from this bridge to Partrishow church which is on the side of a hill in magnificent surroundings   Follow the road a short distance in direction towards Crickhowell (south) and then turn right up the hill at the sign for Partrishow church.]

Pont Escob bridge is the start of an 8 mile somewhat gentle ascent up the valley following the Grwyne Fawr river on the right. This is a surprisingly good road considering the remoteness and seclusion of the valley.

After about two miles the valley becomes heavily wooded on both sides and although the road continues to twist and snake upwards the usual sensation of climb fatigue is hardly noticable because the ascent occurs so steadily and incrementally over a relatively long distance (8 mile valley).

It is in fact a fairly easy mid-gear ride all the way up to the car park at Blaenacwm near the top of the valley. The reservoir is about one and half mile from the car park and can easily be reached on the stone road just past the car park towards the right. Although there is gentle climb up at the start it soon flattens out and the one and half mile stone track to the reservoir is easily rideable

The return route is along the same road back to the Forest Coal Pit junction (there is a part-way alternative mountain track but because of fairly long ride from Blaenafon Ironworks it is preferable to use tarmac road).   Allow 1 hour 20 minutes go and twenty minutes return. Continue the return ride as per Segment 9.

Detour C: Honddu Valley & Llanthony Abbey Ride (14 mile loop)

Continuing from Segment 8:

Turn left at the road junction in Forest Coal Pit and follow the minor road for about quarter mile as far as a four way intersection. Turn right and continue for almost two miles through Cwm Coedycerrig up to the junction of the Llanvihangel-Llanthony minor road just below the Queens Head Inn. Turn left (towards west) continue on this minor tarmac road (Sustrans Cycleway route 42) which follows the Honddu river through the Vale of Ewyas.

Pass Cwmyoy village Hall (Cwymyoy church in distance towards north) and Henlan Baptist chapel. Hatterall Hill on the edge of the Black mountains dominates the northern skyline. Offa's Dyke follows a path along the top of ridge from Hatterall Hill to Hays Bluff.

The ride is flat and easy all the way to Llanthony Abbey where you will find the Half Moon Inn and Abbey Hotel. The return route follows the same minor road back to the Forest Coal Pit junction. Continue the return ride as per Segment 9.

Segment 9 (2 ¼ miles): At the Forest Coal Pit junction head east towards Bettys and Pantygelli. The road now climbs for about quarter a mile passing a sign-posted dirt track on the right leading to top of Sugarloaf. The road eventually flattens out, winds itself around the back of the Sugarloaf passes through the hamlet of Bettws and joins up with the Old Hereford road at Pantygelli.

Segment 10 (3 ¼ miles): At this junction turn right on the minor road which is designated Sustrans cycle route 42 and which follows the west side of the Gavenny valley towards Abergavenny . Pass by the Old Crown Inn and then Triley Court on the right and after just over a mile fork right (watch for it) on to a tarmac lane just after Penlanlas Bungalow. Views over Abergavenny, towards GarnFawr ridge with Blorenge directly in front.

This lane continues for about ½ mile up to a junction just on top of Penypound overlooking Hill College on the left. Cross over and go straight ahead down the lane (Chain road) heading south bearing around to the left at the bottom joining Chapel Road. The road passes through an attractive residential district joining the A40 at the bottom of the hill.
Turn right and then left at the first roundabout (Cantref Inn), right at the next roundabout, pass over Llanfoist road bridge and continue as far as the Waitrose roundabout.

Segment 11 (¾ mile) From the Waitrose

Partrishow ▼

roundabout follow the route back through The Cutting (or past the Cemetery) to Llanfoist Crossing car park as per *Route through Llanfoist*

Segment 12 (3 miles): From Llanfoist follow the north access route through Govilon to the three way junction on lower Gilwern Hill near Ty Cerrig cottage as per *Access Route R.*

Segment 13 (2 miles): From Ty Cerrig continue on the north access route ascending Gilwern Hill to the Lamb and Fox at Pwlldu as per *Access Route Q.*

Segment 14 (2 miles): From the Lamb & Fox follow the road to the Keepers pond and descend the B 4246 road to the Ironworks as per *Access Routes S-W.*

Below Sugarloaf towards Forest Coal Pit ▼

Llanthony Abbey ▼

Detour C: Vale of Ewyas ride: on top of Twyn-y-gaer iron-age fort ▼

Detour B: Up the Grwyne Fawr Valley towards the reservoir ▼

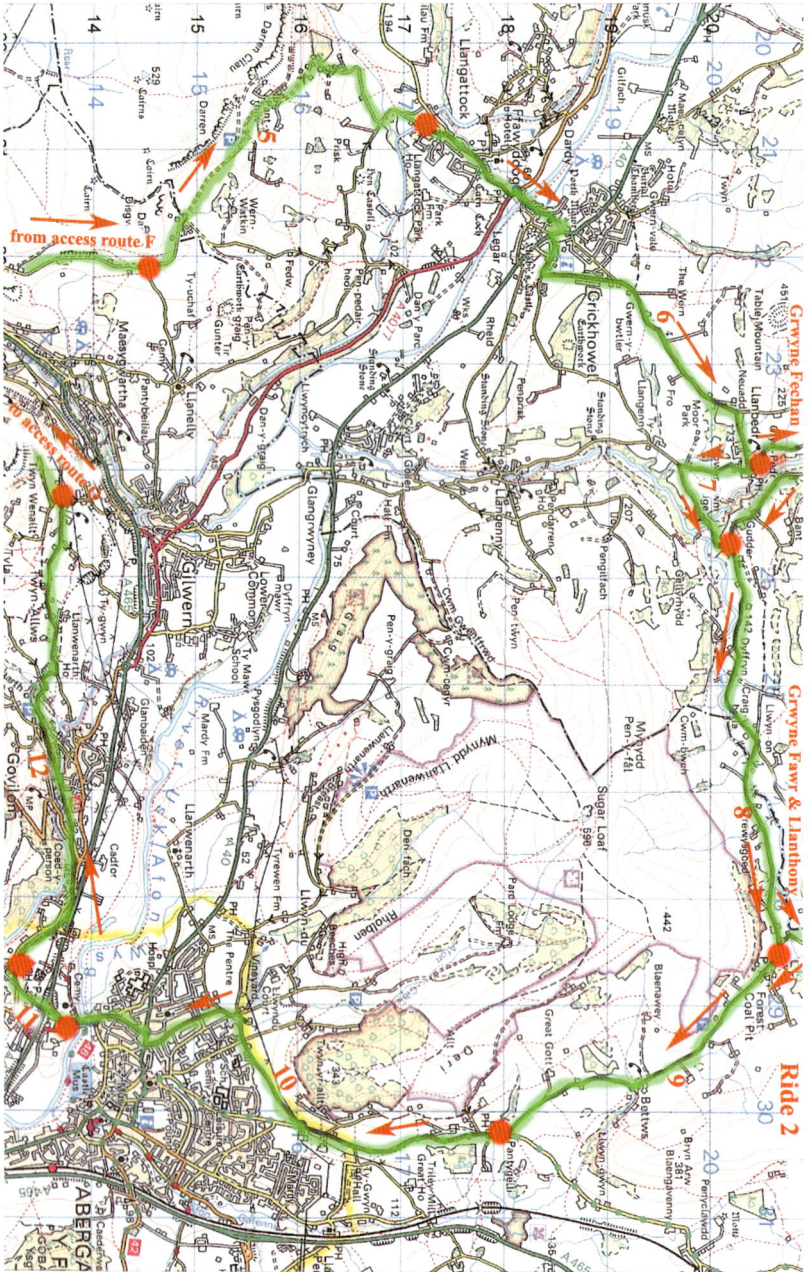

RIDE 2 DETOURS

Grwyne Fawr Reservoir

BLACK MOUNTAINS

Chwarel Fan

Grwyne Fawr Detour

Offa's Dyke

Llanthony

Vale of Ewyas

Pen Garreg

Mynydd Du Forest

Llanthony Detour

Hatterall Hill

Hermitage

Grwyne Fechan Detour

Blaenau

Cwmyoy

Bont

Cwm Milaid

Craig Mawr

Partrishow

Queens Head

Partrishow Hill

Twyn y Gaer Fort

Llanbedr

6

Gudder

Duffryn

8

Forest Coal Pit

9

Cwm Coedcerrig

Ride 3: A short Loop around Gilwern Hill and the Clydach Gorge

The Ride

A short scenic ride skirting over the tops and around sides of mountains, crossing over high railway viaducts that span steep and narrow gorges with far reaching panoramic views.

Route Information	
Start and Finish	**How easy is he Ride**
Blaenafon Ironworks	Fairly easy short ride mostly over flat and gentle inclines with just a couple of short and moderate climbs. Route is completely rideable - a few ruts here and there.
Distance/ Ride Time	**What sort of terrain**
Distance 12 miles: Ride Time 2 hours	Mix of on-road off-road including - minor tarmac lanes, grass/stony mountain tracks/bridle-ways, grass/stony tracks over disused railway beds
Energy Level	**Off-road Grade**
**	G1/G3 the only G3 section is Dynes Incline

The start of the ride from Blaenafon Ironworks follows the west access route through Garn lakes and over the moonscape of Garn-yr-erw mountain.   Once on top there are far reaching views stretching over vast tracts of moorland landscape virtually in all directions – the Beacons Sugarloaf and Coity are all visible.

A short bone shaker ride down Dyne Steels Incline connects with a tramroad route along the east side of Gilwern Hill. There is a fabulous cliff edge ride along the gently descending wide grass track that bends around the hill from north to west passing old Tyler limestone quarries and overlooking Cwm Llanwenerth that disappears into the Usk valley below.

72

Riding along the Tyler looking towards the Sugarloaf ▼

The off-road mountain track soon joins a tarmac lane that descends down to a road-rail crossing on the disused Abergavenny-Merthyr railway trackbed between Gilwern and Clydach Halts.
The ride continues along the gently ascending railway track which twists and winds through some of the most extraordinary and dramatic mountain landscape along the east side of the Clydach Gorge.

Just before Clydach Halt and the Clydach tunnels, the track curves around and passes over a massive eight arch stone viaduct that spans a deep dingle reaching down to the central gorge below. The route continues to weave its way south, over another viaduct, alongside Llanelli quarries, over more railway embankments, bypassing yet more tunnels leading to the old but still recognisable passenger Halt at Gellifellon near Cwm-Nant-du. In the 19C the construction of this railway line was considered to be a major feat of Victorian civil engineering.

At Lower Cwm-Nant-du road-crossing, the route switches to a tarmac lane that ascends the hillside (moderate) through Llanmarch to Waunafon Halt at one time one of the highest railway Halts in the country (1400 feet). From Waunafon there is a gentle descent along a short section of the disused Blaenavon-Brynmawr branch railway (earmarked as an extension to Sustrans cycle route 46) towards the Whistle Inn and then back to the starting point at Blaenafon Ironworks.

Heritage Interest Along Route

Garn-yr- erw- mountain: moon like landscape caused by open-casting in the 1940/50s era; remains of Hill pits on south side

Dyne Steel's Incline Pwlldu: former cable operated inclined railroad on north (Pwlldu) and south (Blaenafon) sides of Garn-yr-erw mountain; used for early transport of minerals between Blaenafon Ironworks and Pwlldu; supplemented tunnel route.

Pwlldu Tramroad Tunnel: route of tramroad under Garn mountain between Blaenafon Ironworks and Pwlldu; linked with Hills tramroad that extended to Garnderris Forge and Llanfoist canal wharf; tunnel mouth can be seen on side of road just below former Welfare Hall

Pwlldu: a one time bustling village built for iron and coal workers but demolished in sixties; there were two terraced rows of houses, two pubs, a shop and chapel; now all that remains is welfare hall (outdoor centre) and Lamb & Fox Inn.

Pwlldu and Tyler quarries; Early Limestone quarries Gilwern Hill; limestone transported to Blaenafon Ironworks through Pwlldu tunnel

Llanelly quarries: near rail-road crossing; supplied limestone for Clydach Ironworks and agricultural use.

Clydach Limeworks: facing Clydach Halt supplied lime for building railway viaducts and tunnels

Clydach Ironworks: not far below Clydach Halt (see West Heritage Ride)

Abergavenny-Merthyr railway; section of disused route including some amazing Viaduct and tunnel architecture east side of Clydach Gorge; important early heads of valley line started middle of 19C ceased middle of 20C; this mountainous section of the historic Merthyr-Abergavenny railway route is earmarked to be upgraded and managed by Sustrans but is already easily rideable.

Bailey's tramroad : The route of the old railway line follows more or less the route of the old tramroad that originally linked Nantyglo Ironworks with Govilon Canal Wharf in the early 19C

Llanmarch 1795 railroad: between Clydach Ironworks and Llanmarch ran mostly along the tarmac road that crosses the old railway path at Llanelly quarries and continues down the hill to a junction near the new Clydach community centre; also series of inclines from Clydach Ironworks to Llanelly Hill built around 1811 to supplement Llanmarch railroad; Blaenafon old stone road is between Llanelli Hill and Pwlldu road

Brynmawr-Blaenafon railway : section of now disused but important branch line serving the Eastern Valley

The Route

Because this is a relatively short ride all the route segments included in this ride are shown on the <u>West Access Route Map,</u> and described under the section <u>Bike Access Routes.</u>

Inns Along Route

Whistle Inn	Garn-yr-erw
Racehorse	Waunafon
Lamb and Fox	Pwlldu
Cwmbrian	Clydach
(near Clydach Station)	

Segment 1 (just over 1 ½ miles): From the Blaenafon Ironworks car-park take the west access route past the Garn Lakes up to the Whistle Inn, as per *Access route A*

Segment 2 (2 mile): From the Whistle Inn cross over Garn-yr-erw mountain to join Pwlldu road just opposite the Lamb & Fox Inn as per *Access route O.*

Segment 3 (1 ¾ miles): From the Lamb & Fox follow the tram road track around the east side of Gilwern Hill, past the Tyla quarry, descending to a three-way junction opposite Ty Cerrig cottage above the Wenault as per *Access route P.*

Segment 4 (1 mile): From Ty Cerrig join the nearby Abergavenny-Merthyr railway trackbed and follow the track up to Clydach Halt as per *Access route N.*

Segment 5 (almost 2 miles): From Clydach Halt continue along the track bed through Gellifellon Halt as far as Crossing Cottage Lower Cwm Nant-gam as per *Access route K.*

Segment 6 (1 ½ miles): From the Crossing at Lower Cwm Nant-gam follow the tarmac lane through Llanmarch ascending the Llanelly Hill minor road to Waunafon as per *Access route D.*

Segment 7 (1 mile): From gate access at old Waunafon Halt follow the Brynmawr-Blaenafon railway trackbed as far as the Whistle Inn as per *Access route B*

75

Segment 8 (just over 1 ½ miles): From the Whistle Inn return along the cycleway past Garn Lakes to Blaenafon Ironworks as per *Access* *route A.*

Railway track over Viaduct at Clydach Halt ▲

Riding along the railway track towards Gellifelon ▼

Ride 4: A short loop around the Blorenge and Punchbowl

The Ride

A short circular mountain ride through "Cordell country" following Hills tramroad around the slopes of the Blorenge with spectacular views over the Usk, Gavenny and Monnow valleys.

Route Information

Start and Finish:

Blaenafon Ironworks

Distance/ Ride Time

11 miles: 2 hours

Energy Level

**

Off-Road Grade
 G1/G2/G3

How easy is the Ride

Easy-Moderate; most of route is over flat and descending terrain with exception of one short wheel-up section near the Punch bowl and a one mile climb up Llanellen road (strenuous in parts) to Foxhunter car park

What sort of terrain

Largely over stone grass mountain tracks that are for most part fairly easy except for a slightly challenging descent down the bridleway track that links the top side of Blorenge with Hills tramroad halfway down.   Dynes incline (G3) is also challenging.

The start of the ride from Blaenafon Ironworks follows the north west access route alongside Garn lakes crossing the moonscape of Garn-yr-erw mountain and descending a stony track (Dyne Steel Railroad Incline) to the Lamb & Fox Inn Pwlldu.

From here there is a short gentle climb along a minor road to the Keepers pond almost at the top of the Blorenge. The old Garnderris feeder pond (Keepers) is now an attractive visitor and sightseeing spot with far reaching views towards Herefordshire and beyond.

The ride continues along an old quarry tram road across the mountain before making a short bumpy descent down the northern slopes of the Blorenge joining up with the historic Hills tram road just below

This tramway is now a wide easily rideable grass track that used to link Garnderris Forge with the canal at Llanfoist Wharf down below on the lower slopes of the Blorenge. An easy detour can be made from here to the site of the old Garnderrys Forge which is a short distance away towards the west on the side of the Keepers road.

The circular ride continues eastwards along the path of Hills tramroad which eventually veers off to the left down an incline towards the canal. However the ride continues along an equally good wide track that begins to curve around the Blorenge towards the south east overlooking the town of Abergavenny. It eventually leads somewhat unexpectedly to a secluded wildlife pond that sits below what looks like a spherical hollow punched into the Blorenge giving it an almost dramatic theatrical appearance.

Wildlife pond Punchbowl ▲

This hollow is the so-called Punch-bowl at one time the apparent site of early fist fights during the Ironworking days.

A short bike-wheel up a steep slope before leaving the mountain track to join a minor tarmac road in the heart of Llanellen valley. A one mile (steep in parts) low gear climb up to Foxhunter car-park at the top of the Blorenge and then a fast easy swoop down to Blaenavon Ironworks.

Heritage Interest Along Route

Garn-yr- erw- mountain: moon like landscape caused by open-casting in the 1940/50s era; remains of Hill pits on south side

Dyne Steels Incline Pwlldu: former cable operated inclined railroad on north (Pwlldu) and south (Blaenafon) sides of Garn-yr-erw mountain; used in 19C for early transport of minerals between Blaenafon Ironworks and Pwlldu; supplemented the Pwlldu tunnel route.

Pwlldu: a one time bustling village built for iron and coal workers but demolished in sixties; there were two terraced rows of houses, two pubs, a shop and, chapel; now all that remains is the welfare hall (outdoor centre) and Lamb & Fox Inn.

Pwlldu Tunnels: the tramroad route between Blaenafon Ironworks and Pwlldu went through a tunnel almost one and a half miles long under Garn mountain; tunnel portal can be seen on side of road just below former Welfare Hall

Cordell Country: a term coined by local author Chris Barber to describe the 19C ironworking landscape around Garnderris made famous by Alexander Cordell in his book "Rape of the Fair Country".

Hills Tramroad: from Pwlldu tunnel and nearby quarries the tramroad routes around Cwm Llanwenarth to Garnderris Forge; from here it continues along the north side of the Blorenge before descending an incline to Llanfoist canal wharf

Keepers pond (Pen-fford-goch): named after Keepers cottage now a popular sightseeing spot on top of Blorenge; originally used as a feeder during 19C for Garnderys Forge

Garnderris Forge and rolling mill: site located on side of B4246 about half mile down from Keepers pond; during 19C it converted pig iron produced at Bleanafon Ironworks into wrought iron; two nearby ponds used to provide water for Forge steam engine; three hundred people lived at Garnderris; there are very few remains.

Punchbowl: nature reserve site on north east side of Blorenge; in 19C it was apparently used as a venue for bare-knuckle fist fights.

Foxhunter car park: commemorates nearby grave of Lt. Col. Harry Llewelyn's famous Olympic show jumping horse Foxhunter (1940-59)

The Route

Because this is a relatively short ride all the route segments included in this ride are shown on the North Access Route Map, and described under the section Bike Access Routes.

Inns Along Route

Whistle Inn   Garn-y-erw
Lamb & Fox   Pwlldu
Riflemans   Blaenafon

Segment 1 (3½ miles): From Blaenafon Ironworks take the access route through Garn Lakes and over Garn-yr-erw to the Pwlldu road opposite the Lamb & Fox as per *Access routes A and O*

Segment 2 (¾ mile): From the Lamb & Fox Inn turn right on to the Pwlldu road heading east and continue up to the junction of Blaenafon road opposite the Keepers pond (Pen-ffordd-goch) as per *Access route S.*

Segment 3 (2 miles): See *Access route b1*. From the Keepers pond head east along the path around the pond joining up with a grass-stony track on the Blorenge mountain; it is mostly rideable in summer but there are some minor waterlogged ruts to dodge in the winter period. Superb views overlooking the Usk valley.

After crossing two piles of loose stones and at about a mile from the pond, a signpost will be seen on left pointing to another bridleway track heading north down the mountain

Turn left on this track which is not that rideable on the top section but gets much better lower down. After about half mile, the downhill track merges with another fairly wide flat grass track (Hills Tramroad) that bends around the mountain from west to east.

[An easy detour can be made to the site of the old Garnderrys Forge by turning left at this point and back tracking to the junction of Blaenavon road. The site of the old Forge and the tramroad path from Pwlldu are on the other side of the road - but no remains of Forge]

Segment 4 (almost 2 ¼ miles): See *Access route b2*. Turn right on to Hill's tramroad passing by a short section of tramway tunnel and following the grass stony track which skirts around the north side of the Blorenge heading east.

After about a mile the tram road track becomes less well defined but continues along the narrow path which bends around the northward facing large bowl and eventually joins up with another well defined wide grass track heading east.

[The actual path of Hill's tramway (not discernable) disappears northwards down the steep incline towards Llanfoist canal wharf at the bottom.]

There are excellent views overlooking Abergavenny and towards the Skirrid. Follow the track which now bends around to the south (easily rideable), Llanellen valley on the left and passing through a gate with a nearby Woodland Trust sign.

Ride 4: A short loop around the Blorenge and Punchbowl

After another half mile the track leads into a hidden but very attractive wild life pond which sits within a shallow valley bowl (Punchbowl).

Take the left-most well defined dirt track and walk the bike up the hill (about quarter mile steepish in parts) passing through the gate at the top.

Follow the track which now flattens out heading towards the west and finally passing through a gate with nearby wildlife sign, joining the minor Llanellen tarmac road.

Segment 5 (1 ½ miles): Ascend Llanellen road (steep in parts) to Foxhunter car-par descending the other side as far as the junction with the B 4246 Blaenafon road as per *Access route U -T.* .

Segment 6 (just over a mile): From the junction with the Blaenafon road descend the hill to the ironworks as per *Access route W*

Around the Punchbowl Wildlife Pond ▼

81

Ride 4: A short loop around the Blorenge and Punchbowl

Riding along the Blorenge track above Hills tramroad▼

Approaching Dyne Steel Incline ▼

Ride 5: Around Longtown and Grosmont Castles

The Ride

An incredibly scenic ride criss-crossing the Herefordshire and Monmouthshire borders. From the Monnow valley to the high plateau on Campstone hill returning along the slopes of the Skirrid; stunning views, unspoilt borderlands, medieval parishes and Norman castles. There is also an option to do a much shorter ride looping back around the Skirrid at Llanvihangel.

At the start of the ride there is an exhilarating long descent either down through Llanellen or Llanover into the village of Llanfoist which is on the border the Blaenafon World Heritage Site. The route then circles through the outskirts of Abergavenny, around the base of Derri hill northwards to the Gavenny valley. A virtually flat and easy ride along the Monnow valley, crossing over Offas Dyke path which can be seen ascending Hatterrall Hill and then disappearing over the top of ridge to Hay Bluff in the north west.

Route Information

Start and Finish

Blaenafon Ironworks

Distance/ Ride Time

Main Ride: Distance 55 miles; Ride Time 5 ½ hours

Ride via optional Skirrid Loop: Distance 31 miles; Ride Time 4 hours

Energy Level *** to ****

Off-road Grade G1/G3

How easy is the Ride

A fairly long but not difficult ride with plenty of down-hill flat and gently ascending sections; a half mile steep low gear climb leaving Longtown; a not difficult low gear one mile moderate climb from Pontrilys; a short low gear climb up Cupids hill to Grosmont. The first 20 miles from the Ironworks to Longtown is mostly downhill and flat give or take a couple of small rises here and there. Ride ends with a moderate 3 mile ascent around Gilwern Hill to Pwlldu and Blaenafon

What sort of terrain

Virtually all tarmac minor roads except for the optional Garn-yr-erw mountain crossing and Dynes Incline (G3).

83

The minor road to Longtown follows the path of the Monnow along the valley floor never loosing sight of the imposing Black mountain ridge that looms upwards to the west. Longtown castle is on the outskirts of the village near the church and has been well positioned by the Normans to defend the English borderlands.

Entrance to Longtown Castle ▼

After a half mile climb up Merddin hill there is an easy laid back ride along a tarmac lane eventually leading to an exhilarating steep descent into the village of Ewyas Harold below. From here the route crosses the Monnow river reaching another high plateau on the Hereford side of the border winding its way through some of the most beautiful rolling hill countryside along the Marches; hardly changed from Elgar times.

If you are feeling energetic there is an option to make a short two mile detour to visit Kilpeck whose extraordinary Romanesque style church with its monster heads still survives from the Norman period. The ride loops around near Crabs Castle skirting through the verdant parkland of Kentchurch with Garway Hill looming in the background. A short climb up Cupids Hill leads to the picturesque village of Grosmont and the remains of the imposing 13C castle which is part of the three-castle Norman defence of the borders.

From Grosmont there is a superb ride over the high plateau of Campstone hill where there are yet again stunning views of the Black mountains as well as the undulating borderlands. The return route skirts around the lower slopes of the Big Skirrid overlooking the Gavenny valley and Black mountain ridges towards the west, linking up with the cycleway route through Abergavenny and on to Llanfoist. From here there is a moderate climb around the west side of Gilwern hill to Pwlldu followed by a fast descent down to the Ironworks.

84

Heritage Interest Along Route

Garn-yr- erw mountain: moon like landscape caused by open-casting in the 1940/50s era; remains of Hill pits on south side

Dyne Steels Incline Pwlldu: former cable operated inclined railroad on north (Pwlldu) and south (Blaenafon) sides of Garn-yr-erw mountain; used in 19C for early transport of minerals between Blaenafon Ironworks and Pwlldu; supplemented tunnel route.

Keepers pond (Pen-fford-goch Pond): named after Keepers cottage now a popular sightseeing spot on top of Blorenge; originally used as a feeder during 19C for Garnderys Forge

Foxhunter car park: commemorates nearby grave of Lt. Col. Harry Llewelyn's famous Olympic show jumping horse Foxhunter (1940-59)

Skirrid Inn Llanvihangel Crucorney: Reputed to be one of the oldest Inns in Wales although present building thought to date from 17C; there was a courtroom and prison cell inside: St Michaels church is close by.

Cloddoch Church: on the road to Longtown close to river; picturesque Hamlet

Longtown Castle 12C Norman castle built by Walter de Lacey to defend English borderlands; impressive ruins - not far from church

Kilpeck Church & Castle: Church built by Hugh de Kilpeck in 12C on site of Saxon church; renowned for its incredible pagan carvings including monster heads, ancient beasts and the Green Man; the remains of Norman castle and moat is just behind the church; Kilpeck was important fortified medieval village.

Kentchurch Church & Court: imposing mid 19C church in England's green and pleasant land; Court opposite was supposed refuge of Owain Glyndwr.

Grosmont Castle: 13C work of Hubert de Burgh; imposing structure with towers and gatehouse surrounded by ditch; church is close by.

Section of Abergavenny-Merthyr railway: built in 1862 and opened by Ironmaster Crawshay Bailey; closed 1958; Govilon station still recognisable; Govilon Llanvihangel tramway predates the railway

Pwlldu Tunnels: the tramroad route between Blaenafon Ironworks and Pwlldu went through a tunnel almost one and a half miles long under Garn mountain; tunnel portal can be seen on side of road just below former Welfare Hall

Pwlldu: a one time bustling village built for iron and coal workers but demolished in sixties; there were two terraced rows of houses, two pubs, a shop and, chapel, now all that remains is welfare hall (outdoor centre) and Lamb & Fox Inn.

The Route

Inns Along Route

Whistle Inn	Garn Lakes
The Pottery (alternate)	Blaenafon
Lamb & Fox	Pwlldu
Crown Inn	Pantygelli
Skirrid	Llanvihangel Crucorny
Cornewall Arms	Clodoch
Crown Inn	Longtown
Temple Bar	Ewyas Harold
Dog Inn	Ewyas Harold
Red Lyon	Kilpeck
Angel inn	Grosmont
Riflemans	Blaenafon

See section "Bike Access Routes" for description and maps of access routes from and to Blaenafon, reference the route segments at beginning and end of ride.

From Blaenafon Ironworks choose either the Llanellen, Llanover or Gilwern Hill access route to Llanfoist. The distances are about the same and they are all easy descending routes. The Gilwern Hill segment is used on the return route to the Ironworks so you may wish to choose one of the other two routes:

Route to Llanfoist via Llanellen:
Segment 1 (3½ miles): From Blaenafon Ironworks take the north west access route through Garn Lakes and over Garn-yr-erw to the Pwlldu road opposite the Lamb & Fox as per *Access route A-O.*

Segment 2 (5 ½ miles): From the Lamb and Fox Inn take the route past the Keepers pond, Foxhunters car-park, down Llanellen valley to Llanfoist Crossing car-park as per *Access routs S-T-U-V.*

Alternative Route to Llanfoist via Llanover:
Segment 1 (just under 2 ½ miles): From Blaenafon Ironworks take the north-east access route along Llanover road to the second cattle

grid as per *Access route X-Y.*

Segment 2 (5 ½ miles): From the second cattle grid descend Llanover valley to the canal and follow the towpath and minor road to Llanfoist Crossing car-park as per *Access route Z.*

Alternative Route to Llanfoist via Gilwern Hill

Segment 1 (3 ½ miles): From the Ironworks take the north west access route through Garn Lakes and over Garn-yr-erw to the Pwlldu road opposite the Lamb & Fox as per *Access route A-O.*

Segment 2 (5 ¼ miles) From the lamb & Fox descend the tarmac lane around the west side of Gilwern Hill joining the cycleway near Govilon to Llanfoist Crossing car-park as per *Access route Q-R..*

Continuing the Ride from Llanfoist

Segment 3 (just over ½ mile): From Llanfoist Crossing car park pass through the Cutting to Waitrose roundabout near Llanfoist Bridge as per *Access Route through Llanfoist*

Segment 4 (just under 2 miles): From the Waitrose roundabout pass over the Bridge turning left at the Merthyr road roundabout continuing up to the Brecon road roundabout. Turn right and then almost immediate left on to Chapel road. Continue northwards gently climbing up through Chapel road all the way to the top where it merges with Pentre road.

Bear right at the top go along Chain road a short way as far as the crossroads at the base of Twyn-yr-allt mountain and just above the Hill Residential College. Go straight ahead gently climbing Chain Lane in a northerly direction as far as the junction with Old Hereford road (minor road designated as Sustrans route 42).

Segment 5 (3 ½ miles): From this junction continue on Old Hereford road still heading north passing by Triley Court and the Old Crown Inn Pantygelli. The road skirts around the base of the Sugar loaf and Bryn Arw in the Gavenny valley and after about 3 miles the road forks left and right near the railway bridge close to Pen-y-clawdd.

Take the left fork and continue on Sustrans route 42 for another half mile up to the junction of the Llanthony road at Lower Stanton farm.

Segment 6 (just under 2 miles): Turn right at the Lower Stanton farm junction (leaving Sustrans route 42) continue along the flat Honddu valley road for just under a mile up to the junction with the Honddu bridge at Llanvihangel Crucorney. The church and the famous Skirrid Inn are just up the hill on the right.

For those wishing to do the shorter loop around the Skirrid turn right at the Bridge in Llanvihangel, left at the top of

hill and follow through to the main Hereford road. Cross over the A road and ascend the hill through Llanteems. Watch out for a lane on the right signposted Offa's Dyke footpath. From here follow the return Skirrid route as per Segment 11

Continuing the main Longtown ride:

Cross over the bridge and continue northwards on this minor road which is sign-posted to Longtown, passing by Offas Dyke path. Continue on the Longtown road for about one and a half miles up to the junction with Pandy road not far from the Alltyryns Hotel (superb old stone Manor house and close to the point where the Honddu and Monnow rivers merge.

Segment 7 (just under 4 ½ miles): From the junction with the Longtown Pandy road continue on the minor tarmac road along the Monnow valley towards Longtown. The road is flat and easy with some small undulating sections. Hatterrill Hill ridge is on the left and Offas Dyke skirts along the top of this ridge all the way to Hays Bluff. Pass through the village of Cloddoch, bear left near the Crown Inn Longtown and continue straight ahead for just over half a mile as far as Longtown castle.

Segment 8 (5 miles): From Longtown castle go back through the village to the Crown Inn. Turn left at the Inn and then turn right at the sign post to Ewyas Harold. Cross over the Monnow river and Escley Brook and make a moderate half mile climb - low gear at the bottom and mid gear toward top. Once over the top continue for a half a mile and then turn right towards Balls Cross.

After passing Journeys End farm where there are wide reaching views, there is a long steep exhilarating descent down to the village of

Ewyas Harold and on to the bridge over the Dulus brook in front of the Temple Bar and Dog Inns. St Michaels church is just behind the Dog Inn.

Segment 9 (8 ¼ miles): Turn right in front of the Temple Bar Inn and then bear right on the B4347 to Pontrilas. Cross over the A 465 T (Abergavenny Hereford road) continue to a road fork and bear left on to the road sign-posted to Orcop and Garway Hill.

A one mile gentle to moderate climb (mid gear) and then a flat stretch. After another mile pass by the left fork to Kilpeck [If you have the energy make a short detour to Kilpeck – just over two miles and visit the famous church and castle]. Bearing right in the direction towards Orcop continue for just over half mile and then turn right on to single track tarmac lane at Crabs Castle.. Watch for it there is no sign – easily missed.

Follow this lane through Kentchurch deer park gently descending for almost two miles as far as the tee junction in Kentchurch.

The church and entrance to Kentchurch Court is just down on the left. Turn right at the tee and left again at the junction with the B 4347.

Cross over the Monnow bridge make moderate low gear climb up Cupids Hill and follow the road through Grosmont village to the castle which is just opposite the church.

Segment 10 (5 miles): From Grosmont castle turn right and go back up through the village turning left at the signpost to Abergavenny, make a short climb to the tee junction and turn left towards Llanvihangel Crucorney. The road skirts along a high plateau with incredible views of the Black mountains, Skirrid and the rolling hills of the borderland. Gently climb up towards top of Campstone Hill.

After about two miles bear right at the fork sign-posted towards Pandy. Follow this flat section of road along Campstone Hill passing by two turnings on the left (watch out for them). The third left turning on to a single lane (easily missed) is the one you take. It is near Offa Dyke path crossing and there is a footpath signpost at the junction indicating the path.

Segment 11 (5 ¾ miles): From the Offas Dyke path turn-off follow the lane through towards the Skirrid mountain turning right on to an unsigned lane after a mile (watch out for a horse and rider signpost).

Follow the flat and gently descending lane along the slopes of the Skirrid with excellent views over the Gavenny valley.

After about three miles bear left near New Court farm and continue past the Craft centre up to the junction with the minor road to Llantilio Pertholy. Turn left at the junction and follow road up to junction of the B 4521 (Skenfrith road). Cross over the road and continue straight ahead past the Golf course up to the tee junction in front of Tredillion House.

Segment 12 (just over 2 ½miles): From Tredilion house follow the cycleway route through Abergavenny to the Waitrose roundabout near Llanfoist bridge as described in *Ride 6 segment 9.*

Segment 13 (½ mile) From the Waitrose roundabout follow the route back through The Cutting to Llanfoist Crossing car park as per *Segment 3 of this ride.*

Segment 14 (3 miles): Continue through Govilon and on to the three way junction just at bottom of Gilwern Hill near Ty Cerrig cottage as per *Access route R*

Segment 15 (2 miles): Ascend Gilwern Hill (easy-moderate) to the Lamb and Fox at Pwlldu as *per Access route Q*

Segment 16 (2 miles): From the Lamb & Fox follow the road to the Keepers pond and descend the B 4246 road to the Ironworks as per *Access routes S-W.*

Riding into Grosmont ▼

View riding along Skirrid lane ▼

View riding along top of Campstone ▼

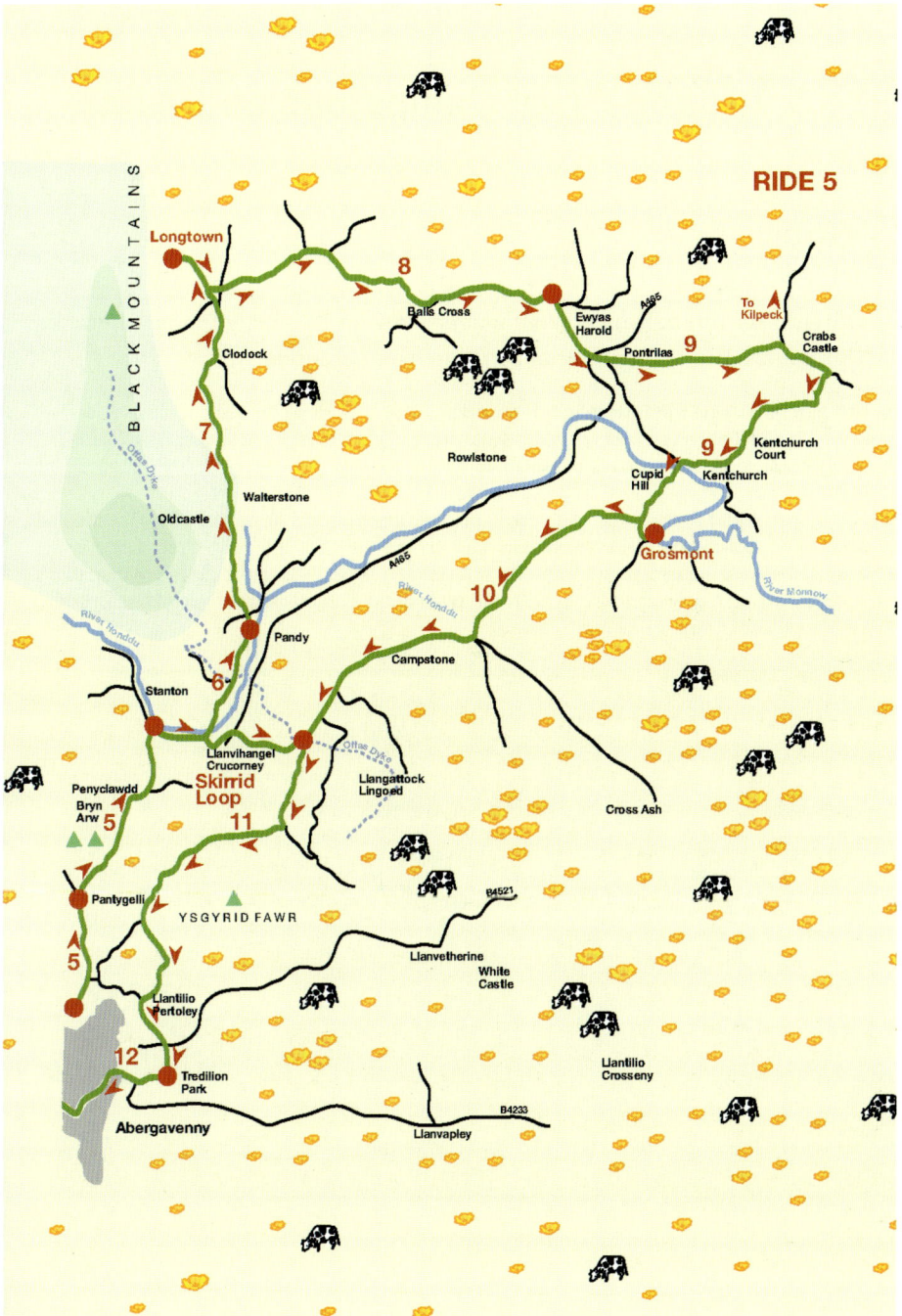

RIDE 5

BLACK MOUNTAINS

Longtown

8

Balls Cross

Clodock

Ewyas Harold

A465

To Kilpeck

Crabs Castle

Pontrilas

9

7

Rowlstone

9

Kentchurch Court

Walterstone

Cupid Hill

Kentchurch

Oldcastle

Offa's Dyke

A465

River Honddu

Grosmont

River Monnow

River Honddu

Pandy

10

Campstone

6

Stanton

Llanvihangel Crucorney

Offa's Dyke

Penyclawdd Bryn Arw

5

Skirrid Loop

Llangattock Lingoed

Cross Ash

11

Pantygelli

YSGYRID FAWR

B4521

5

Llanvetherine

White Castle

Llantilio Pertholey

Llantilio Crosseny

12

Tredilion Park

Abergavenny

Llanvapley

B4233

Ride 6: Around Great Campstone and White Castle

The Ride

A leisurely ride through rural Monmouthshire with its ancient inns, churches and Norman castles that have changed little over centuries.

The first part of the ride from Blaenafon Ironworks to Pandy is along the same route as Ride 5 – descending the Llanellen or Llanover valleys and crossing Offers Dyke path near Llanvihangel Crucorney on the edge of the Black mountains.

The ride loops around towards the east near Pandy, not far from the junction of the Honddu and Monnow rivers, ascending a narrow tarmac lane to the top of a hill near Great Campstone. There are some amazing panoramic views from this high plateau; the imposing Black mountains dominate the western side contrasting with the undulating borderlands between Herefordshire and Monmouthshire towards the north east.

Route Information

Start and Finish:

Blaenafon Ironworks

Distance/ Ride Time

Distance: 44 miles, Ride Time 5 hours

Alternative Two-Castle route: Distance 58 miles, Ride Time 5 ½ hours

Energy Level

***
**** alternative return route

How easy is the Ride

A medium distance, moderate but not difficult ride with plenty of flat and up-down sections, moderate and gentle climbs with a couple of short steep bits. Ride via alternative Two-Castle route avoids Gilwern Hill ascent but is a longer ride.

What sort of terrain

Virtually all tarmac minor roads with exception of grass stony mountain tracks over Garn-yr-erw (alternative access route).

Off-road Grade
G1/G3

The next section is an easy laid back ride through country lanes far from the madding crowd and far from any sign of urban life. Through the picturesque ancient parish of Llangattoc Lingoed the reputed homeland of Henry Morgan the famous Welsh Buccaneer; St Cadoc's Church and the Hunters Moon date back to the 12/13C.   The ride from here through Bont to White castle follows a patchwork of minor country roads criss-crossing hills and dales in a never ending rural landscape.   This is a very secluded part of Monmouthshire with nothing but scattered farms, rolling hills, pastureland and complete silence.

The Norman castle is not white but still retains much of its former architectural splendour rising up on a small hill in a show of strength and power. The Normans were not the only ones to defend the borderlands; the path of the earlier Saxon Dyke also skirts along the side of White castle.

From the castle there is a fast descent down towards the village of Llantilio Crossenny just above the river Trothy; its ancient church and rural setting looks like a scene from centuries past.   The route back to Abergavenny follows a section of a quiet B road through Llanvaply parish, linking up with a lane through Tredillion park north of Little Skirrid (Ysgyryd Fach).

An easy Sustrans route around Abergavenny castle along the meadows bank of the river Usk crossing through the Cutting to join the cycleway at Llanfoist   The route along the old railway track through Govilon links up with the mountain lane ascending the west side of Gilwern Hill above the spectacular Clydach valley through Pwlldu descending the other side of the hill to the Ironworks.

There is also an option to try out a slightly longer ride taking in Raglan castle and returning along an easier southern route through Bettwys Newydd and Chainbridge to the canal towpath joining up with the cycleway to Blaenafon at Pontypool.

White Castle Moat ▼

Heritage Interest Along Route

Garn-yr- erw mountain: moon like landscape caused by open-casting in the 1940/50s era; remains of Hill pits on south side

Dyne Steels Incline Pwlldu: former cable operated inclined railroad on north (Pwlldu) and south (Blaenafon) sides of Garn-yr-erw mountain; used in 19C for early transport of minerals between Blaenafon Ironworks and Pwlldu; supplemented tunnel route under Garn mountain.

Keepers pond (Pen-fford-goch pond): named after Keepers cottage now a popular sightseeing spot on top of Blorenge; originally used as a feeder during 19C for Garnderys Forge

Foxhunter car park: commemorates nearby grave of Lt. Col. Harry Llewelyn's famous Olympic show jumping horse Foxhunter (1940-59)

Skirrid Inn Llanvihangel Crucorney: Reputed to be one of the oldest Inns in Wales although present building thought to date from 17C; there was a courtroom and prison cell inside: St Michaels church is close by.

Llangattoc Lingoad: 13C Hunters Moon Inn and very impressive 12C church; Henry Morgan the famous 17C buccaneer is reputed to have hailed from these parts.

Offa's Dyke: path of the famous Saxon dyke can be seen near Llanvihangel Crucorney and White castle

White Castle: early 12C built by Normans and includes inner and outer wards; part of the three-castle complex to protect northern Gwent; substantially refortified in 13C; impressive remains with outer wall and moat around inner ward; under responsibility of CADW.

Llantilio Crossenny church: imposing grey stone building dating from the 12C; in the midst of stunning rural landscape

Llanvapley church: just off the B road opposite the old Red Hart Inn

Abergavenny: see Towns & Canal section

Section of Abergavenny-Merthyr railway: built in 1862 and opened by Ironmaster Crawshay Bailey; closed 1958; Govilon station still recognisable; Govilon Llanvihangel tramway predates the railway

Pwlldu Tunnels: the tramroad route between Blaenafon Ironworks and Pwlldu went through a tunnel almost one and a half miles long under Garn mountain; tunnel portal can be seen on side of road just below former Welfare Hall

Pwlldu: a one time bustling village built for iron and coal workers but demolished in sixties; there were two terraced rows of houses, two pubs, a shop and, chapel, now all that remains is welfare hall (outdoor centre) and Lamb & Fox Inn.

Inns Along Route

Whistle Inn	Garn-yr-erw
Lamb and Fox	Pwlldu
The Skirrid Inn	Llanvihangel Crucorny
The Pandy Inn	Pandy
Park Hotel	Pandy
Hunters Moon	Llangattoc Lingoad
Bridge Inn	Llanfoist
Riflemans Arms	Blaenafon

The Route

See section "Bike Access Routes" for description and maps of access routes from and to Blaenafon, reference the route segments at beginning and end of ride.

The first part of the Ride from Blaenafon Ironworks to just outside Pandy is along the same route as Segments 1-6 of the previous Ride 5

Segments 1-6 (17 miles): Follow segments 1-6 of Ride 5

Segment 7 (just under 3 ½ miles): Turn right at the Longtown-Pandy road junction crossing another bridge over the Honddu proceeding up to the junction of the main Hereford road near the Pandy Inn. Cross over the Hereford road joining the minor road on the opposite side; go along Glanhonddu Close and past the Park Hotel before starting a one and half mile climb up to the tee-junction at the top which is about a hundred metres above valley floor (near Wern-

gounsel farm). It is a moderate climb up with just a couple of low gear steep bits at the bottom.

Turn right at the tee-junction. Superb panoramic views all around including Hondu valley, Black mountains, Skirrid mountain, Monnow valley, and rolling borderlands of Monmouthshire and Herefordshire,.

Proceed along this road for quarter mile, turn left at the next junction sign-posted to Llangatoc Lingoed. A gentle descent for just over half mile to a bridge at bottom and then a short climb and flat section into the picturesque village of Llangattoc Lingoed.

Segment 8 (5 ¼ miles): At Llangattoc Lingoed pass by the church and the the thirteenth century Inn the Hunters Moon. Follow the minor road around bearing right at top of small hill and then forking left after about quarter mile.

There are some gentle and moderate (not difficult) climbs since the road crosses two shallow valleys. Bear right at the junction with the Old Inn (house), and continue through Bont up to the next tee-junction which is about 2 miles from Llangattoc Lingoed. Bear right at this junction (signposted to Llanvetherine) and continue for quarter mile up to next junction.

[From this point it is theoretically possible to take a dirt track leading to the B 4521 (Skenfrith road) and then to White castle, but unfortunately the track has become sunken and waterlogged virtually impassable and not recommended.]

Turn left at this junction and continue for another half mile up to the junction with the B 4521. Turn right on to the B road (very little traffic) and after a mile turn left at the White Castle signpost following this minor road right into White castle.

Segment 9 (8 ¾ miles): From White castle descend the minor road for just under one and half miles up to the junction of the old Monmouth road (B 4232). Cross over and take the road almost opposite leading to the 12C church at Llantilio Crossenny.

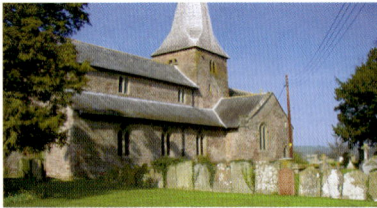

From the church follow the road down through the village of Llantilio Crossenny as far as the

minor road junction near Hostry House (used to be the Hostry Inn). The minor road straight ahead soon joins the old Monmouth road. The minor road left heads south towards Raglan.

There is an option to do a longer ride via Raglan Castle returning to Blaenafon Ironworks via Pontypool. This alternative loop starts from this junction. If you want to try this alternative two-castle ride turn left at this junction and follow the route description for Two Castle Ride given at end of this section.

To continue the main ride from the Hostry junction keep straight ahead returning back to the old Monmouth road. Turn left heading towards Abergavenny arriving at Llanvapley village after about two miles.

Llanvapley church is on right just opposite the location of the old Red Hart Inn which is now a private residence. Go through Llanvapley, make a half mile climb (moderate) and after about a mile turn right on to a minor road near a sign "Emmas Field" just after a postbox on the left hand side of the old Monmouth road.

Continue on this minor road with the Skirrid ahead and towards the right. Good views all around. Pass by Werngochlyn farm and continue up to junction of another minor road near Tredillion fruit farm (which is a little over two miles from the junction of Emmas field). Cross over this minor road and continue a descent southwards on a lane for about a mile, passing by the Golf course on the right as far as Tredillion Court House on the left.

Segment 10 (just over 1 ½ miles): From Tredilion Court house follow the lane down passing under the railway bridge crossing over the Gaveny river bridge up to the junction with

Skenfrith road in Abergavenny. Turn left and left again at the four castle cycleway sign on to old Ross road. Continue along Old Ross road turn left at the junction with Old Monk street and proceed to mini-roundabout. (From now on follow the Sustrans cycleway signs)

Segment 11 (1 mile): At the mini roundabout on Old Monk street turn right on to Holywell road and continue to the junction of the A40T road. Cross over the main road near the Abergavenny Hotel, keep straight ahead turning on to Mill street estate through the access gate.

At the end of Mill street turn left below Abergavenny castle near a water wheel (heritage monument) and follow path down to the triangular Sustrans cycleway signpost (Bank of Scotland provided black signpost). Pass through the nearby gate leading to Castle meadows and follow the cycleway track along the banks of the Usk to Llanfoist road bridge. Cross over the bridge and proceed to the nearby Waitrose roundabout.

Segment 12 (½ mile) From the Waitrose roundabout follow the route back through The Cutting to Llanfoist Crossing car park as per *Segment 3 of this ride.*

Segment 13 (3 miles): Continue along the cycleway through Govilon and on to the three way junction just at bottom of Gilwern Hill near Ty Cerrig cottage as per *Access route R*

Segment 14 (2 miles): Ascend Gilwern Hill to the Lamb and Fox at Pwlldu as per *Access route Q*

Segment 15 (2 miles): From the Lamb & Fox follow the road to the Keepers pond and descend the B 4246 road to the Ironworks as per *Access route S-W.*

Optional Two-Castle Ride

From Llantilio Crossenny there is an option to take an alternative route south to Raglan Castle returning through Bettwys Newydd and Chainbridge joining the canal just near Penperlleni. From here it is an easy 5 mile ride along the canal towpath to Pontypool followed by a relatively easy 10 mile ride along the railway line cycle-way to Blaenafon Ironworks. Be aware there is a steep half mile climb up Clytha Hill before descending to Bettwys Newydd The energy grade for this relatively long ride is high (****). The round trip distance is 58 miles.

Route: From the Hostry junction at Llantilio Crossenny (segment 9 above) take the minor road (lane) left and follow this around for about three and half miles up to the cross roads just near Tregare. Keep straight ahead (south) and follow this lane for two miles. Good views of Raglan castle on the left. The lane leads directly to the A40 Raglan roundabout [To access Raglan castle either proceed a short way down the dual carriageway a short distance and take the sign-posted entrance on the left or alternatively go through Raglan village turn left at the church and proceed to the dual carriageway crossing just opposite the castle access. It is an allowed cross over point but there are no pedestrian lights.]

To continue the ride from Raglan follow the route for Ride 7 segments 6, 5 and part of segment 4 (in reverse direction) via Bettwys Newydd to Chain Bridge. On the other side of the Bridge take the minor road west towards Nantyderry turning left at the first crossroads a short distance away. Follow this minor road through to the junction of the A4042 at Goitre village. Cross over to the lane directly ahead and continue a short way to the canal bridge. Follow the canal towpath to Pontypool joining the Sustrans cycleway over the railway line just near Griffithtown Hospital. Continue along the cycleway to Blaenafon Ironworks (see Ride 11 Mamhilad to Pontypool to Blaenafon).

Above Llanfihangel towards Ewyas Vale ▲

Riding through Llanfihangel Crucorny ▼

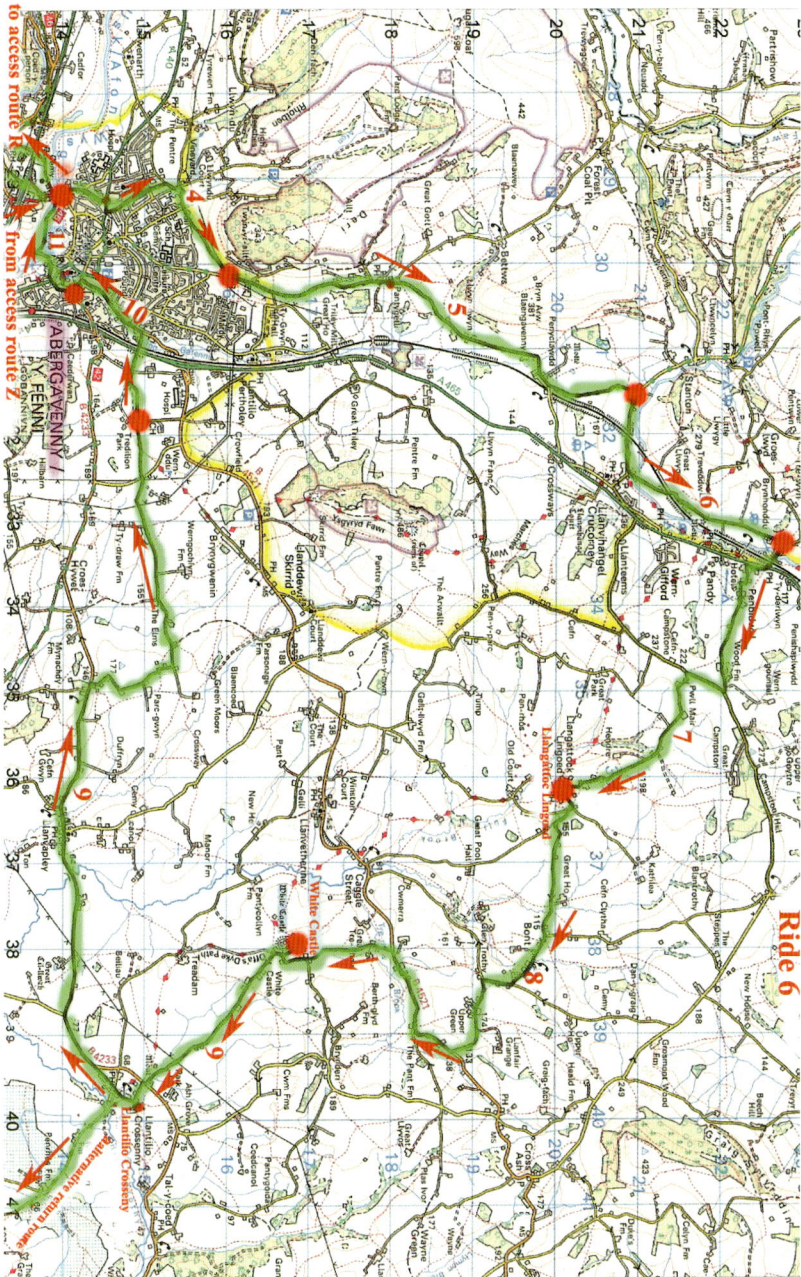

Ride 7: Around Raglan Castle and Llanarth

The Ride

Another relaxing summertime bike ride around castles, manors and forts that date back to the iron-age and Norman periods; ride through the ancient land of medieval Lords, Barons and Bishops

The ride begins from the Ironworks along the north-east access route over the open moorlands of Garn Fawr dropping down through the wooded slopes of Upper Llanover to Pencroesoped in the Usk valley below.

The route then continuous along a quiet tarmac lane that crosses over the canal winding its way through hedgerows and fields to the junction of the Nantederry lane not far from Upper Hendre.

<table>
<tr><td colspan="2" align="center">**Route Information**</td></tr>
<tr><td>**Start and Finish**</td><td>**How easy is the Ride**</td></tr>
<tr><td>Blaenafon Ironworks</td><td>Loop B: Moderate: most of ride is fairly easy going but there are several hills to negotiate;</td></tr>
<tr><td>**Distance/ Ride Time**</td><td>Loop A: Moderate: shorter and fewer hills to negotiate</td></tr>
<tr><td>Distance:
Via Loop A 27 ¼ miles: Via Loop B 37 miles</td><td>Ride ends with moderate ascent around Gilwern Hill</td></tr>
<tr><td>Ride Time:
Via Loop A 4 ½ hours; Via Loop B 5 ½ hours</td><td>**What sort of terrain**</td></tr>
<tr><td>**Energy Level**</td><td>Virtually all tarmac lanes</td></tr>
<tr><td>***</td><td>**Off-road Grade**
Not applicable</td></tr>
</table>

From here there is an option to try out a shorter loop via Pant-y-Goitre to Llanarth or alternatively do the longer more interesting ride through Bettws Newydd looping back to Llanarth at Raglan castle.

The shorter Loop A ride passes through Cross Llanfair joining the Usk road just near Pant-y-Goitre and not far from the old church of Llanfair Kilgeddin where there is some interesting Arts and Craft wall decoration.

From here the route passes over the stone-arched Pant-y-Goitre bridge following the river Usk along a minor road towards Clytha park. There is a short section of B road just near the access to Llansantfraed Court Hotel before joining the minor Llanarth road through very attractive rural countryside as far as Pit Clytha just near the imposing access to Llanarth Court.

The longer Loop B ride passes through the small parish of Nantyderry crossing over a wide section of the river Usk at Chainbridge – an impressive structure with green iron girders but no chains. From here there is a steep climb up to the parish of Bettys Newydd and then another climb up Clytha Hill to the ancient but still recognisable iron-age fort of Coed Bynydd.

There are superb views of rolling countryside from the top of Clytha hill towards Llanarth and Llantilio Crossenny in the north. A nice easy descent down the other side of Clytha Hill and then a fairly flat stretch along a tarmac lane between hedgerows and open fields, descending down into Raglan after a few miles.

Raglan Castle ▼

The ride loops around at Raglan and follows a tarmac lane towards the north, where there are some exceptional views of the medieval castle whose massive stone structure stands out in stark contrast to the surrounding green countryside; even today it still exudes an aura of power and strength.

The route heads west about two miles north of the castle not far from Tregare continuing through the quiet hamlet of Bryngwyn and then Great Oak where the large and splendid Llanarth Court (now a Hospital) can be seen in the distance through the surrounding parkland. The tarmac lane sweeps around the perimeter of Llanarth Court parkland through Pit Clytha to join a minor road just near the impressive stone entrance to the Court.

The ride continues past the church in Llanarth village, criss-crossing rolling countryside to the parish of Llandewi Rhydirch where it joins Sustrans route 42 along a tarmac lane to the old Monmouth B road. It is not long before the seven hills surrounding Abergavenny begin to appear in the distance and soon there is a fast and exhilarating descent down into the town. The route around Abergavenny castle and along castle meadows leads to the village of Llanfoist just below the historic canal wharf.

From here the return ride follows the northern access route to Blaenafon climbing the west side of Gilwern Hill above the Clydach Gorge through Pwlldu descending the other side of the hill to the Ironworks.

Riding around Llanarth Park ▼

Heritage Interest Along Route

Chainbridge (Pont Kemeys): Built in 1906 it has curved iron girders; it replaced an earlier bridge that was supported by chains. The original Chain bridge was erected beginning of 19C and had replaced an earlier oak bridge.

Pant-y-goitre (Llanfair Kilgeddin) bridge: early 19C handsome stone bridge spanning the Usk with three elliptical arches

Llanfair Kilgeddin church: attractive church with unusual internal wall decoration

Bettwys Newydd church: very attractive grey stone building dating from Norman times – opposite Alice Springs golf course entrance

Coed Bynydd: site of an early iron-age fort with very visible banks and ditches: Near-by Clytha Castle and park

Raglan Castle: built in 15C on site of Norman castle – flamboyant display of strength and power - although battered by Cromwell in civil war it is still in really good shape and dominates the surrounding landscape

Bryngwyn St Peters church: local sandstone construction; parts inside date from from 13C

Llanarth Court: erected around 1770 on site of former house that was part of Manor of Llanarth in Norman times (Bradney): Llanarth Park laid out in 1792 by Samual Lapidge in Capability Brown style; now a hospital

Llanarth Church: on south end of village probably dating from 16C

Abergavenny: see Towns & Canal

Section of Abergavenny-Merthyr railway: built in 1862 and opened by Ironmaster Crawshay Bailey; closed 1958; Govilon station still recognisable; Govilon Llanvihangel tramway predates the railway

Pwlldu: a one time bustling village built for iron and coal workers but demolished in sixties; there were two terraced rows of houses, two pubs, a shop and, chapel, now all that remains is welfare hall (outdoor centre) and Lamb & Fox Inn: Pwlldu tramroad tunnel portal can be seen near road just below Welfare Hall

Keepers pond (Pen-fford-goch pond): named after Keepers cottage now a popular sightseeing spot on top of Blorenge; originally used as a feeder during 19C for Garnderys Forge

103

The Route

Inns Along Route

Pottery	Blaenafon
Goose & Cuckoo	Llanover
Foxhunter	Nantyderry
Chainbridge Inn	Kemys
Black bear	Bettws Newydd
Village Inns	Raglan
Bridge Inn	Llanfoist
Lamb and Fox	Pwlldu
Riflemans Arms	Blaenafon

See section "Bike Access Routes" for description and maps of access routes from and to Blaenafon, reference the route segments at beginning and end of ride.

Segment 1 (2 ¼ miles): From Blaenafon Ironworks take the north-east cycle exit route along Llanover road as far as the second cattle grid as *per Access route X-Y.*

Segment 2 (3 miles): Turn right at the cattle grid go through a gate leading to a 2 meter compacted dirt track. [Note this track belongs to the Forestry Commission who have allowed the track to be used as a public footpath].

After a quarter of a mile cross over a style and then follow the track down for about half a mile up to a junction where it continues straight ahead and another track bends around to the left.

This is also the junction of the old Llanover to Cwmavon Parish road which can be seen going north and south at the junction of Forestry tracks. Take either the Parish road (stony track not easy to ride) going south or the easy descending Forestry track to the left. Both routes arrive at the same point.

After about half a mile both the the Forestry track and parish road join a tarmac lane just above the Goose and Cuckoo Inn (cross style on Forrestry track).

From the Goose and Cuckoo descend the hill for just under half mile and take first turning right (watch out for it). Follow the tarmac lane through a very attractive part of Llanover for just over a mile up to the junction with the Mamhilad minor road at Pencroesoped.

Segment 3 (3 miles): From this junction turn left and immediate right go over the canal bridge; follow this tarmac lane for half a mile up to junction of the busy A4042. Cross over to another lane on opposite side; continue along the tarmac lane as far as the junction with a minor road near Upper Hendre close to a railway Bridge.

From this junction choose either the shorter Loop A ride or the main Loop B ride around Raglan castle

Loop A: Upper Hendre to Llanarth (3 ¾ miles): Turn left at this minor road junction (near road bridge over railway) and continue in a northern direction for just over 1 ½ miles (keeping straight ahead at Cross Llanfair) up to the junction with the Usk road near Pant-y-Goitre bridge.

Turn left, cross over bridge, turn right and follow minor road up to the junction with the A 40. Turn right and after a short distance turn left on to the minor road sign-posted to Llanarth.

Follow this minor road up to the junction with the Pit Lane. The entrance to Llanarth Court (now Hospital) can be seen just ahead. This completes Loop A. Continue the ride at Segment 8,

Loop B: Upper Hendre to Llanarth via Raglan (13 ½ miles)

Segment 4 (3 ¼ miles): Turn right at this minor road junction (near road bridge over railway), bear left after about half mile and follow this minor road into the village of Nantyderry. Picturesque stone cottages and Foxhunter restaurant on right. Go over the railway bridge follow lane for about a mile keeping straight ahead at the crossroads. Follow the lane a short distance into Chainbridge.

Chainbridge Inn is on bank of river Usk adjacent to Bridge. Pass over the bridge and take immediate left on to a tarmac lane sign-posted to Bettwys Newydd. A moderate to steep climb for about three quarters of a mile leads to the village of Bettwys Newydd. There is a Motte and Baily on the hill just above the village but you need to look for it. The church is just along the road from the Black Bear Inn and just opposite the Golf course.

Segment 5 (4 ¼ miles): From the Black Bear Inn proceed along the lane in the same direction (roughly north east) make a short climb, bear left and continue the climb up Clytha Hill. The wooded mound of Coed y Bwnydd stands out clearly on the left.

Almost at the top of the hill a stile and signpost marks the access to the site of the Coed y Bwnydd Iron-age hill fort. Well worth a look. Descend the other side of hill keeping left at the road fork. Good panoramic views at the high point but unfortunately Clytha Castle obscured by trees.

After about a one mile descent, turn right at the junction and continue on this lane towards the east (easy riding) for almost one and half mile. Raglan castle and Raglan village will soon be seen in the distance. At the junction near Castle View farm fork left and continue down to the Usk road junction.
.

Segment 6 (3 miles): At the Usk road junction turn left in direction towards Raglan (sign posted Cycleway 30). To visit Raglan village take the right hand turn-off after about a mile. Raglan village still retains lots of character - three pubs, church and old Courthouse. To access the castle turn left at the church and proceed to the dual carriageway crossing just opposite the castle access. (It is an allowed pedestrian cross over point but there are no pedestrian lights - take care)

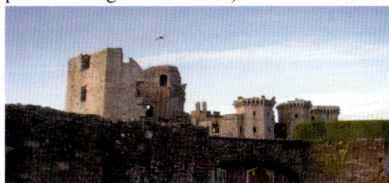

Continuing the ride from the castle proceed to the A40 roundabout and take the second exit on the B4598 (towards Abergavenny). Go a couple of hundred yards on the B4598 and then turn right on to a tarmac lane sign-posted to Llantilio Crossenny. This is a beautiful two mile stretch with superb views of Raglan castle standing in the midst of rolling countryside.
Continue on the lane up to the crossroads near Tregare.

Segment 7 (3 miles): At this crossroads turn left heading west, continue for about a mile to Bryngwyn forking right near the church. After a short distance turn left and then right at the tee-junction. Continue on the lane through Great

Oak up to the next tee junction just on the boundary of Llanarth Court park.

Good views of Llanarth Court and surrounding parkland..   Follow the lane around for about mile westwards through the Pit up to the tee-junction of the minor road to Llanarth.   This completes Loop 2.   Continue the ride at Segment 8 below.

Segment 8 (just over 3 ½ miles): At the Llanarth road junction continue northwards towards Llanarth village passing the Llanarth court gatehouse (St Michaels Catholic church) on the right.

Follow this minor road for just under a mile into Llanarth village with St Tilio Church on the right.

Stay on the minor road for just under a mile and then turn left on to a lane sign posted to Coed Morgan.   Follow for over a mile up to tee junction signposted left to Coed Morgan and straight ahead to Llandewi Rhydderch village.

Continue west on the lane which is now signposted as Sustrans route 42 into the village of Llandewi Rhydderch..

Segment 9 (just under 3 ½ miles): Bear right through the village and then turn left just outside

the village following the Sustrans route 42 sign. Climb up the hill to the junction of the B 4233 (old Monmouth road).

Turn left towards the west and follow this road which continues to climb for another half mile before beginning a fast and long descent into Abergavenny.

Good views of the hills around Abergavenny; the two Skirrids towards north, Rholben, Dewi Allt, and Llanwenerth more or less ahead, and the Blorenge towards the left.   The old Monmouth road eventually terminates at a mini-roundabout at the junction of Lower Monk street and Holywell road .

Segment 10 (1 mile) From the mini- roundabout take the route around Abergavenny castle

and the meadows to the Waitrose roundabout as described in *Ride 6 segment 11.*

Segment 11 (½ mile) From the Waitrose roundabout follow the route back through The Cutting to Llanfoist Crossing car park *as per Route through Llanfoist*

Segment 12 (3 miles):   Continue along cycleway through Govilon and on to the three way junction just at bottom of Gilwern Hill near Ty Cerrig cottage as *per Access route R*
.
Segment 13 (2 miles): Gently ascend Gilwern Hill to the Lamb and Fox at Pwlldu as per *Access route Q*

Segment 14 (2 miles): From the Lamb & Fox follow the road to the Keepers pond and descend the B 4246 road to the Ironworks *as per Access route S-W.*

Over Chainbridge▼

Riding towards Tregare from Raglan ▼

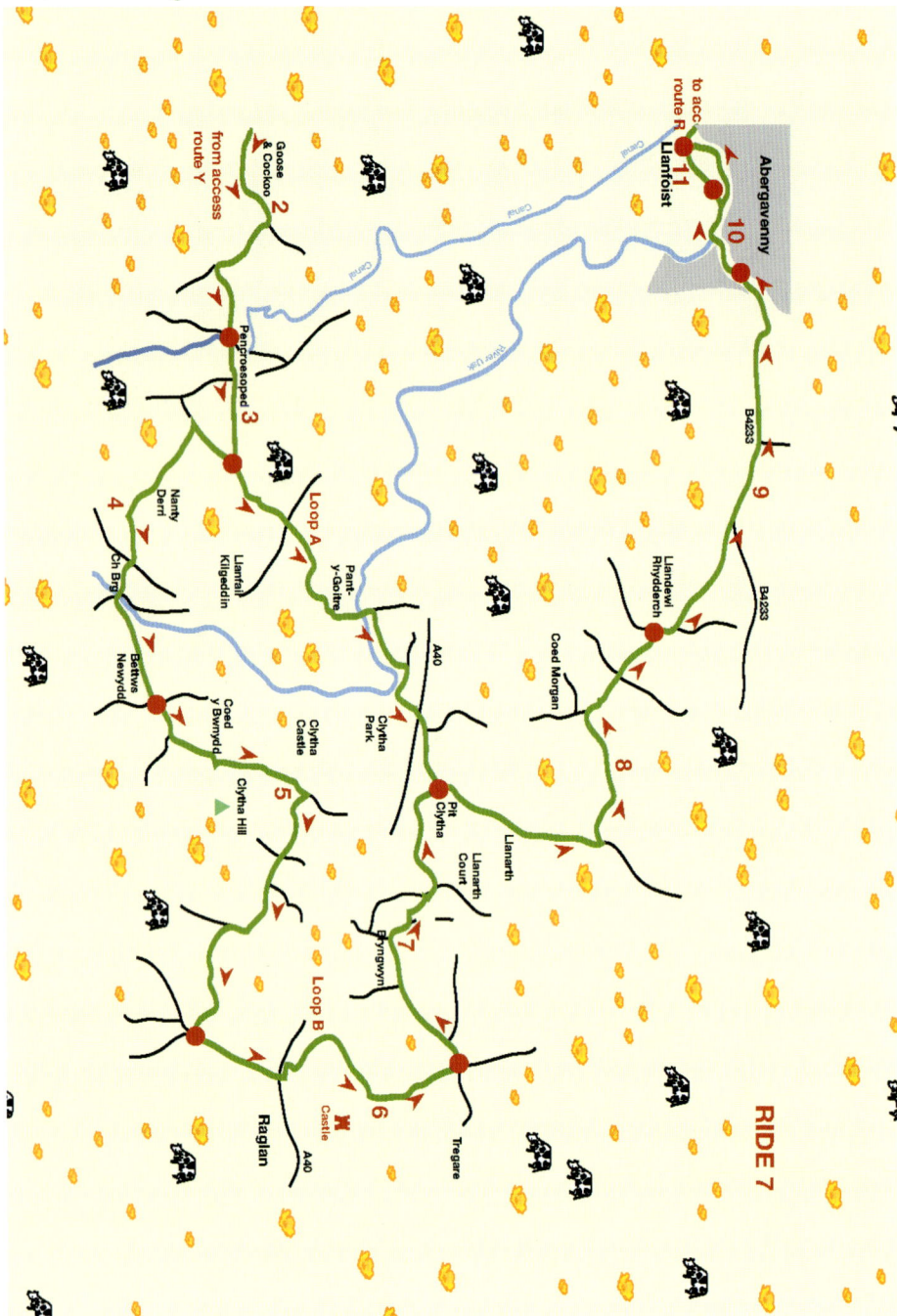

RIDE 7

Ride 8 Through the Vale of Usk to Llandegfedd Reservoir

The Ride

A scenic ride through the rural heartland of south-east Gwent. Easy cycling along the flatlands of the lower Usk valley looping back around at Llandegfedd reservoir. An opportunity to try out alternative routes between Usk and Llandegfedd.

Route Information

Start and Finish

Blaenafon Ironworks

Distance/ Ride Time

Distance:
Via Loop A 32 ½ miles; Via Loop B 42 miles

Ride Time
Via loop A 3 ½ hours; Via Loop B 4 ½ hours

Energy Level

Loop A **
Loop B ***

Off-road Grade
 G1

How easy is the Ride

Moderate but plenty of easy, flat and descending sections through the Usk valley; gentle easy ascent along railway track into Blaenafon. A couple of short steep climbs to negotiate around the Llandegfedd area particularly for Loop B but less so for Loop A.

What sort of terrain

Virtually all minor tarmac lanes with some B-road sections; off-road dirt track between Llandegfedd Village and Coed-y-paen (Loop B). Long section of off-road cycleway Blaenafon-Pontypool

---

The ride begins from the Ironworks along the north-east access route over the open moorlands of Garn Fawr dropping down through the wooded slopes of Upper Llanover to Pencroesoped in the Usk valley below.

The next section is really easy going, cycling idly along virtually flat country lanes through Chainbridge and then along the quiet B road that follows the river into the town of Usk. Nothing but lime green fields, hardwood trees, grassy tumps, rounded mounds, and distant mountain ridges.

Riding along these country lanes at 15 mph is never visually boring. The landscape may seem to linger forever and a day, but each time you turn a corner the whole scene changes in shape, form and colour. If time permits there is also an iron-age hill fort to look at on a hill near the village of Llancayo on the road to Usk.

Loop A routes through the town of Usk and over the stone arched bridge to the village of Llanbadoc a short distance away. There is a two to three mile gentle-moderate ascent mostly mid-gear from Llanbadoc to the top of the hill near the Golf course that overlooks the reservoir. From here it is an easy going scenic ride sweeping around the north side of the reservoir towards Glascoed village and then westwards towards the residential outskirts of New Inn.

Llandegfedd Reservoir ▼

Loop B is an alternative longer route along minor roads and country lanes that follows the river Usk down a wide flat and open section of the valley through the village of Llantrisant to the small and picturesque hamlet of Newbridge-on-Usk.

From here it circles back through Llangybi village and along a country lane up hill and down dale through secluded rural countryside with occasional glimpses of the lower Usk valley towards Caerleon.

It is a roller coaster ride into the village of Llandegfedd which is the start of a good off-road section through open fields ending with a superb descent through a densely wooded forest and a short tarmac lane section into Coed-y-paen village.

From Coed-y-paen the ride is along a minor road around the south perimeter of the reservoir which looks like a spectacular natural lake trapped between the the hills. The reservoir is also a centre for outdoor leisure activities such as sail boating and fishing. Leaving the reservoir there is a short but strenuous low gear climb before dropping down into the outskirts of New Inn.

The final leg back to the Ironworks is over an easy eight mile stretch of the old Blaenafon-Pontypool railway track that is now part of Sustrans cycle-way route 46.

Heritage Interest Along Route

Usk & Pontypool: see Town & Canal section

Capel Newydd: Iron Cross marking site of early 16C chapel (Capel Newydd); nearby is Blaenafon – Pontnewenydd early mule- pack track used at start of Ironworks

Llancayo Windmill: tapering tower visible from B 4598; early 19C but sails and machinery are gone.

Llancayo Hillfort: very impressive remains of iron age fort with triple banks and ditches; turn off B 4598 not far from Llancayo windmill continue along this lane towards Trostrey for a mile watch out for an unsigned track through gate near stream on the right; this leads to the iron-age campsite

Llangybi Castle: ruins of large medieval 14C castle; historians conclude castle was abandoned unfinished although it was occupied in 17C holding out against Cromwell's forces

Llandegfedd reservoir: largest reservoir in county completed in 1966 to supply Cwmbran with water. The road is over the Dam on south side.

Griffithstown Railway Museum: history of the Monmouthshire railway with lots of memorabilia; located just off the Sustrans route 46 cycleway (railway track-bed)

Pontypool Blaenafon high level railway; at the Pontypool end the high level line joined the low level line at Trevethin junction ; from here the Mon Railway & Canal company extended the line in 1876 to Talywaun which was later extended to Blaenafon by the LNWR (London & North West railway company); the line crosses the massive Ffrwd valley viaduct at Talywaun; it is now a superb tarmac cycleway (Sustrans route 46);

Loop A Over Usk Bridge ▼

Loop B Riding towards Newbridge-on-Usk from Llantrissant ▼

Inns Along Route

The Pottery	Blaenafon
Goose & Cuckoo	Llanover
Goetre Arms	Goetre
Chainbridge Inn	Chainbridge
Three Salmons Inn	Usk
New Court Inn	Usk
Greyhound	Llantrissant
NewbrdgHotel	Newbrdg-on-Usk
White Hart Inn	Llangybi
Farmers Arms	Llandegfedd
Carpenters Arms	Coed-y-Paen

The Route

See section "Bike Access Routes" for description and maps of access routes from and to Blaenafon, reference the route segments at beginning and end of ride.

Segment 1 (2 ¼ miles): From Blaenafon Ironworks take the north-east cycle exit route along Llanover road as far as the second cattle grid as per *Access route X-Y.*

Segment 2 (3 miles): From the second cattle-grid on Llanover road take the route down through Llanover valley to Pencroesoped as per Ride 7 Segment 2.

Segment 3 (4 miles): From the junction at Pencroesoped turn right and continue south for about half a mile in direction towards Mamhilad; after passing the access to Goetre Wharf take the next unsigned turning left which is a single access lane. (just over a mile from Pencroesoped).

Continue down this lane and keep straight ahead at the cross roads a short distance away; cross over the canal bridge following the lane all the way to the junction of the A 4042 road in front of the Goetre Arms Inn. Cross over the A 4042 and take the minor road in the direction towards Chain Bridge. Superb views towards the south and west - the Folly above Pontypool can be clearly seen in the distance.

After about one and half miles turn right at the cross roads which leads on to the junction of the B4598 Usk road at Chain Bridge.

Segment 4 (3 ½ miles): Cross over Chain Bridge and follow the B road in the direction towards Usk passing by the Alice Springs Golf course, an old stone round tower (windmill without sails), and Llancayo village from where the B road continues to Usk as Sustrans cycle route 42 up to the junction at the Three Salmons Inn (the castle is on top of hill on the left).

There are two alternative scenic routes between Usk and around Llandefedd reservoir to New Inn. Try out either loop on a different day.

Loop A: Llanbadoc-Glascoed Loop

Segment A1 (2 ¾ miles): At the Three Salmons Inn junction turn right and follow the road through Usk town crossing over the Usk Bridge and turning left on to the minor road in the direction towards Caerleon. Follow this road for about a mile into Llanbadoc turning right on to a lane near the church and which is signposted as Cycleway 30 to Llandefedd reservoir.

It is a gentle to moderate (mainly mid gear) climb for about a mile up to a left-right fork which is sign-posted towards the right in the direction of the golf course and cycleway 30. Take the right fork and make a one mile moderate climb up to the junction with the Glascoed road. [if you wish to make a detour to the Carpenters Arms Coed-y-paen and access close to the reservoir bear left at this junction and follow the lane for just over a mile]

Segment A2 (3 ½ miles): At the junction with the Glascoed road turn right and continue on this minor road to the village of Glacoed. Good view of the reservoir from the Golf Course on left. At the crossroads in Glascoed village go straight ahead in direction towards Pontypool and Cwmbran.

The reservoir can occasionally be spotted amongst the hills towards the left. Follow this lane all the way around until it eventually joins with Jerusalem lane on the outskirts of New Inn. The first turning on the right off Jerusalem lane is Chester Close and the second turning is Golf road. Proceed to the Golf road junction and continue the ride to the canal as per segment 5 below.

.

Loop B: Newbridge-on-Usk - Coed-y-paen Loop

Segment B1 (3 ¼ miles): From the Three Salmons Inn junction at Usk cross over the road keeping straight ahead which is sign-posted Sustrans route 42. Keep on the Llantrisant road, pass by the New Court Inn and HMS prison on the outskirt of Usk.

It is a flat and easy ride down a wide part of the Usk valley through Llanllowell. Cross under the A449T road, pass by the Greyhound Inn Llantrissant, bear right at the turn-off to Llantrissant village, cross under the A449T road once again and continue to the village (church on left).

Segment B2 (1 ¾ miles) From Llantrissant village continue on a long flat section of road alongside the river Usk as far as the right hand turn-off to Newbridge-on-Usk (sign post missing). There are wide sweeping views down the valley and along Wentwood Ridge towards the south east. [*Ride 9 continues from this junction.*]

Turn right on this minor road and follow through to the picturesque village of Newbridge-on-Usk. The Newbridge Hotel is just near the bridge.

Segment B3 (2 ¼ miles): From Newbridge-on-Usk follow the road through Tredunnock (St Andrews church on right) as far as the GlanUsk-Llangybi crossroads. Turn right at the crossroads and after just under half a mile turn right at the junction of the Usk-Caerleon road and follow this road for about a mile into Llangybi village.

Segment B4 (2 ½ miles):.At Llangybi turn on to Ton road which is just opposite the White Hart Inn. Continue on this lane which is a bit up and down.for about 3 miles into Llandegfedd village. (Note that within this section there is one rather steep very low gear climb for about quarter mile.) The Farmers Arm inn at Llandegfedd village is just down the hill from the church.

Segment B5 (just over 2 ½ miles): From Llandegfedd village there is now an off-road section which starts just off the lane leading to Court Perrot near the church. Follow this stony track a short distance up to a track crossing and go straight ahead through the gate. Walk and part ride for about quarter mile turning left on to good flat grass-stone track which eventually winds around into a wooded section.

A superb ride over an excellent track through the Forest before joining a tarmac lane once again. Turn left at the junction with the tarmac lane and then left again; continue for about three quarters a mile into Coed-y-paen. The Carpenters Arms is just opposite the church near the junction.

Segment B6 (2 ¾ miles): From the Carpenters arms proceed to the T-junction, turn right and follow the lane towards the west keeping straight ahead bearing right at the next fork (sign-posted Cwmbran left). At the top of the rise there are wide spreading views towards the west above New Inn and Sebastopol in the valley below.

About half way down the hill there is a car park on the right overlooking the reservoir below. This is a good rest spot and the best location to view the reservoir.

Continue the ride down the hill passing by the jetty at the bottom. There follows a short steep (strenuous) low-low gear climb for about

quarter of a mile and then a fairly easy down-hill and flat ride up to the junction with Jerusalem Lane in New Inn. Turn right on to Jerusalem lane and follow the lane for just over half a mile up to the turn-off of Golf Road on the left. Continue at Segment 5.

Final Part of Ride from New Inn to Ironworks

Segment 5 (just under 2 miles): Descend Golf road for about half a mile down to the junction with the main Pontypool-New Inn road (The Highway). Turn left on to the Highway and after a short distance turn right (sign-posted Panteg Public hall with Disability Advice Project shop on corner) down toward the Polo Grounds.

Continue on this link road passing the rugby grounds on left and crossing over the Avon Lwyd river, the railway line and the new A4042T road. Watch out for the Sustrans cycle-way route 46 signpost just after the new road-bridge crossing and turn right on to the cycleway. Follow the cycleway along the old railway path crossing over the junction of Stafford road and continuing along route 46 up to the junction with the Cwmynyscoy roundabout just outside Pontypool.

Segment 6 (1 ½ miles) From Cwmnyscoy roundabout follow the purpose built and well signed cycleway (Sustrans route 46) around the south side of Pontypool as far as the small road crossing just near Pontnewynydd. This is the start of the old railway track route to Blaenafon.

Segment 7 (just under 8 miles): Follow the tarmac cycleway along the old railway track through Talywaun and Varteg to Blaeanfon as per *south-east access route*

.

Defensive ditches Llancayo Hill Fort near Usk ▼

Loop B   Just outside Newbridge-on-Usk ▼

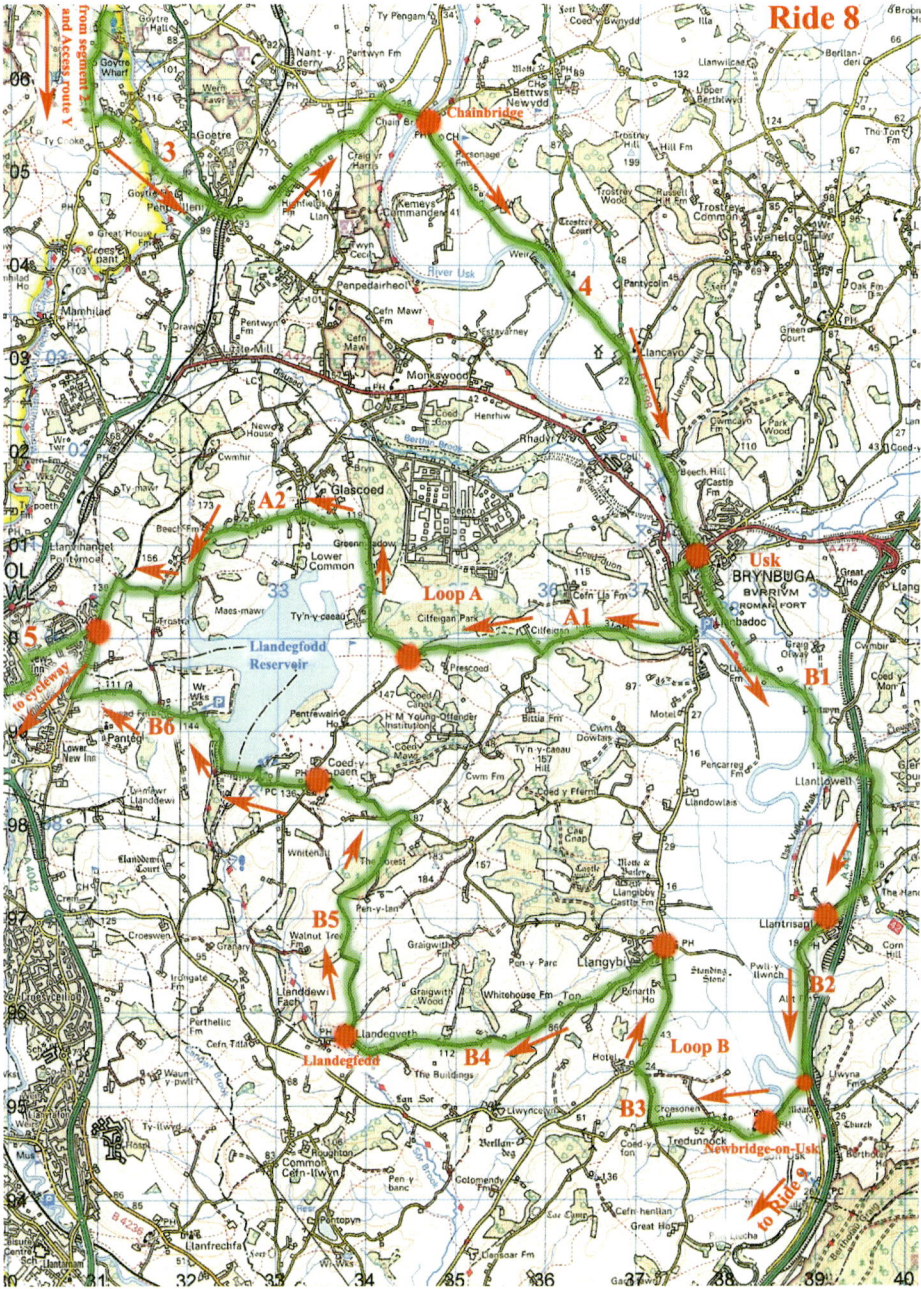

Ride 9: Newport Coastal Plain and Caerleon Loops

The Ride

A fabulous ride down the lower Usk valley looping back through the Caldicot Levels just above the Sea Wall. Blaenafon may be 1000 feet above sea level but here is a 50 mile plus traffic-free ride that is almost flat and descending from start to finish. It is the longest ride in the series graded as relatively easy.

The first part of the ride from Blaenafon Ironworks follows the same route as Ride 8 swooping down through rural Llanover and biking along virtually flat country lanes to the village of Llantrisant in the lower Usk valley.

Route Information

Start and Finish

Blaenafon Ironworks

Distance/ Ride Time

Ride via Loop A: Distance 57 ¼ miles: Ride Time 5 ½ hours.

Ride via Loop B: Distance 42 ½ miles: Ride Time 4 ½ hours

Energy Level
**

How easy is the Ride

Fairly easy given the distance; long down hill section from Blaenafon to Usk valley; almost all flat along the lower Usk valley to just near Caerleon; long flat stretches through the Gwent Levels; easy return ride along towpath and gently ascending railway track to the Ironworks.

What sort of terrain

Minor tarmac lanes with some B road sections; canal towpath and railway track off road sections

Off-road Grade

G1

The easy riding continues down the wide valley below Wentwood escarpment following the river Usk that weaves its way through woods and pastures down into Caerleon. Just past

Kemeys House the minor road forks west and east. From here there is an option to continue the ride along the flatlands of the Severn Estuary to Newport (Loop A) or alternatively try out the shorter loop through Caerleon (Loop B).

The Loop A route skirts around the south east side of Wentwood escarpment and above the busy A 449 dual carriageway. Through Cats Ash and around Llanbeder (Langstone) to the village of Llanmartin where there are the ruins of Pencoed Castle - an early Tudor mansion. Cross over a bridge above the M4, and follow the rural lanes through Bishton into Greenmoor. At this point the ride joins Sustrans Route 4 through the Gwent levels towards Nash and over the historic Transporter Bridge in Newport.

There is a slightly longer but more interesting alternative route to Nash through the coastal villages of Whitson and Goldcliff near the muddy banks of the Severn. The ride toward the sea wall passes alongside several of the many drainage canals that are a dominating and attractive feature of the Levels landscape and seem to be just about everywhere.

The Levels are completely flat wherever you look and cycling is easy and relaxed almost like a biking holiday in Holland. Don't be confused if you can't see the sea cycling towards Goldcliff village. It is hidden by the massive stone embankment that stretches right along the coast protecting all the inland villages and settlements from flooding.

At Goldcliff take a trip down to the sea wall where there are wide open views across the Severn to England.

Sea Wall Goldcliff ▼

Following Sustrans Route 4, cross over the Usk on the Transporter Bridge gondola and join the designated cycleway that routes through the attractive riverside front to Newport Castle a short distance from the Mon & Brecon canal.

The Loop B optional ride starts just past Kemeys House and follows the river Usk into the Roman Fortress town of Caerleon, home of the Second Augustan Legion from around AD 75. The museum is a good starting point for visiting all of the ancient sites. The ride continues through open rolling countryside along Malthouse Lane to the Three Blackbirds in Llantarnum and then down Pentre Lane to join the towpath along the Mon & Brecon canal.

The final section from either Llantarnum or Newport it is a relatively easy ride along Sustrans Route 46 tarmac cycleway following the canal towpath and old railway track to Blaenafon Ironworks.

Riding alongside the drainage canal near Bishton ▼

Heritage Interest Along Route

Newport, Usk, Pontypool and Canal: see Towns & Canal section.

Iron Cross: marking early chapel (C*a*pel Newydd) on Garn Fawr near Blaenafon.

Kemys House (private): Kemeys Inferior (off minor Llantrissant road) impressive house dating back to the Kemys Lordship in middle ages; Kemys Folly (private) on top of Wentwood ridge.

Pencoed Castle Llanmartin: remains of Tudor mansion – from Old Barn Inn continue east past church and take next lane on the left.

Whitson Court (private): impressive late 18C mansion on outskirts of Whitson.

Whitson Church: evocative piece of architecture – it has a leaning tower capped with a strange looking spike; currently up for sale and door is locked; there is apparently an inscription inside commemorating great flood early 17C when sea wall was breached drowning 2000 people; this inscription can also be found in other churches along the Levels..

Goldcliff: name relates to gold like reflections off the cliffs along the shoreline – note these cliffs are long gone; original site of 12C Benedictine Priory but hardly any trace of remains.

Sea Wall: huge stone embankment reconstructed between 1950s and 1970s extending along the Gwent Levels coastline; `originally built by Romans extending 20 miles between Rhymney and Sudbrook; Caerleon Museum houses an original Roman Inscription stone from sea wall discovered near Goldcliff.

Old Pontypool-Newport Railway Line: in the 19C there were two separate lines operated by the MRCC (later GWR); the one line went from Pontypool through Sebastopol, Pontrhydyrun, Upper Pontnewydd, Cwmbran, Llantarnam to Newport Mill St; the other ran further east between Lower Pontnewydd, Llantarnam, Ponthir, Caerleon to Newport Mill St; the cycleway between Sebastopol and Pontypool (near canal) is over the old west-side route that continued from Sebastopol through Blaendare Rd Halt to Crane St Station as well as Pontypool Road Station.

Caerleon Roman Heritage Sites
Museum: houses artefacts discovered around the roman sites;
Amphitheatre: remains of arena used for gladiatorial sport and troop training;
Roman Baths: impressive remains of baths complex enclosed in modern building;
Roman Barracks: remains of Roman legionary barracks used for housing troops.

The Route

The first part of the ride between Blaenafon

Ironworks and Newbridge-on-Usk follows exactly the same route as Ride 8 LoopB. From Blaenafon it descends the Llanover valley to Goitre and Chainbridge, continuing through Usk and Llantrissant along the Usk valley basin towards Newbridge on Usk.

Inns Along Route

Pottery	Blaenafon
Goose & Cuckoo	Llanover
Goetre Arms	Goetre
Chainbridge Inn	Chainbridge
Three Salmons	Usk
New Court	Usk
Greyhound	Llantrissant
Bell Inn, Bull Inn	Caerleon
Old Barn Inn	Llanmartin
Farmers Arms	Goldcliff
Three Blackbirds	Llantarnam

Segments 1-2-3-B1-B2 Ride 8 (17 miles): Follow the Ride 8 route segments from Blaenafon Ironworks as far as the right-hand turn-off to Newbridge-on-Usk on the minor road from Llantrissant.

Segment 4 (2 ½ miles): From the Newbridge-on Usk turn-off continue straight ahead along a good flat section close to the river as far as the right hand turn-off to Caerleon.

There are two alternative loops to choose from. Both Loop A and B start from this location. Try out either loop on a different day

Loop A: Through the coastal plain to Newport and the Mon Brecon canal (14 ¼ miles)

Segment A1 (just over 5 ¾ miles): From the Caerleon turn-off keep straight ahead and follow minor road up to the tee-junction in the small hamlet of Cats Ash on the outskirts of Langstone.

Turn left and follow the lane into the hamlet of Llanbeder (now part of Langstone). Take the right hand lane just after Langstone Primary school and follow this back around to the junction with the A48 in Langstone. Cross over the A48 and follow the B 4245 into the village of Llanmartin turning right on the minor road towards Underwood just after the Old Barn Inn. Cross over the bridge above the M4, turn left on to Bishton lane and follow this to the village of Bishton.

Go through the village take the turn-off on the left towards Redwick, go under the Railway tunnel at Bishton Crossing and continue along a long flat section near an attractive tree lined drainage "canal". Cross over an "A looking" road and follow the lane to the minor road junction near Greenway farm. At this point you will see the Sustrans sign for Cycle Route 4 towards Redwick and Newport.

Segment A2 (2 ¼ miles): At the Greenway junction turn right on the minor road towards Newport.

Follow Sustrans route 4 along the flat open landscape of the Caldicot Levels through Bowleaze for just over 2 miles to the Newport-Whitson road junction.

From here choose either the shorter A3 route to Pye corner or the more interesting coastal route A4 via Goldcliff

Segment A3 (2 miles): From the Whitson junction bear right towards Newport and follow Sustrans route 4 via Broadstreet Common to Pye corner on the outskirts of Nash. Continue the ride at Segment A5.

Segment A4 Coastal route (just under 5 ½ miles): At the Whitson junction near sub-station bear left towards Whitson passing Whitson Court on the left.

The old church of Whitson is towards the left just before entering the village.

At Goldcliff make a short excursion down to the sea wall and then continue around through Goldcliff Village and the outskirt of Nash to Pye Corner. Watch out for the Sustrans Route 4 sign on the western side of the Pye tee-junction.

Segment A5 (2 ¼ miles): From Pye corner follow Sustrans Route 4 signs along an off-road track that connects with a designated cycleway along side of road all the way to the Newport Transporter Bridge. Cross over the Usk on the Transporter Gondala (free for cyclists) to join the purpose built cycleway on the other side.

Segment A6 (just under 3 miles): From the west side of the Newport Transporter Bridge follow the Sustrans route 46 towards the west

along the side of the road not far from the river heading towards the new bridge. The cycleway passes close by the new road bridge and George St road bridge; it routes through the attractive riverside front to Newport Castle which is in the centre of Newport and a central point for pedestrian access to the town.

From the castle continue west following the route 46 cycle-way signs alongside the river and then over a road-crossing to the start of the Mon & Brecon canal at Barrack Hill. Proceed along the canal towpath a short way to the canal junction near the M4 bridge.

Segment A7 (just over 2 miles): Follow the canal towpath north to the Pentre Lane canal road bridge. Continue ride at Segment 5 below.

Loop B: Through Caerleon to the Canal (almost 7 miles)

Segment B1 (3 miles): Continuing from end of Segment 4. At the Caerleon turn-off on the minor road from Llantrissant, turn right, go under the A449T and follow the lane which stays close to the Usk river for most of the way to Caerleon. This is another easy flat section emerging at the Bell Inn on the eastern side of river. Cross over bridge pass the Hanbury Arms and turn left up the one way street (if congested with cars walk on pavement).

The Caerleon museum centre and Tourist Office are just past the Bull Inn on the right. This is good central point from which to visit the Roman sites.

Segment B2 (just over 3 ¾ miles) From the Museum follow the road around to the junction with the B 4236. Turn left towards Cwmbran and follow this B road for just under half a mile, watch out for a lane on the left just near Ponthir Tyre Service. Turn left on to Malthouse lane and follow this all the way around to the Three Blackbirds Inn crossing over the new dual carriageway (A4042) and the minor Llantarnum road. From the Blackbirds continue along Pentre Lane to the canal towpath access just

below the bridge over the A4051. Continue the towpath ride at Segment 5 below

Segment 5 (15 miles): The return ride from the the Pentre Lane canal junction is along Sustrans cycle route 47 (tarmac canal towpath). The cycle route is well signed all the way. Follow the canal towpath to Griffithstown and then continue along the old railway track via Pontypool to Blaenafon Ironworks as per *south-east access route.*

Riverside cycle route near Newport Castle ▼

Sustrans cycleway route 4 crosses Transporter Bridge Newport ▼

Riverside cycleway crosses the road near the new Bridge Newport ▼

Along the cycleway near the castle looking towards old Town Bridge Newport ▼

Usk Valley bike route approaching The Village part of Caerleon ▼

Riding through Roman Caerleon ▼

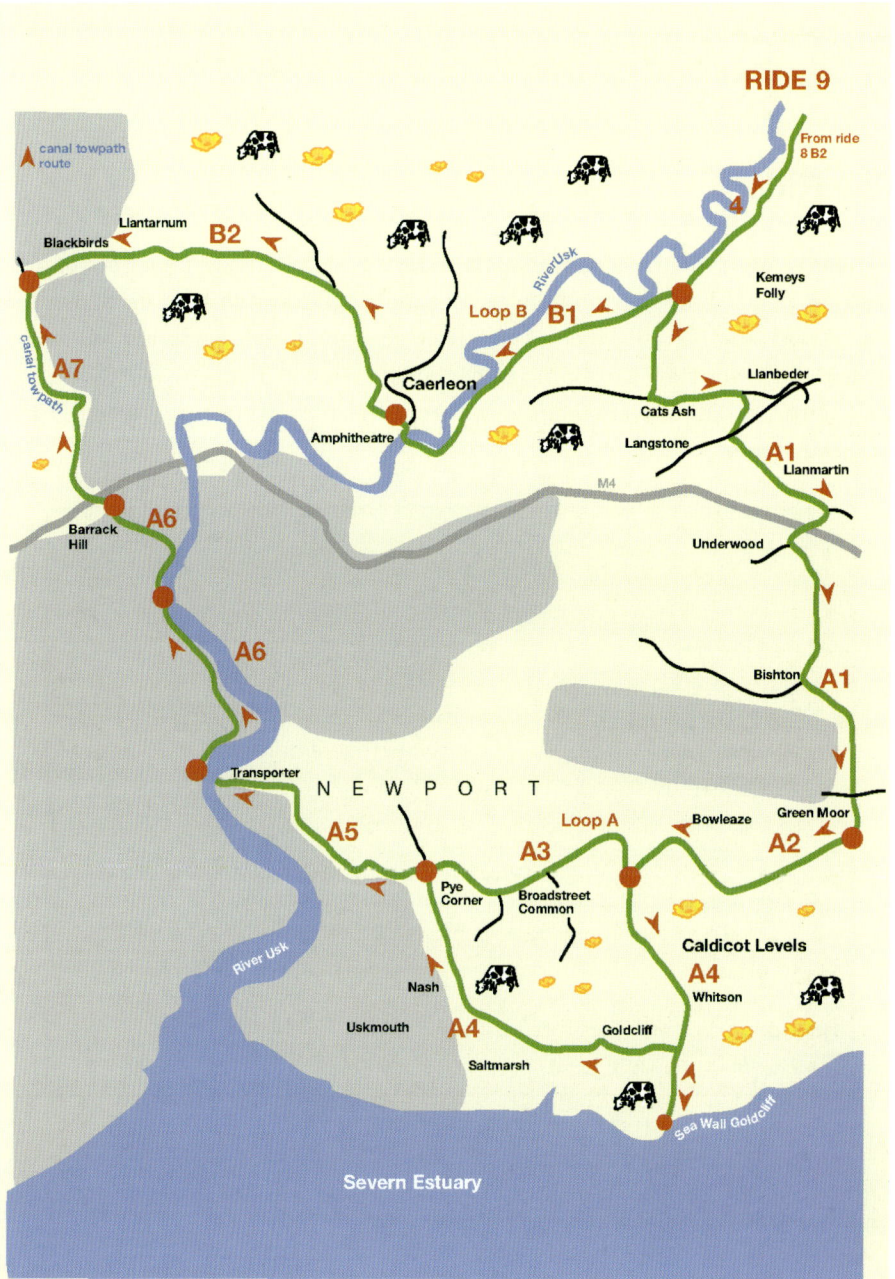

Ride 10: Loops around the Folly above Pontypool

The Ride

Two fairly short relatively easy loops around the historic Folly Tower south east of Blaenafon.   An opportunity to try out the ridge-top ride high up above the Avon Lwyd and Usk valleys or alternatively descend through a forest sweeping around the lower slopes of Garnwen ascending back up to the Folly.   On a clear day there are literally stunning views from the top of the ridge towards the Severn Estuary.

Route Information

Start and Finish

Blaenafon Ironworks

Distance/ Ride Time

Ride via Loop A: Distance 19 miles; Ride Time 3 hours

Ride via Loop B: Distance 21 ½ miles; Ride Time: 3 ½ hours

Energy Level
**

Off-road Grade
Mostly G1 with one G2/G3 section

How easy is the Ride

Easy-Moderate. Fairly easy Loop A ridge-top ride to the Folly; easy-moderate Loop B ascent south-east side of Folly; one challenging off-road descent through Cwm wood; easy Loop B Mamhilad minor road section; easy return cycleway route;

What sort of terrain

Mostly off-road mountain and woodland tracks with some tarmac sections; off-road mountain tracks are typically grass-stone surfaces with occasional ruts.

The ride starts from the Ironworks along the north-east access route over the open moorlands of Garn Fawr to the cattle-grid at the top of Upper Llanover.

From here there is an option to take the ridge-top route (Loop A) to the Folly or alternatively descend through Craig-yr-allt forest (Loop B) almost 250 metres down to the Mamhilad minor road sweeping back around the lower Usk valley and ascending back up to the Folly.

The Loop A ride begins along a wide grass track over the open moorlands of Garn Clochdy just above the top of the Craig-yr-allt forest. Towards the top east side of the forest there is a further option to try out a steep descent down the mountain and along a challenging stone track through Cwm Wood to connect with the Loop B route along Mamhilad minor road.

The Loop A ridge-top ride however continues eastwards over a grassy but bumpy part of the mountain (easy to ride) sweeping around towards a wide open flat grassy area of Garn-wen just above the Holy Well. You soon arrive at a Triangulation Point (small stone marker) at the top of Garn-wen ridge where there are some amazing panoramic views for miles around.

Loop A ride over Garn-wen looking back towards Blaenafon ▼

From this high point the track gently descends the ridge skirting well above Pontypool Golf course emerging at the top of Little-Mountain almost opposite the Folly Tower.

The Loop B ride to the Folly begins from the cattle-grid at the top of Upper Llanover swooping down along a wide woodland track through Craig-yr-allt forest to connect with a leafy but steepish stone track through Cwm Wood to the Mamhilad minor road.

There follows an easy ride along a relatively flat minor road through Lower Llanover following the course of the Mon & Brecon canal into the village of Mamhilad. Crossing over the canal

129

near the Star Inn the route ascends the north-east side of Garn-wen along a tarmac lane that changes to a stone track towards the top.

The tarmac lane also passes the start of the so called Roman road that winds its way up to the Folly almost directly above. Although it is possible to wheel a bike up the Roman road to the Folly it is unfortunately steep and muddy and not recommended. Continue to gently climb the wide stone dirt track (rideable) that leads to the top of the ridge near a Microwave radio tower. From here the route is along a wide public footpath leading directly to the Folly tower.

End of Loop B ride approaching the Folly ▼

The Hanbury family could not have chosen a better location to build an 18C summer retreat high up above the valleys overlooking a vast expanse of largely rural landscape.

From the top of this ridge there is an exhilarating descent down Folly Lane through Penygarn to the northern entrance of Pontypool Park. There are a number of alternative routes through the Park but the track down the hill circling around towards the east near the Bandstand leads to the large iron gates on the east side of the Park. From here it is only short distance to the canal towpath at Pontymoile canal wharf..

The final leg back to the Ironworks is over an easy eight mile stretch of the old Blaenafon-Pontypool railway track that is now part of Sustrans cycle-way route 46.

130

Heritage Interest Along Route

Pontypool town and Park: see Town & Canal section
Mon & Brecon canal: see Town & Canal section

Iron Cross: marking early chapel (Capel Newydd) on Garn Fawr near Blaenafon; near-by Blaenafon – Pontnewenydd early mule track used at start of Ironworks

Roman road: descends hill from Folly; thought to be built by Romans but some suggest it may have medieval origins.

Folly Tower: originally an 18C summer house of the Hanbury family; dismantled during war because of its close proximity to nearby Ordinance factory; rebuilt in 1994 and opened by Prince Charles. Open to visitors during the summer months.

Pontypool Blaenafon high level railway; at the Pontypool end the high level line joined the low level line at Trevethin junction; from here the Mon Railway & Canal company extended the line in 1876 to Talywaun which was later extended to Blaenafon by the LNWR (London & North West railway company); the line crosses the massive Ffrwd valley viaduct at Talywaun; it is now a superb tarmac cycleway (Sustrans route 46);

The Route

Inns Along Route

The Pottery	Blaenafon
Goose & Cuckoo	Llanover
Star Inn	Mamhilad Road
Horseshoe Inn	Mamhilad Road

Segment 1-2 (2 ¼ miles): From Blaenafon Ironworks take the north-east cycle exit route along Llanover road as far as the second cattle grid as per *Access route X-Y* (see section Bike Access Routes North for description and map).

From here choose either the Loop A over-mountain ride to the Folly via Segment 3A or the Loop B Mamhilad road ride to the Folly via Segment 3B.
There is also an option to access the Loop B ride via Segment 3A and Segment 3a.

Loop A Ride (and alternate route to Loop B via Segment 3a)

Segment 3A (1 ½ miles): At the Llanover road cattle grid go through a gate leading to a 3-metre Forestry Commission hard-compact dirt track heading east. Follow this track a short distance and bear right at the fork on to the upper track. Continue on this track until it crosses another north-south track (old Llanover-Cwmavon Parish road) just near a gate access to Garnclochdy mountain.. The track continuing eastwards is the private track to Garn-llech farmhouse.

Go through the mountain gate heading south for about quarter mile and then watch for grass track heading east not too far above the stone wall. Turn left on to track which crosses a couple of small streams and is not far above Craig-yr-allt wood. It is easily ridable and there are excellent views over Llanover towards the north..

After almost a mile you will arrive at a clearing just at the corner of the forest where there are wide open views north and also towards the east.

From here there is an option to continue the Loop A over-mountain ride to the Folly as per Segment 4A below or alternatively try the alternate route to Loop B via Segment 3a.

Segment 4A (2 ½ miles): Just at the clearing at the end of forest straight ahead towards the east

you will see lots of grassy mounds with several tracks.

Take your pick of tracks but keep heading east. Very shortly the Folly can be seen in distance slightly left.

Eventually you will see the track heading south near a stone wall and then bending around to the east once again over a flat easy-to-ride section of mountain top. Superb views towards the south overlooking the British and Coity-Varteg mountain ridges.

Follow the track to the end of ridge where there is a small triangulation point

Good views of the Folly towards south-east and towards the southern ridge.

Follow track down to wall and then descend towards another wall at the bottom.

The track continues east between two walls just above Pontypool Golf course . Pass through a gate descend a small hill cross over a stream and ascend the track to another good wide stone track. Follow this around until it joins top of Folly Lane near the Folly.

Alternate route to Loop B via Segment 3a

Segment 3a (just over ½ mile): Continue from Segment 3A. At the clearing just above the forest look out for the lower track which descends towards the east and then bends around towards the north. Excellent views towards Llandegfedd reservoir and the Severn estuary.

Descend this track which emerges at a gate on the edge of the wood. Pass through the gate and follow a wide woodland track which is challenging in parts. It eventually emerges in a clearing just near a small pond.

This is the same end-point as Segment 3B. Continue the ride to the Folly at segment 4B.

Loop B Forest track option to Mamhilhad road to Folly

Segment 3B (2 miles): Continuing the ride from Segment2. At the Llanover road cattle-grid go through a gate leading to a 3-metre Forestry Commission hard-compact dirt track heading east.

Follow this track for a quarter of a mile as far as gate and stile. Cross over the stile and continue along track for a further half a mile up to a fork in a clearing (one track continues straight ahead and the other bends around to the left). This is also the crossing point of the old Parish road from Llanover to Cwmafon.

Stay on the Forestry track heading east. This is an excellent 1 ½ mile forest ride but you will need to cross two gates about half way.

At the end of this forest track there is barrier gate in a clearing not far above a farmhouse. Just past the gate bear right on to the ascending forest track which soon leads to another barrier gate and ascending dirt track.

Just beyond the barrier is a short section of tarmac road that leads to clearing near a pond. This is also the same end-point as Segment 3a. Continue the ride at Segment 4B.

Segment 4B (4 ½ miles): From the clearing near the pond look out for the track descending through the forest towards the north

Follow this track down which is about 2 metres wide and very stony. It is a fairly challenging ride but gets better towards the bottom. After about half a mile the dirt-stone track joins a tarmac lane near Pen-y-Stair farm and this lane leads on to the junction with the Pencroesoped – Mamhilad minor road.

Turn right on to the minor road in the direction towards Mamhilad. Pass by the Horse Shoe Inn, cross over canal bridge 65 and after a further half mile turn right on to a lane just near the Star inn and attractive church opposite

Follow this lane which soon crosses canal bridge 62 . There follows a half mile mid to low gear climb up to the turn-off of the Roman road (narrow stony track – need to watch for it). It is possible to wheel the bike up the Roman road to the Folly but track can be rutted and steep in parts therefore not recommended.

Continue instead on the tarmac lane which changes to a gritty grass track after a short distance. Follow the track which is rideable for most of the way up to the top of the mountain above Pontypool.

Pass through the gate turn right pass through another gate that leads to a public footpath (wide track). Walk the bike on the footpath for less than quarter of a mile to the Folly passing through one open gate and crossing one stile. From the Folly there are outstanding panoramic

views in all directions.

Segment 5 (just under 4 miles): Leaving the Folly cross over the gate/stile to the small car park and access to Folly Lane. Descend Folly Lane for three-quarters of a mile, turn left at the bottom on to Ridgeway and Caerwent road which joins with St Cadocs road. Proceed down St Cadocs road turning left at the bottom on to Penygarn road.

Follow this road down for about half a mile passing by an Infants school and American gardens on left and then turning left on to Channel View. Follow this around to Park Crescent which leads to the north entrance of Pontypool Park. Inside the Park follow the new gravel track with the Dry Ski Slope directly ahead.

The gravel track bears right winding its way

Loop A Riding along Garnwen above Lasgarn ▼

down the hill above the Rugby ground. At the bottom just in front of the Bandstand turn left and follow track eastward towards the Lake continuing as far as the ornamental iron Park Gates at the exit to Rockhill road.

Turn right, then left on to Fountain road passing an old fountain and Victorian lamp-post.

Follow this road around to Pontymoile canal wharf passing over the canal bridge and turning right on to the towpath. After just under half a mile watch out for a turning left off the canal towpath just opposite Griffithtown Hospital. Take this turning left which leads on to the old Monmouthshire railroad now Sustrans cycle-way route 46. Turn left and follow the cycle-way a short distance crossing over Stafford road proceeding to Cwmynyscoy roundabout

Segment 6 (9 miles): The final route from Cwmynyscoy roundabout to Blaenafon is via the new purpose built cycle-way through Pontypool (Sustrans 46) and along the tarmac path of the old railway line (Sustrans route 46) all the way to the Ironworks.

Loop A Riding over Garnwen looking towards Llandegfedd ▼

Loop A Riding over Garn Clochdy looking towards Skirrid ▼

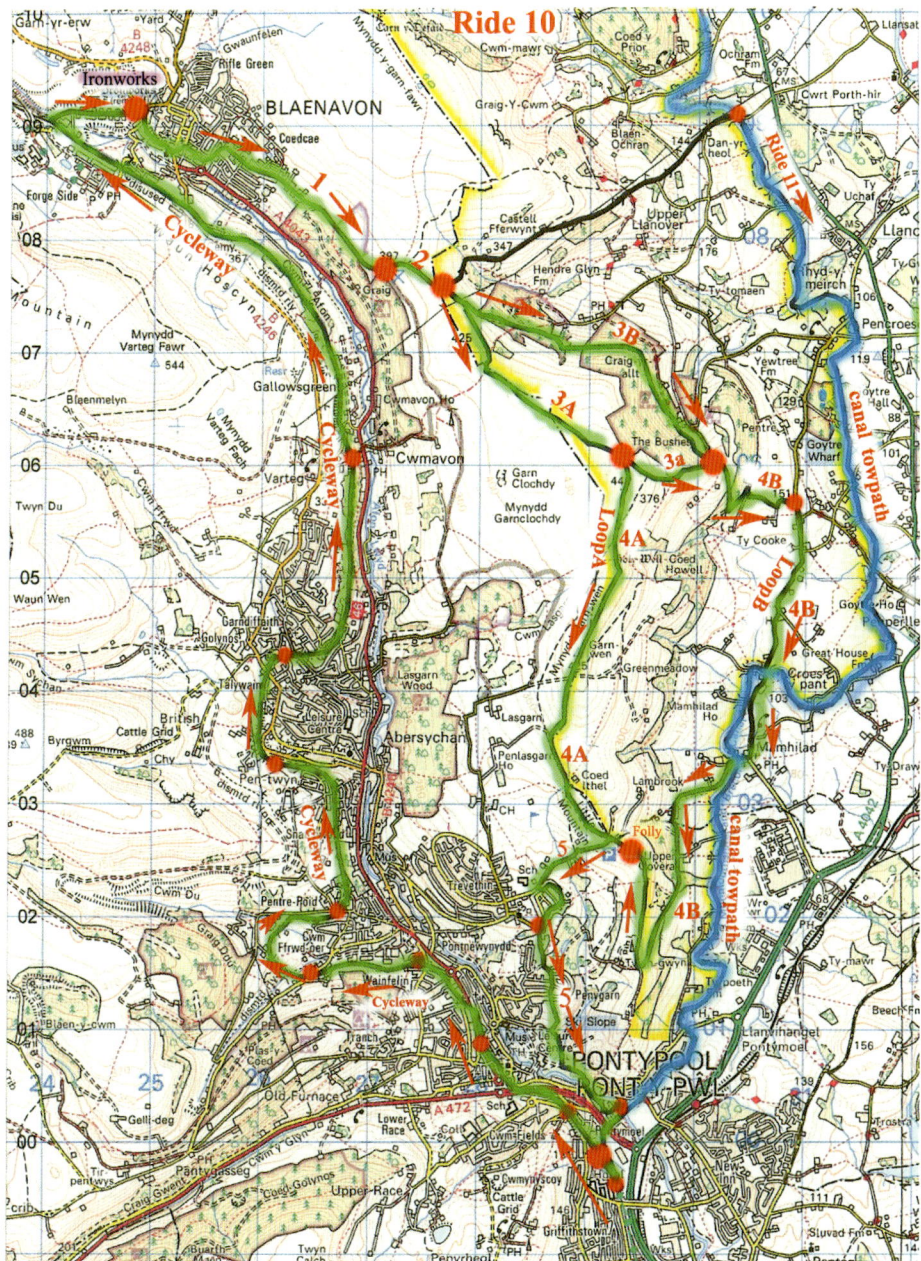

Ride 11: The Canal Loop

The Ride

Probably the most laid back and easiest ride of the series following a long stretch of canal towpath that circles around the base of the hills between Gilwern and Pontypool. Some of the most spectacular canal landscape in Britain. It will appeal to those who enjoy longish rides but don't like hills.

The first part of the ride from the Ironworks is along the west access route through Waunavon to the top end of the Clydach Gorge just outside Brynmawr. From here there is an exhilarating 3 mile descent down Blackrock road (virtually traffic-free) through the Gorge linking up with the canal towpath at Gilwern. This is the start of a 15 mile easy ride along the canal towpath to just outside Pontypool.

The first four miles of towpath, passes through the historic and picturesque wharfs of Gilwern, Govilon and Llanfoist and around the lower slopes of the Blorenge whose towering presence dominates the south side of the canal. The next section of canal twists and turns through Llanellen and Llanover passing under numerous stone bridges and crossing several aquaducts.

Route Information

Start and Finish

Blaenafon Ironworks

Distance/ Ride Time

Distance: just over 34 miles

Ride Time: 3 ¾ hours

Energy Level
  *

How easy is the Ride

Very easy: Virtually all flat and descending. The final section along the cycleway is an easy gentle ascent to the Ironworks.

What sort of terrain

Canal towpath varies between well compacted surfaces to undulating grass dirt tracks see segment 5 below; the whole section is easily rideable during summer; some muddy parts during winter; the remainder are minor roads

Off-road Grade   G1

The scenery riding along the towpath can change dramatically from one moment to the next. Along some of the leafy tree line sections the sunlight flits in an out like a silent movie but turn around the bend and it suddenly changes to wide open views of rolling hills and high ridges. This is lazy summer time cycling at its best.

The towpath continues along a very attractive woodland part of the canal weaving its way into Goitre Wharf whose moorings are usually jam packed with colourful barges. From here it hugs the side of the mountain making a major wiggle towards the south-west before arriving at Mamhilad.

Riding along the Towpath near Mamhilad ▼

At Mamhilad the 18C Folly Tower on the mountain ridge above Pontypool can easily be seen from the towpath. After crossing an impressive looking aqueduct over the Avon Lwyd river and passing by the old Toll house at Pontymoile wharf, the towpath connects with the Sustrans route 46 cycleway along the old Monmouthshire railway track bed near Griffithtown.

A purpose built cycle-way routes through the south side of Pontypool, crossing several road bridges and joining up with a tarmac track along the old Blaenafon-Pontypool railway line (Sustrans route 46). From here there is an easy gentle climb along the tarmac track-bed above the heavily wooded Avon Lwyd valley crossing over a spectacular viaduct at Garndiffaith before arriving back at Blaenafon Ironworks.

Heritage Interest Along Route

Waunafon Halt: on the old LNWR Brynmawr-Blaenafon railway opened in 1869; at 1498 feet it was second highest station on standard guage railway in Britain; closed to passengers 1941.

Black Rock region*: Black Rock road* is the old Govilon-Merthyr turnpike road of 1812; the *1794 Clydach Railroad* (horse drawn) ran just below Black Rock road crossing over to the Mysgwartha road near Cheltenham (Clydach) village and terminating at Gilwern canal wharf; *Blackrock limekilns* can be seen on side of Blackrock road; there was a branch line to the Kilns from Clydach railroad; *Machine House* (private house) on Mysgwartha road used to weigh the iron and coal for assessing the appropriate tolls for carriage on the railroad and canal;

Mon & Brecon Canal - *Gilwern to Pontypool section:* see section Towns & Canals

Pontypool: see section Town & Canals

Pontypool Blaenafon high level railway: at the Pontypool end the high level line joined the low level line at Trevethin junction ; from here the Mon Railway & Canal company extended the line in 1876 to Talywaun which was later extended to Blaenafon by the LNWR (London & North West railway company); the line crosses the massive Ffrwd valley viaduct at Talywaun; it is now a superb tarmac cycleway (Sustrans route 46);

The Route

See section "Bike Access Routes" for description and maps of access routes from and to Blaenafon, reference the route segments at beginning and end of ride.

Most of the route for Ride 11 is shown on Ride 10 Map. The beginning of Ride 11 route is shown on the Access Routes West Map (Segments A B D E J) .

Segment 1 (just over 1 ½ miles): Follow the west access route from Blaenafon Ironworks around Garn lakes to the Whistle as per *Access Route A.*

Inns Along Route

Whistle Inn	Garn-yr-erw
Racehorse	Waunafon
Drum & Monkey	Blackrock
Rock & Fountain	Blackrock
Navigation/Bridge/Lyon	Gilwern
Bridge/Lyon	Govilon
Star Inn	Mamhilad

Segment 2 (just under 2 ½ miles): Continue on the west access route through Waun-afon and Llanmarch to the road railway crossing at Lower Cwm Nant-gam as per *Access Route B-D*

Segment 3 (just over 1 mile): Continue on the west access route along the old railway track-bed to the top of the Heads of Valley roundabout at Brynmawr and from here to the junction of the Llangatoc and Black Rock roads as per *Access route E and route through Brynmawr*

Segment 4 (just over 4 miles Descend Black Rock road to Gilwern Wharf on the Mon & Brecon canal as per *Access route J*

Segment 5 (15 ¾ miles): Turn on to the canal towpath at Bridge 104 heading towards Gilwern. There is now an easy flat 15 mile ride along the towpath to just beyond Pontypool wharf.

The main sections of the tow-path ride are as follows:

Gilwern Wharf-Govilon Wharf: good smooth compact grit towpath track for most part easy riding;

Govilon Wharf-Llanfoist Wharf: good smooth compact grit towpath track – easy riding;

Llanfoist Wharf - Llanover moorings (bridge 87): compact dirt towpath track; surface smooth for large part but can be undulating, bumpy and sometimes stony. Easily rideable in summer but in winter can be muddy in parts;

Llanover Mooring-Goitre Wharf: good compact smooth hardcore grit towpath track easy riding:

Goitre Wharf-Mamhilad: towpath track can be a little bumpy leaving Goitre wharf but gradually improves and from about bridge 67 is reasonably flat and smooth all the way to Mamhilad.

Mamhilad-Pontymoil wharf: good smooth compacted towpath track – easy riding;

Pontymoile Wharf-Griffithstown: Good smooth hardcore towpath track – easy riding.

From Pontymoile wharf continue on the towpath for about half a mile and watch out for a left hand track that leads to the Sustrans cycleway route 46 over the old railway track (just in front of Griffithtown hospital on the right). Turn left on to the cycleway.

Segment 6 (9 miles): Continue along the cycleway following the Sustrans Route 46 signs through Pontypool and on to Blaenafon Ironworks as per *south-east access route*

141

Riding along the towpath near Goitre ▼

Riding along the towpath Goitre Wharf ▼

142

Ride 12: Loops around the north side of the Avon Lwyd Valley

The Ride

Three very short loops over mountain bridleways, woodland trails, and disused railway trackbeds; descending the northern ridge above the Avon Lwyd valley to the cycleway on the south side; it will appeal to those who like off-road riding with some bike wheeling.

The ride from the Ironworks begins along the north-east access route following the tarmac Llanover mountain road as far as a Bridle-way junction not far from the site of the Capel Newydd Cross.   The route then skirts east along the slopes of Garn Clochdy mountain over a wide dirt track that was once used as a packhorse trail during the early Ironworking period.

Route Information

Start and Finish

Blaenafon Ironworks

Distance/ Ride Time

Distance:
Via Loop 1: Distance 6 ½ miles; Ride Time 1 hrs
Via Loop 2 : Distance 11 ¾ miles; Ride Time 2 hr
Via Loop 3 : Distance 19 miles, Ride Time 3 hrs

Energy Level

Loop1 *; Loop 2 *; Loop 3 **.

How easy is the Ride

All loops are fairly easy and quite short, with mix of riding and bike wheeling – but mostly riding. Some short climbs and push-ups.

What sort of terrain

Largely off-road with some tarmac minor roads; dirt/stone mountain bridleway – parts of over-mountain track between Llanover road and Waterworks road badly waterlogged particularly in spring/winter; better in summer Some wheeling on Loop3

Off-road Grade
G1/G2

Some parts of the trail are however susceptible to heavy water-logging during springtime and even in the summer months there will be a need to do some clever dodging around the sides. There are superb open views down the Avon Lwyd valley and over the tops of the settlements

143

dotted on the southern side of the mountain.

Loop1 is the shortest of the three ride options, descending Garnclochdy on an old Parish road at a point just above the site of the old Forge in Cwmavon and connecting with the southern side of the Avon Valley via the Snail Creep. The Creep is a winding steep stony track climbing up the side of the mountain and crossing the now disused high level Blaenafon-Pontypool railway track (cycle-way) over a bridge near the old Varteg station. The wheel up the Creep is however quite short and not difficult. The return leg is an easy short ride along the Sustrans cycle-way to the Ironworks.

Riding along the cycleway looking towards Forge Row Cwmavon ▼

Loop 2 goes a little further east along Garn Clochdy before swooping down the side of the valley on a single track tarmac lane (Waterworks road), passing a disused but picturesque mountain reservoir and crossing the Avon Lwyd river over the Rising Sun bridge. On the south side the ride passes under the massive nine arch stone Viaduct that crosses the Ffrwd valley, gently climbing up a tarmac road (Viaduct road) to join the Sustrans cycle-way along the old railway track on top of the Viaduct. The return ride from the Viaduct is along the tarmac railway track (cycleway) to Blaenafon Ironworks.

Loop 3 is the longest of the three ride options going even further east and starting just above the disused reservoir on top of Waterworks road. There are also two alternative routes to choose from for the first part of the loop.

The longer mountain route skirts around Garn Clochdy descending a large open grassland common down the side of Garnwen mountain to the top of Lasgarn Lane high up above Pontypool. In late summer this part of the mountain Common looks like fields of gold that stretch for miles..

Riding down Garnwen mountain track towards Lasgarn Lane▼

The shorter woodland route is a bike wheel along a trail through Lasgarn wood crossing open fields and emerging on Lasgarn Lane about a mile above Pontypool Golf Club.

From Lasgarn lane there is fast descent down through Trevethin and Penygarn to the northern entrance of Pontypool Park. The route through the Park joins up with the canal towpath at Pontymoile Wharf and from here it is an easy ride along the Sustrans cycleway to Blaenafon Ironworks.

Riding along an old packhorse trail Garn Clochdy ▼

Heritage Interest Along Route

Capel Newydd: Iron Cross marking site of early 16C chapel (Capel Newydd); nearby is Blaenafon – Pontnewynydd early mule- pack track used at start of Ironworks for conveying iron to Newport

Llanover Parish Road: old stone road (track) linking Llanover and Cwmafon;

Snail Creep: an old stone road (track) descending a steep hillside from Varteg to Cwmafon; a vehicle actually ascended the Creep in the 1920's; the only way down prior to Shop road.

Cwmafon: 18C Forge near Afon Lwyd just west of the Westlake building and associated with Varteg Ironworks and most likely Blaenafon Ironworks - but no remains; Forge Row built for workers in the Forge and now refurbished but under private ownership – located just above the Forge; Cwmafon House (private) is a large mansion style house built for the Ironmaster; nearby Westlake Brewery built in 1900 by Charles Westlake who utilised local spring water for brewing the beer.

Pontypool: see section Town and Canal,

Pontypool Blaenafon High-Level Railway; at the Pontypool end the high level line joined the low level line at Trevethin junction ; from here the Mon Railway & Canal company extended the line in 1876 to Talywaun and was later extended to Blaenafon by the LNWR (London & North West Railway Company); the line crosses the massive Ffrwd valley viaduct at Talywaun; it is now a superb tarmac cycleway (Sustrans route 46);

Pontypool Blaenafon Low-level Railway: built by the Monmouthshire Railway company and opened in 1854; it went through Pontnewynydd, Abersychan and Cwmafon and followed the route of the old tramroad (1796) between Blaenafon Ironworks and the canal head at Pontnewynydd; shut down during the Beeching era.

The Route

Inns Along Route

The Pottery	Blaenafon
The Westlake Inn	Cwmafon
The Rising Sun	Cwmfrwdd
The Yew Tree	Trevethin

Segment 1(2 miles)*:* From Blaenafon Ironworks take the town route up to the first cattle grid crossing on Llanover road continuing as far as the packhorse trail turn-off on the right just above the Capel Newydd cross as per *Access route X*

Segment 2 (¾ mile): Turn on to the old packhorse trail which is severely rutted and waterlogged for most of the first half mile particularly in winter and spring. It is however possible to wheel the bike around the side of the badly waterlogged areas but be prepared. The track does get better just at the end of the wood where it becomes rideable.

After about another half a mile, and just before the TV mast, the track crosses another north-south track which is an old parish road to Llanover. There is a bridle-way signpost at the cross-road of tracks.

From this location choose either the Loop 1 ride below or continue at Segment 3 towards Loop 2 and 3 rides.

Loop 1: Up the Snail Creep to Varteg Station (¾ mile)

Following on from Segment 2.
At the bridleway signpost on the cross-roads of tracks, turn right heading towards south and descend the mountain (TV mast now on left). After a short distance - about 150 yards, take the bridle-way fork on the left (watch for the sign) and follow this path around until it joins the top part of a concrete access track just below the TV mast.

Descend the concrete access lane to the bottom near a bench seat and pass through the gate.(alternatively instead of forking left you can continue straight down the stony bridle-way track to join the concrete lane near the bench seat at the bottom).

Cross over a tarmac lane and continue a short way down the bridle-way (stony track) which joins a tarmac lane leading to the bridge over the Avon Lwyd river. Pass over the bridge, cross

over the A4043 Blaenafon road and turn up Snail Creep Terrace just near the Westlake Arms.

The start of the Snail Creep is on the right hand side and is signed as a bridle-way. Wheel the bike up this steepish twisting dirt stone track for just under quarter mile until it meets the Sustrans cycleway along the old Blaenafon Pontypool railway line.

Cycletrack Segment (2 ¾ miles): At the Snail Creep junction of the cycleway follow the cycleway track in a westerly direction passing through old Varteg Station (wooden sculptures), and Gallows Green to Blaenafon Ironworks.

Continuing from Segment 2 towards Loop 2 and 3

Segment 3 (2 ¾ miles): From the crossroads of tracks follow the old packhorse track heading east passing the radio mast on the right.

As indicated above the first part of the track does get severely waterlogged and unfortunately this is the case for the remaining three quarters mile up to the point where it joins the rideable dirt road near Havod Wenog Farm.

Some parts are rideable; there are several small footbridges over the worst water-logged sections of track.

147

From Havod Wenog farm continue down the dirt track for just under half mile as far as the gate access at top of Waterworks lane (metalled road).

From the gate access at top of Waterworks lane choose either Loop 2 or Loop 3

Loop 2: From Waterworks road Reservoir to Talywaun (1 ¼ miles)

From this gate descend Waterworks lane a short distance as far as an old reservoir on the left. From the reservoir continue the descent down Waterworks lane, passing some farms and crossing over the Rising Sun bridge at the bottom and then on to the junction of the Blaenafon road.

Cross over the road with care and proceed up Vicarage Lane almost immediately opposite. Cross over the next road and continue up Vicarage lane until it meets Harpers road. Cross over Harpers road and on to Viaduct road opposite.

Proceed up Viaduct road passing by Victoria Village Chapel on left, and after about half mile the road passes under the magnificent eight arch stone Viaduct that spans the Frwdd valley (trains used Viaduct up until the 1940's).

After the Viaduct, turn left over the Frwdd

bridge and after passing Pisgar church turn left and left again up to the access of the Sustrans Blaenafon-Pontypool railway track.

Cycleway Segment (4 ¾ miles): Continue west over the Viaduct gently ascending the cycleway passing through Garndiffaith and Varteg Station all the way to Blaenafon Ironworks.

Loop 3: Around Garn Wen Mountain or through Lasgarn Wood to Pontypool

This loop has two alternative routes; Segment 4A is a mountain route around Garn Wen joining the top of Lasgarn Lane; Segment 4B route is through Lasgarn Wood arriving just below the top of Lasgarn Lane. Try either route on a different day.
Start either Segment 4A or 4B route after completing segment 3 above.

Segment 4A Option: (just under 1 ¾ mile): At the gate access on top of Waterworks lane turn left on to the mountain track which begins as a stony road between two stone walls soon emerging on to the mountain common (Garnclochdy).

Once on the common you need to watch out for the track which is not so well defined at the beginning but nevertheless is discernable. It heads up through the gap in the ferns towards the north. Keep in sight Pen-y-ddoyga farm ahead on the right.

The track eventually bends around towards the wall and almost level with the farm. Just past the farm a well defined track continues to head north close to the wall. It eventually winds itself eastwards around the top of the stone wall enclosure about quarter of a mile or more above

Pen-y-ddoyga farm.

It soon emerges through a large area of open grassland (Garn-wen) and begins to gently descend towards the south east. The grass track changes to a hard compact gravel stone track that skirts above Garn Wen farm on the right.

After a short distance it emerges at a cattle grid and gate and the start of Lasgarn Lane (metalled road). Descend Lasgarn Lane for a quarter of a mile as far as the footpath sign and stile just opposite Lasgarn Farm. This is the same end point as segment 4B below. Continue the ride at segment 5.

Segment 4B Option: (¾ mile): From the gate access on top of Waterworks road descend a short distance as far as an old reservoir on the left. (You now need to wheel the bike for just under a mile on a public footpath until it reaches the junction of Lasgarn Lane.)

Leave Waterworks road and take the well defined track heading east, cross over the style at end of reservoir, follow the well defined dirt track up through the woods for about quarter mile until it joins with another well defined track on the right and heading east (easily missed - watch for stones on left).

Follow this track which after a short distance merges with another well defined track heading east, and then after a short distance (less than quarter mile) watch out for a footpath (easily missed) climbing up on the left. Take this footpath and after maybe 50 yards it joins another very well defined wide track.

Bear right (east) on to this track and immediately on the left there is a sign with a public footpath going up the hill a short distance to meet a stile. Haul your bike over the stile and wheel the bike on this footpath over fields for

less than half mile crossing another three styles up to the junction of Lasgarn Lane just opposite Lasgarn farm. Continue at segment 5.

Segment 5 (3 ½ miles): From the footpath junction on Lasgarn Lane just opposite Lasgarn Farm continue for about a mile passing Pontypool Golf Club on the left until it meets the junction of Church Avenue Trevethin.

Turn left on to Church Avenue, go down hill and keep straight ahead at the roundabout bearing left on to Penygarn Road. Pass Trevethen Church, Yewtree Inn, Penygarn Infants school and American Gardens.

Continue to descend Penygarn road a short distance turning left on to Channel view through to Park Crescent and the north entrance of Pontypool park. Enter the Park and follow the new gravel track with the Dry Ski Slope directly ahead. The gravel track bears right winding its way down the hill above the Rugby ground.

At the bottom just in front of the Bandstand turn left and follow track eastward towards the Lake continuing as far as the ornamental iron Park gates at the exit to Rockhill road.

Turn right then left on to Fountain road passing an old fountain and Victorian lamp-post. Follow this road around to Pontypool canal wharf passing over the canal bridge and turning right on to the towpath.

After just under half a mile watch out for a left-turning off the towpath just opposite Griffithtown Hospital. Turn left on to the old railroad now Sustrans cycle-way route 46 looping back towards Pontypool. Follow the cycle-way crossing over Stafford road joining up with the cycleway bridge at Cwmynyscoy roundabout.

Cycleway Segment (9 mils): The final route from Cwmynyscoy roundabout to Blaenafon is via the new purpose built cycle-way through Pontypool (Sustrans 46) and along the tarmac path of the old railway line (Sustrans route 46) all the way to the Ironworks as per *south-east access route.*

Approaching top of Trevethin from Lasgarn Lane ▼

Mountain track towards Lasgarn lane ▼

Above Lasgarn in winter ▼

150

Ride 12 Loops around the north side of the Avon Lwyd valley

Riding by Trevethin Church ▼

Riding through Pontypool Park ▼

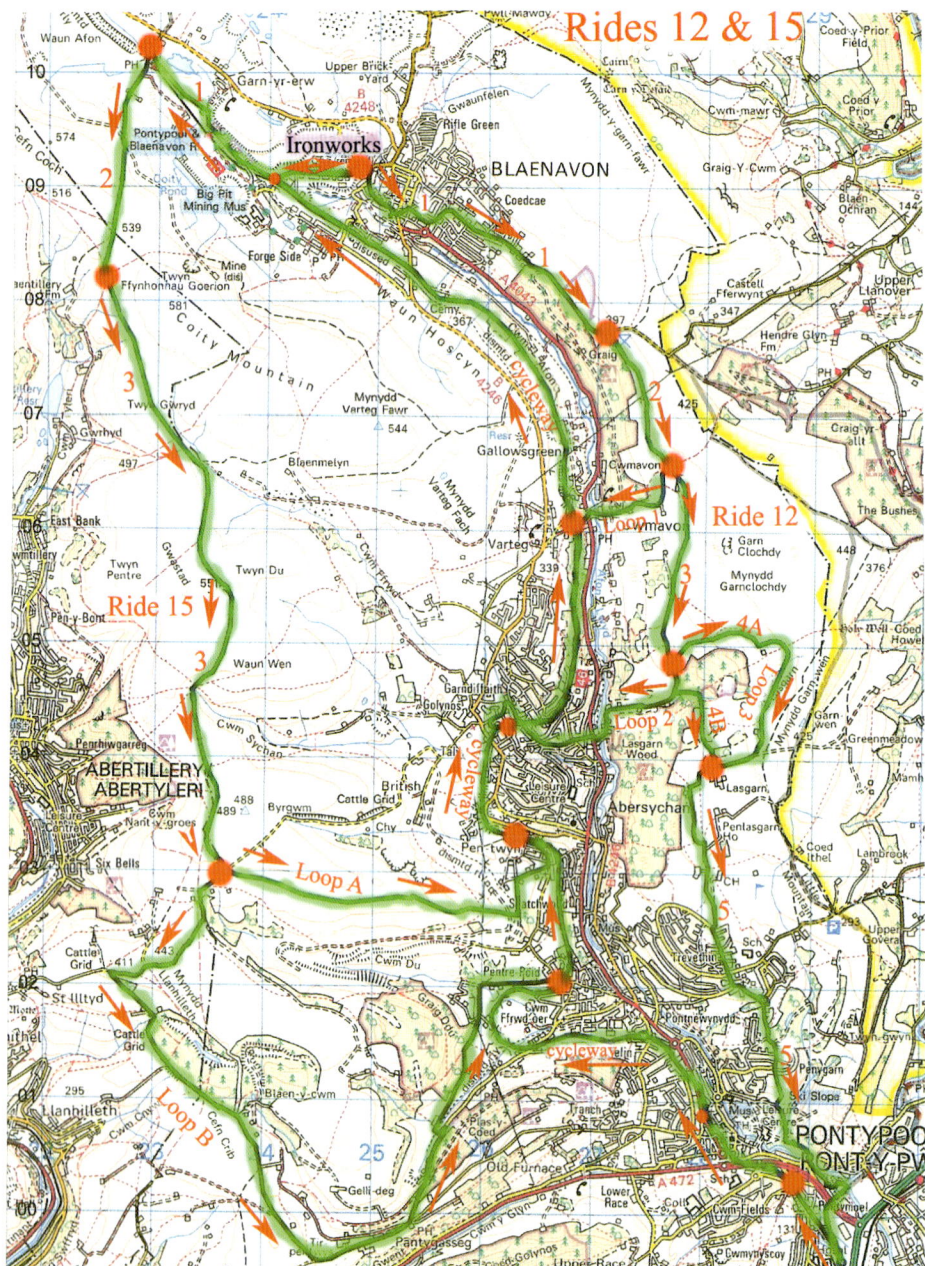

Rides 12 & 15

Ironworks

BLAENAVON

Ride 12

Ride 15

Loop A

Loop B

Loop 2

Loop 3

Ride 13: Through Llanellen and Llanover to Gallows Green

The Ride

A short largely off-road ride criss-crossing the remote rural countryside of Upper Llanellen and Llanover; biking over moorland tracks, woodland trails and tarmac lanes through virtually unspoilt landscape on the fringe of the World Heritage Site.

The ride from Blaenafon Ironworks begins along the northern access route crossing over Garn-yr-erw mountain and circling past the Keepers pond to Foxhunters car park at the top of the Blorenge.

Not far down from the Foxhunters, the route switches to an off-road bridleway track descending south-east along the slopes of Garn Fawr mountain eventually joining a rough tarmac lane near a farmhouse in Upper Llanellen.

Route Information

Start and Finish	How easy is the Ride
Blaenafon Ironworks	Easy-Moderate. There are a couple of steep climbs but they are short; some bike wheeling along gently ascending off-road stone tracks but they are short and not difficult; not many miles but need to allow 3 hours ride time to cater for off road sections
Distance/ Ride Time	
Distance: 15 miles Ride Time: 3 hours	
Energy Level	**What sort of terrain**
**	Largely off-road plus some tarmac lanes; off-road sections are grass/stony bridleways, mountain tracks - occasional ruts.
Off-road Grade	
G1/G2 (short G3 section)	

From the farmhouse the ride continues down through Llanellen criss-crossing the slopes of Graig-y-cwm partly on-road and partly off-road eventually arriving at Upper Llanover.

This is a particularly remote part of the countryside. With the exception of a few scattered stone farmhouses there is literally nothing but fields, clumps of woodland, streams, hedgerows, rolling hills and mountain ridges; a rural retreat for those seeking an escape from urban living.

There follows a mid to low gear climb up through the Llanover valley past the Goose & Cuckoo Inn continuing along an old Parish stone road that ascends through forestry woodland eventually arriving on the slopes of Garn Clochdy mountain.

Along the ridge there are wide open views towards Varteg mountain in the south and down the Avon Lwyd valley towards the Severn.

It is a is reasonably easy bridleway descent down the side of the Garn Clochdy mountain to Cwmavon at the bottom of the Avon Lwyd valley and from here it is a fairly short bike-wheel up the steep and twisting Snail Creep that soon crosses the Blaenafon cycleway near the old Varteg station just below Gallows Green.

Once on the cycleway it is an easy return ride following the old railway track back to the Ironworks

Approaching the Keepers Pond from Pwlldu road ▼

Heritage Interest Along Route

Garn-yr- erw mountain: moon like landscape caused by open-casting in the 1940/50s era; remains of Hill pits on south side

Dyne Steels Incline Pwlldu: former cable operated inclined railroad on north (Pwlldu) and south (Blaenafon) sides of Garn-yr-erw mountain; used in 19C for early transport of minerals between Blaenafon Ironworks and Pwlldu; supplemented tunnel route under Garn mountain.

Pwlldu: a one time bustling village built for iron and coal workers but demolished in sixties; there were two terraced rows of houses, two pubs, a shop and, chapel, now all that remains is the welfare hall (outdoor centre) and Lamb Inn.

Keepers pond (Pen-fford-goch pond): named after Keepers cottage now a popular sightseeing spot on top of Blorenge; originally used as a feeder during 19C for Garnderys Forge just below.

Foxhunter car park: commemorates nearby grave of Lt. Col. Harry Llewelyn's famous Olympic show jumping horse Foxhunter (1940-59)

Cwmafon: 18C *Forge* near Afon Lwyd just west of the Westlake building and associated with Varteg Ironworks and most likely Blaenafon Ironwork - but no remains; *Forge Row* built for workers in the Forge and now refurbished but under private ownership – located just above the Forge; *Cwmafon House* (private) large mansion style house built for the Ironmaster; nearby *Westlake Brewery* built in 1900 by Charles Westlake who utilised local spring water for brewing the beer.

Pontypool Blaenafon High-Level Railway; at the Pontypool end the high level line joined the low level line at Trevethin junction ; from here the Mon Railway & Canal company extended the line in 1876 to Talywaun which was later extended to Blaenafon by the LNWR (London & North West Railway Company); the line crosses the massive Ffrwd valley viaduct at Talywaun; it is now a superb tarmac cycleway (Sustrans route 46);

The Route

Inns Along Route

The Whistle	Garn-yr-erw
Lamb & Fox	Pwlldu
Goose & Cuckoo	Llanover
Westlake	Cwmafon

See section "Bike Access Routes" for description and maps of access routes from and to Blaenafon, reference the route segments at beginning and end of ride.

Segment 1 (4 miles): From Blaenafon Ironworks take the northern bike route through Garn Lakes over Garn-yr-erw mountain to the Lamb & Fox and along Pwlldu road to the Keepers pond as per *Access routes A-O-S*

Segment 2 (1 miles): From the Keepers Pond follow _Access route T_ to Foxhunter car park just opposite the Radio masts at the top of the Blorenge.

Descend Llanellen road for approximately a mile as far as a small pull-in on the right hand side. Look out for the bridleway descending the Llanellen valley to the south. (you can also pick up the bridleway which is actually a better track about quarter mile above this small pull-in on the right).

Segment 3 (¾ miles): Follow this track a short way down the mountain to join a wider more discernable bridleway; the track is rutted, sometimes stony and muddy in parts, but it gets better and becomes easier to ride; it descends the mountain slope eventually emerging through a gate at the top of a single track tarmac lane near a farmhouse.

Segment 4 (1 ¾ miles): Descend the tarmac lane; there is a valley on either side and the landscape gets more green and lush towards the bottom.

Pass through another two gates and at the last gate near Cwm Uchaf farm turn right on to a short steep concrete track which joins another single track tarmac lane near another farm.

Go through the gate on the right (sign indicating track has been provided by Brecon Beacons and

Llwyndu volunteers) and follow the dirt track (bridleway) for just under a mile up to the point where it joins a tarmac lane near Craig-y-cwm farm (please ensure you walk the bike through Craig-y-cwm access gate).

Alternatively from the Brecon Beacons sign follow the tarmac lane down the hill turning right at the bottom and then making a very steep climb (need to walk) for just under half a mile to reach the same point just outside Craig-y-cwm farm gate.

Segment 5 (3 ½ miles): From the tarmac lane just near Craig-y-cwm farm gate go along the lane a short distance south east and then turn right on to the stone grass track (could be an old Parish road). Gently ascend (wheel the bike) along this track for just over half a mile up to the junction with a single track tarmac lane (Blaenafon Llanellen road).

Turn left and after a short distance turn right (watch for it) on to another lane continuing the descent as far as the junction with the Goose & Cuckoo lane. Turn right and follow the flat and gently ascending lane for half a mile up to the second fork. Continue straight ahead in a southerly direction making a moderate to steep low gear climb for a further half a mile up to the Goose & Cuckoo Inn.

From the Inn continue south a short distance up to gate and style which provides access to a dirt stone parish road on left and a hard core 3-metre forestry track on the right. Either wheel the bike for about quarter mile up the stone parish road

as far as a junction of forestry tracks or alternatively take the easier (rideable) but longer forestry track around to the same point.

From this track junction at the clearing wheel the bike up the stone Parish road which continues to ascend southwards passing through a gate near the top of Garn Clochdy mountain.

The parish road is now mostly rideable over a flat and descending section up to the cross roads of tracks with several bridleway signs not far from the TV mast.

The remaining part of the route below is the same as the Loop 1 section of Ride 12.

Segment 6 (¾ mile) At the bridleway signpost on the cross-roads of tracks, go straight ahead and continue descending the old Parish road (bridleway) towards the south (TV mast now on left). After a short distance - about 150 yards or so, take the bridleway fork on the left (watch for the sign) and follow this path around until it joins the top part of a concrete access lane just below the TV mast.

Descending Cwm Mawr Llanellen ▼

near a bench seat and pass through the gate.(alternatively instead of forking left you can continue straight down the stony bridleway track to join the concrete lane near the bench seat at the bottom - but not really rideable).

 Cross over a tarmac lane to rejoin the bridleway. Descend the bridleway a short distance to meet a tarmac lane that crosses the Avon Llwyd river at the bottom of the valley. Pass over the bridge, cross over the A4043 Blaenafon road and turn up Snail Creep Terrace just near the Westlake Arms. The start of the Snail Creep is on the right hand side and is signed as a bridleway. Push the bike up the Creep (steepish stone track) for just under quarter mile until it meets the Sustrans cycleway along the old Blaenafon Pontypool railway line.

Cycleway Segment (3 ¼ miles): At the Snail Creep junction continue on the Sustrans cycleway climbing gently in a westerly direction passing under Snail Creep Bridge, through the old Varteg Halt (wooden sculptures),   along Gallows Green and above the town of Blaenafon terminating at the Ironworks.

Descending the bridleway track Llanellen▼

Approaching Keepers pond from Pwlldu road in February ▼

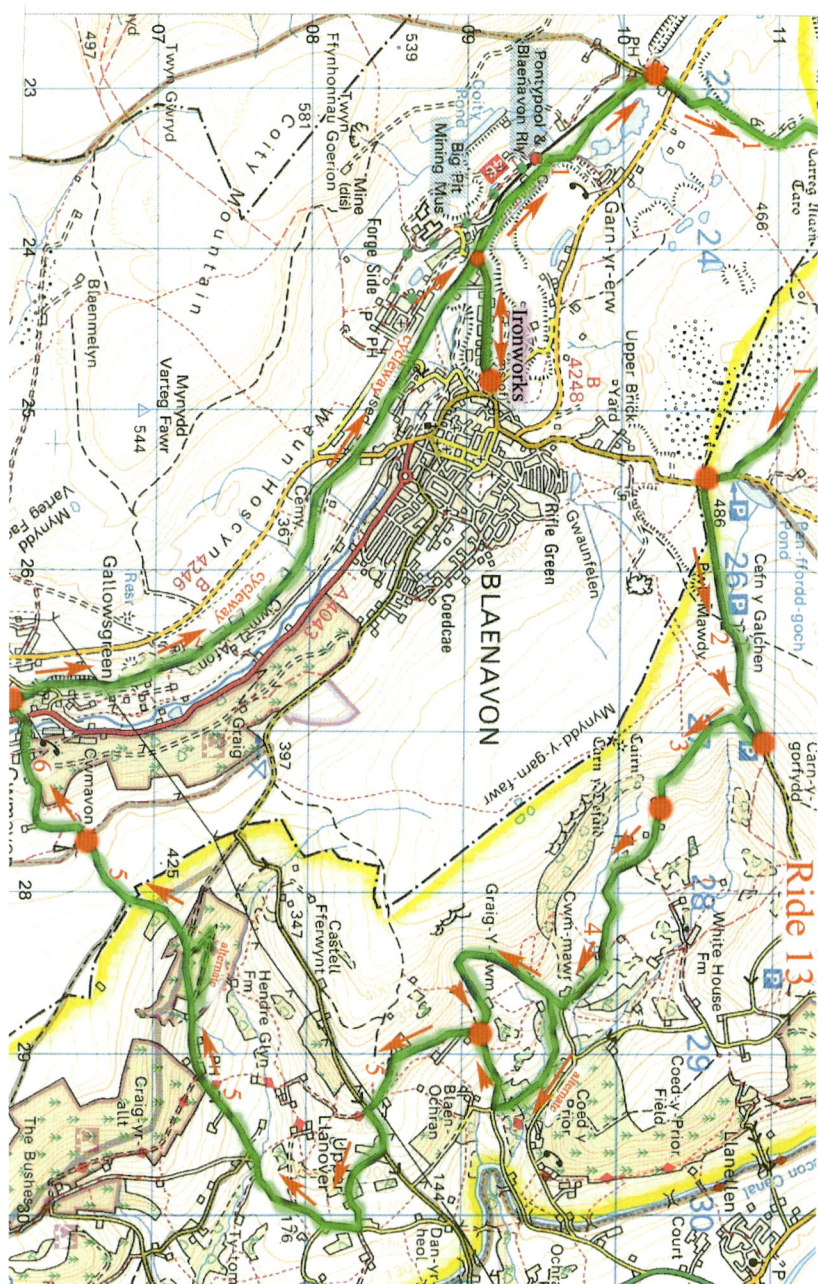

Ride 14: Three Loops over Henllys mountain to the canal

The Ride

A largely off-road ride from the Ironworks to the top of Henllys mountain high up above Cwmbran and Newport; an opportunity to try out three highly scenic loops down to the canal. On the west side a superb down hill ride through the spectacular forested valleys above Cwmcarn to the canal at Pontywaun; on the south side an exhilarating descent down to the canal at Penrhiw; on the east side a challenging down-hill off-road ride to the canal at Llantarnam.

Route Information	
Start and Finish	**How easy is the Ride**
Blaenafon Ironworks	Moderate. Quarter mile strenuous low gear section bottom part of Prescoch lane; half mile strenuous low gear section above Upper Cwmbran; Loops are all long descents; almost 25 miles of easy flat towpath and railway track riding; tiny bit of bike wheeling
Distance/ Ride Time	
Ride via Cwmcarn Loop: Distance 44 miles; Ride Time 5 hours	
Ride via Penrhiw Loop: Distance 40 miles; Ride Time 4 ½ hours	
Ride via Henlys Church Loop: Distance 34 ¾ miles; Ride Time 4 hours	**What sort of terrain**
	Long section of canal towpath and cycleway over railway trackbed; some minor road sections; mountain bridleways and public access tracks; one mile stretch of public access footpath over mountain.
Energy Level	
***	**Off-road Grade**
	G1-G3

The first eight miles of ride is an easy gentle descent along the south-east access route following the Sustrans cycleway along the tarmac railway track-bed to Pontypool. From here there is a short steep on/off-road climb up the hill joining the mountain road at the Lamb Inn Penyrheol

160

high up above Griffithtown and Sebastapol. The route sweeps around the slopes of Twyn Glas past the Mountain Air Inn eventually dropping down to the Siloam Baptist church in the rural outskirts of Upper Cwmbran.

From the church there is steep climb up a tarmac lane that connects with an off-road track high up on the slopes of Maen mountain and virtually on top of the large extensive development of Cwmbran and the lower Avon Lwyd valley. From here a short section of public footpath (track) links up with a public access dirt track that gently climbs up to a wide open grass Common on top of Henllys mountain not far from the ancient iron age fort of Twmbarlam   From this vantage point there are some massive panoramic views across the Severn Estuary to Bristol and beyond.

From the top of Henllys there are three optional rides down to the canal towpath in the Ebbw and Avon Lwyd valleys below.

The Cwmcarn Loop is probably the most exciting and dramatic of the three options. From the top of Henllys the ride follows a 5 mile scenic tarmac route swooping down through the green forested glens of Cwmcarn dropping down almost 1000 ft to the canal in the Ebbw valley below. You could easily be riding through parts of Canada or Scandanavia.

Cwmcarn Loop: start of descent from top of Henllys through Cwmcarn forest▼

The Penrhiw Loop may not be quite as spectacular but nevertheless follows a scenic and long easy descent down to the canal near Pontymister a few miles east of Cwmcarn.

The Henllys church Loop begins with a short challenging down-hill section of dirt stone track followed by a gently descending ride over tarmac lanes through the rural unspoiled countryside of Henllys vale to the Mon & Brecon canal.

Henllys Church Loop: descending mountain track towards church and canal▼

The seven mile picturesque section of canal between Cwmcarn and Rogerstone is cut into the northern slopes above the Ebbw river with good views over Risca to the southern mountain ridges.

From Rogerstone there is an exhilarating descent down the amazing series of fourteen locks joining up with a virtually flat section of towpath that tracks the M4 to a junction just outside Newport.

The next eight mile section is another easy and relaxing ride along the canal towpath in a north west direction through Cwmbran to Pontypool passing by pubs and attractive landscape features. Rather surprisingly the canal route still retains a magical picture-book quality given the wide spread of urban development that has mushroomed up around it.

Near Pontypool the route switches from the canal towpath to the railway track cycleway and the start of an easy gently ascending nine mile ride back to Blaenafon Ironworks.

Heritage Interest Along Route

Pontypool Blaenafon High-Level Railway: at the Pontypool end the high level line joined the low level line at Trevethin junction ; from here the Mon Railway & Canal company extended the line in 1876 to Talywaun and was later extended to Blaenafon by the LNWR (London & North West Railway Company); the line crosses the massive Ffrwd valley viaduct at Talywaun; it is now a superb tarmac cycleway (Sustrans route 46);

Twmbarlwm Iron Age Fort: the highest hill fort in Gwent on top of Twmbarlwm mountain; reputed to be the burial ground of an ancient British Chieftain

Cwmcarn Forest Drive: scenic drive through heavily wooded slopes of Cwmcarn; popular tourist attraction with visitor centre, campsite and picnic facilities; site of Cwmcarn Colliery Pit No 2 sunk in 1914 just above the lake; mountain bike circuit and purpose designed tracks.

Pontypool and Newport: see Town & Canal section

Henllys church: medieval church standing in open rural countryside

Mon & Brecon Canal: see Town & Canal section

Griffithstown Railway Museum: history of the Monmouthshire railway with lots of memorabilia; located just off the Sustrans route 46 cycleway (railway track-bed)

The Route

Inns Along Route

Castle		Pontywaun
Philanthropic		Pontywaun
Prince of Wales	towpath	Risca
Halfway	towpath	Cwmbran
New Bridge Inn	towpath	Cwmbran
Old Bridge Inn	towpath	Cwmbran

There are three suggested optional routes from Henllys mountain to the canal. Try out each of the loops on a different day.

Blaenafon Cycleway Segment (9 ¼ miles): Follow the south east exit route along the cycleway to Pontypool and Cwmnyscoy roundabout as described in _Bike Access Routes_

Segment 1 (3 miles): Cross over the roundabout on to the road leading up to Cwmynscoy. Turn almost immediately to the left on to a tarmac lane (Prescoch Lane).

There is a steep quarter mile climb (strenuous), flattening out on top and changing to a dirt track (partly rideable) which shortly merges at a tarmac lane tee-junction. Turn right and loop immediately around to the left emerging at the junction of the mountain road near the Lamb Inn Penyrheol.

Turn left on to the mountain road and climb for a half mile (easy) to the Mountain Air Inn followed by a fast three quarter mile descent down to junction of Upper Cwmbran road near the Siloam Baptist Church. Turn right (signed no-through road) and make a steep low gear half mile climb (strenuous). Just near the top there are two tracks bearing left off the tarmac lane.

Segment 2 (just under 2 miles): Take the uppermost grass stony track heading south and follow for half a mile up to a gate.

Need to lift bike over gate. The next one mile is a public access footpath (well defined track) with four stiles. Follow track around to left, slightly boggy area, pass by a farm on left and continue to walk bike up good grassy track.

After the fourth style it rejoins a wider rideable track (road used as a public path).

Stunning views towards the east looking over Cwmbran, Newport and the Severn. Follow this grass track for just under half mile up to a fork (farm down on left) near a tree line. Take right fork and gently climb (rideable) the grass and hard packed dirt stone (slightly rutted) track up to the top near the start of a conifer grove to left.

At this point there are several tracks on right and left near a public access footpath sign.

Take the track heading slightly right which ascends up towards the rise. After a short distance the track leads to the top of the mountain where there are wide open views towards Twmbarlwm straight ahead, Newport and the Severn (south east) and the heavily wooded steep Cwmcarn valley towards the south west.

Once on top of the Common look out for a well defined track towards the west heading down towards the Cwmcarn valley.

For those choosing the Cwmcarn Loop continue the ride as below. For those choosing either the Henllys or Penrhiw Loops continue the ride at Segment 3.

Cwmcarn Loop (just over 5 ½ miles to Pontywaun bridge)

From the open Common on top of Henllys mountain take the track going down to the south west. (bending to right) towards Cwmcarn valley. After a short distance (maybe 100 yards) the track leads to a gate and style and to a tarmac lane bending around from the west to the south.

This is the top of the spectacular 7 mile Cwmcarn Forrest drive that winds itself along the wooded slopes and steep narrow valleys to the north of Cwmcarn village. It is now one of the key tourist attractions in the area.

At this point there is the option to take the designated mountain bike trail but due to the overall length of this ride (from Blaenafon Ironworks and back) it is suggested to use the Forest Drive tarmac road that descends for more than 5 miles all the way to the bottom of the Ebbw valley.

Turn left and head south down the scenic Forrest drive passing the picnic area, Pay Lodge, Visitor Centre, site of Cwmcarn colliery and lake, eventually meeting the junction of the B 4591 near Cwmcarn village.

Turn left and continue for half a mile up to Pontywaun canal bridge passing the Castle and Philanthropic Inns. The turn off to Halls road terrace at the Bridge marks the start of the canal towpath cycleway.

From Pontywaun Bridge follow the Sustrans route 47/46 cycleway along the canal towpath and railway track-bed all the way back to Blaenafon Ironworks as described in the cycleway segments below.

Penrhiw & Henlys Church loops

Segment 3 (1 ¼ miles): From the open Common at the top of Henllys mountain follow the wide grass track straight ahead towards Twmbarlwm. (mountain with unmistakable mound of Iron-age fort).

Bearing slightly left continue along the track until it meets a stony track heading down to the south east (Twmbarlwm is now west of this point). Descend the dirt stone track down a short distance up to the point where it joins a tarmac lane.

From this location choose either the Penrhiw Loop or the Henllys Church Loop..

Penrhiw) Loop (1 ½ miles to the canal bridge)

Continuing from segment 3. Descend the tarmac lane towards the south (direction Risca) for about half mile to the cattle grid and then turn right on to a stony grass track that soon changes into a tarmac lane.

The tarmac lane descends the hill for about ¾ mile down to the junction of Holly road (extensive views westwards along the Ebbw valley). At the Holly road junction turn right and then left on to Mount road (Moriah Hill) until it meets the bridge over the Crumlin arm of the Mon & Brecon canal near Pontymister.

From the canal bridge follow the Sustrans route 47/46 cycleway along the canal towpath and Railway track-bed all the way back to Blaenafon Ironworks as per the Cycleway Segment below.

Henllys Church loop (4 ¼ miles to canal bridge)

Continuing from segment 3. At the junction with the tarmac lane proceed more or less straight ahead joining a wide stone track which now points roughly south east in the direction towards Cwmbran.

There follows a steep descent (just over quarter mile) over a loose stone dirt track which is a challenging mountain bike ride. There are good views of Pant-yr-eos reservoir towards the south (right) as well as Newport

The stone track joins a tarmac lane which continues down the hill passing Cwrt Henllys and Henllys church, emerging at a junction with the Castell-y-bwch road.

Turn right then immediate left towards Bettws then immediate left again on to a single track tarmac lane. Continue through a wooded area (Coed Craig y Ceiliog) for just over a mile up to a tee-junction. Turn right follow the lane which joins Pentre lane leading to the canal road bridge.

From the Pentre Lane canal road- bridge follow the Sustrans route 46 cycleway along the canal towpath and railway track-bed all the way back to Blaenafon Ironworks as per the Cycleway Segments below.

Cycleway Segment along Canal Towpath: Pontywaun to Newport (7 miles)

The *Cwmcarn loop* joins the canal at Pontywaun bridge. At the Pontywaun canal bridge continue along the towpath which is well signed as Sustrans route 47 in the direction towards Newport.

The next bridge one mile along the towpath is close to the unsigned burial site of miners who died in the Risca colliery disaster end of 19C (cross over bridge look towards the fence line by clump of trees signed Pontywaun garden suburb).

Follow the cycleway along the towpath through a very scenic section of the canal which passes through Crosskeys, Risca, and Pontymister. There are extensive views over the Ebbw valley

towards the wooded area of Coed Mawr and Fox Hill in the south.

The *Penrhiw Loop* joins the canal towpath at Pontymister. Follow the canal cycleway through Pontymister for a further 3 miles through Rogerstone up to the Fourteen Locks canal centre not far from Highcross. The Ynysfro reservoir can be glimpsed on the left.

From the canal centre there is a terrific descent down through the extraordinary system of stone constructed locks to the M4 tunnel at the bottom.

The towpath continues along a fairly flat section for just over a mile through the bottom of Allt-yr-yn and Ridgeway joining up with the Pontypool spur of the canal at a junction near the Crindau M4 bridge (about a mile from the centre of Newport)

Cycleway Segment along the Canal towpath-railway track: Newport to Pontypool (8 miles)

From the canal junction at the Newport M4 bridge continue north-west on the Sustrans route 46 cycleway towpath towards Cwmbran.

The next two miles of towpath routes via an attractive section of Bettws and Malpas, gently climbing up an eight lock section through to Llantarnam towards the outskirts of Cwmbran. Twmbarlwm mountain can be seen towards the west.

About two miles from Newport junction is the Pentre road crossing which is where the *Henllys Church Loop* joins the canal towpath.

For the next couple of miles the cycleway makes a number of road crossings including Two-Locks road and Bellview road and also switches left right and left again. At the road crossing near the Halfway Inn the canal disappears and will re-emerge after about half a mile near B & Q's Cwmbran.

Follow the cycleway which is clearly signed down towards the Green Forge Way road-crossing with Cwmbran town centre on right and B & Q's directly ahead. Cross over Green Forge Way follow the cycleway to just near B & Q's where the canal re-emerges.

Continue along the towpath passing the New

Bridge-End Inn, crossing Maindy Way, ascending yet another three Locks, and passing the Old Bridge End Inn.

You have now come 5 miles from Newport junction. Continue to gently climb past old locks which have been converted into a series of picturesque waterfall steps. Proceed on the towpath passing another four locks, crossing over Five Locks Close up to the point at which the Sustrans cycleway leaves the canal bearing right on to lane. You are now in Sebastopol.

Turn on to lane and follow it down for about quarter mile and then turn left on the old tarmac railway track which is signed Sustrans 46. Pass by Griffithstown Railway Museum on the left, cross over Station road, New Inn road, the canal, and Stafford road and then follow the cycle-way down to the Cwmynyscoy roundabout.

Cycleway Segment Pontypool to Blaenafon (9 ¼ miles)

Follow the south east access route along the cycleway (Sustrans 46) through Pontypool to Blaenafon Ironworks as described in *Bike Access Routes*

Cwmcarn Loop: descending Cwmcarn Forest Drive ▼

Henllys Church Loop: descending mountain track towards church and canal ▼

Cwmcarn Loop: descending bottom of Forest Drive past Lake ▼

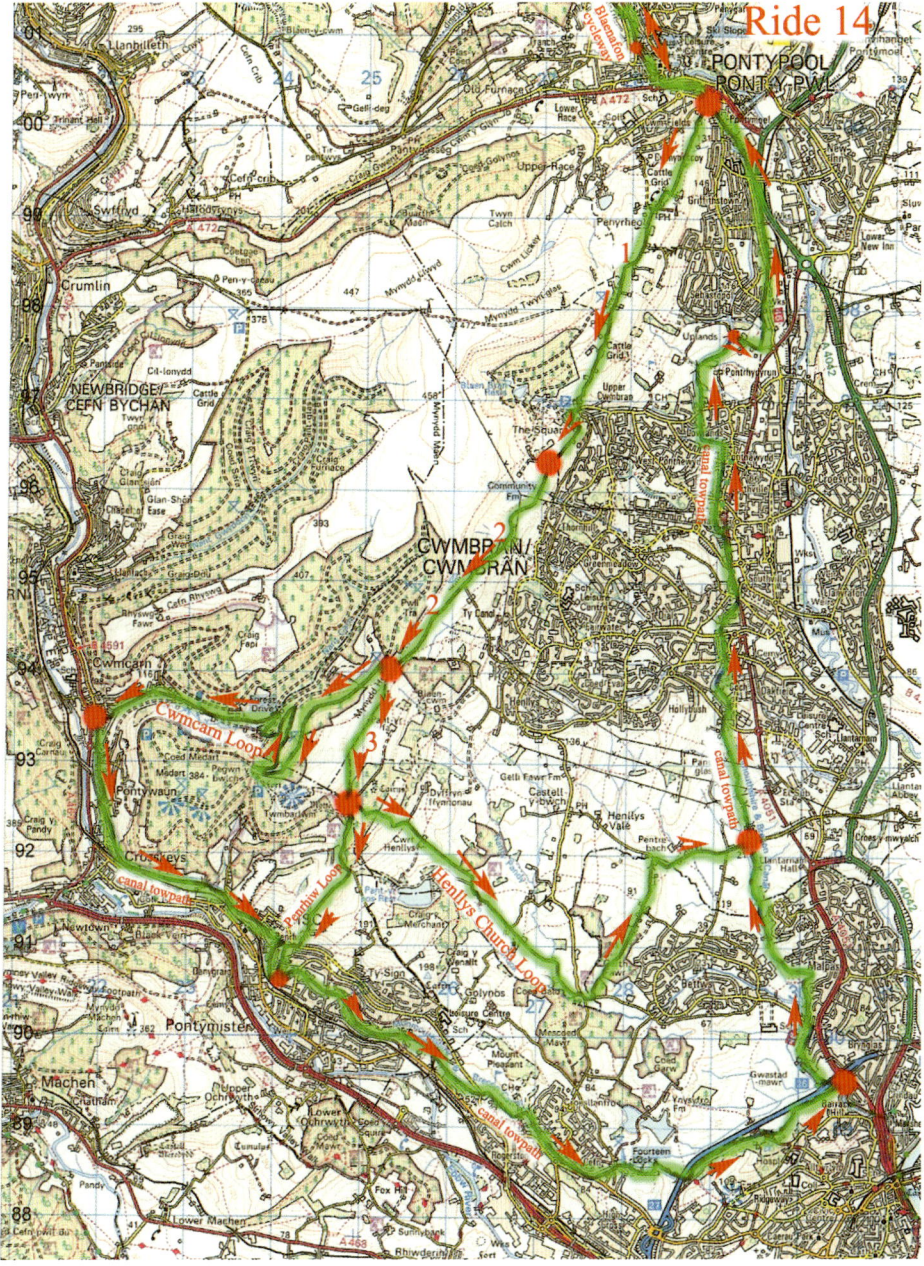

Ride 14

PONTYPOOL
PONT Y PWL

CWMBRAN/
CWMBRÂN

Cwmcarn Loop

Henllys Church Loop

© Crown Copyright

Ride 15: Looping over the southern mountain ridge towards the Avon Lwyd valley

The Ride

A short but lively mountain-top ride through heather and grass moorlands high up above the Avon Lwyd and Ebbw valleys. Looping around from the top of the ridge to the Blaenafon cycleway.

Loop A is an exhilarating off-road descent along the ridge between the valleys of Cwmbyrgwm and Cwmnantdu. Loop B takes a wider on-road route around Llanillith mountain before descending the Cwm Ffrwd-oer valley.

<table>
<tr><td colspan="2" align="center">**Route Information**</td></tr>
<tr><td>**Start and Finish**</td><td>**How easy is the Ride**</td></tr>
<tr><td>Blaenafon Ironworks</td><td rowspan="3">Moderately easy; one steep bike-wheel climb up the Coity at the start of ride; afterwards it is mostly flat and descending. Loop B has one short steep climb just before Tirpentwys; easy return route along tarmac cycle-way</td></tr>
<tr><td>**Distance/ Ride Time**</td></tr>
<tr><td>Ride via Loop A: Distance 14 ¼ miles: Ride Time 2 ½ hours
Ride via Loop B: Distance 19 miles: Ride Time 3 hours.</td></tr>
<tr><td>**Energy Level**
</td><td>What sort of terrain**</td></tr>
<tr><td>**Off-road Grade**
G1/G2</td><td>Mostly off-road; includes long sections of stony and occasionally rutted tracks over mountains – all rideable; Loop A is over a hard grass track; Loop B is over minor tarmac roads; cycleway is tarmac.</td></tr>
</table>

The ride begins from the Ironworks along the west access cycleway route to the Whistle Inn just above Garn lakes. The route then switches to an off-road stone track that winds its way up the side of Coity mountain in a southerly direction.

Once on top of the mountain it is a relatively easy off-road ride following a 4 mile stretch of bridleway track that hugs the top of the ridge above Cwmtillery Abertillery Six Bells and Llanilleth. The bridleway ride is best undertaken in summer when the track is dry and hard.

There are literally breathtaking views stretching over the eastern and western valleys towards the Severn Estuary

From this high vantage point the floors and sides of the steep narrow valleys are completely hidden and all that can be seen for miles around is a vast panorama of undulating mountain tops as far as the Severn; it looks like one big national park. The valley bottoms that were once swirling in smoke and blackened with coal tips have vanished into the past.

Riding along Bridleway on Gwastad ridge looking towards south ▲

The bridleway eventually leads to the mountain tarmac road between the British and St Iltyds. The two optional loops start from this road.

Loop A follows the bridleway around to the north-east where again there some incredible views over the top of Pontypool and towards Llandegfedd reservoir. A steep down-hill ride over the mountain ridge leads to the route 46 cycleway near Pentwyn

Loop B follows a wide easy loop along a minor tarmac road around Llanilleth mountain through the mountain top settlements of Tirpentwys and Pantygasseg joining up with the route 46 cycleway near Pentre Piod.

The final part of the route is an easy ride along the cycleway following the old railway line

Ride 15 Looping over the southern mountain ridge towards the Avon Lwyd valley

through Garndiffaith and Varteg all the way to to Blaenafon Ironworks.

Heritage Interest Along Route

Pontypool Blaenafon high level railway; at the Pontypool end the high level line joined the low level line at Trevethin junction ;   from here the Mon Railway & Canal company extended the line in 1876 to Talywaun which was later extended to Blaenafon by the LNWR (London & North West railway company); the line crosses the massive Ffrwd valley viaduct at Talywaun; it is now a superb tarmac cycleway (Sustrans route 46);

British Ironworks: located through Big Arch near the cycleway (old railway) not far from the road-crossing at Pentwyn; the British Ironworks started 1826: all that remains are the quadrangle of 19C office buildings/workshops and the 19C Beam Pumping Engine-House that served the Ironworks Colliery.

Site of Tirpentwys Colliery: located on left side descending Pantygasseg road; pit was sunk in 1878 ; it had two shafts and fine 19C buildings; closed in 1969, colliery buildings dismantled but site is greened and landscaped

Pontypool: see section on Towns & Canals

Loop A descending the bridleway above Pontypool ▼

The Route

See section "Bike Access Routes" for description and maps of access routes from and to Blaenafon, reference the route segments at beginning and end of ride.

The route of Ride 15 is shown on the map of Ride 12

Segment 1 (1 ½ miles): From Blaenafon Ironworks follow the west access route around Garn lakes to the Whistle Inn as per *Access route A*

Segment 2 (1 ¼ miles): Go past the Whistle Inn heading south towards Coity mountain. After a short distance the track becomes a public footpath. Cross over the stile (need to haul bike over stile but not difficult) and wheel bike up the mountain path crossing over a tarmac road (old quarry road – now private) almost halfway up. It is a fairly steep ascent over a wide stone track but is fairly short and not too bad.

At the top the track is an easily rideable bridle-way. Follow the grass track heading south descending gently as far as the gas pipeline fence which extends right across the mountain. There are views over the other side towards Cwmtillery straight ahead.

Go through the fence access towards a stone wall. On the southern side of the pipeline

access turn left on to the bridleway which heads towards the east and can be seen following the fence-line over the rise. After a couple of hundred yards another bridleway branches to the right (south) heading down to Cwmtillary. This junction is just above Blaen-tillery farm (can't see it)

Segment 3 (just under 4 miles): At this bridleway junction continue heading east in the same direction as the pipeline fence. The bridle-way path follows the pipeline fence all the way along mountain top and therefore you cannot get lost.

After passing over a small rise (bike wheel) the bridleway becomes a wide hard compacted dirt-stone track, rutted in parts with a couple of muddy bits but easily navigable. Don't stray from line of fence.

The track is rideable and mostly flat or gently descending. Stunning views of the Avon Llwyd valley stretching down to the Severn estuary as well as the Ebbw valley looking towards Newport and Cardiff. Just beyond Abertillery (below you) there are incredible views down the steep Cwm Nant-y-groes towards Six Bells and the junction of the two Ebbw valleys.

173

After riding almost 4 miles look out for a minor tarmac road (Talywaun- St Illtyd) towards the south-east. Watch out for a small clump of trees and brick building on the left and also watch where the bridleway track swings around to the left off the main track. Take this left bridle-way track which after a short distance joins up with the mountain road.

From this location there are two alternative loops back to the Ironworks. Try either loop on a different day.

Loop A: Descend Byrgwm mountain (just over 2 miles)

From the junction of the bridleway track and mountain road take the bridleway track which continues on the south east side towards the stone wall. Near the wall the bridleway swings around to the left. Follow the grass track which is rideable and soon there are absolutely incredible views above Pontypool, Llandegfedd reservoir, the Folly and the Usk valley.

There is a now a steep descent down the grass bridleway but is easily rideable. Towards the bottom go through two gates and the bridleway then meets another wide hardcore east-west track. Cross over this track and follow the bridleway straight ahead. Cross over another wide descending track and stay on the path straight ahead slightly right; the last short section through woodland is a bike wheel as far as Pentwyn road.

Turn left and follow Pentwyn road a short distance to the junction of the Sustrans route 46 cycleway at the road crossing. [There is an alternative better way to the cycleway but some parts are not shown as a public right of way. Where the bridleway meets the first east-west track turn left go through two gates near a farm, descend the road, turn left down another track at the next farm, go past Pentwyn rugby ground and follow track down to the route 46 cycleway junction.]

Follow the cycleway back to the Ironworks as per the final segment below

Loop B: Around Llanilleth mountain (6 ¾ miles)

From the junction of the bridleway track and St Illtyd mountain road turn right on to the road and continue south for a mile turning left on to a tarmac lane just near a Radio mast. Follow this around for about two miles towards Tirpentwys

There is one short but steep low gear climb to negotiate. At the tee-junction in Tirpentwys turn left over a cattle grid and follow through to Pantygasseg. Bear left near what used to be the Mountain View Inn Pantygasseg.

Descend the hill for about half a mile and watch out for a small turning on the left signposted Abergelli cottages. Turn left and follow the tarmac lane around the top of Cwm-ffrwd-oer for about a mile joining the Route 46 cycleway near Pentre Piod – look out for long corrugated shed. near the cycleway.

Follow the cycleway and after about a mile you arrive at the Pentwyn road-crossing. This is the same point at which Loop A joined the cycleway. Continue to Blaenafon Ironworks as per final segment.

Final Segment along Cycleway (5 ½ miles)

From the Pentwyn road-crossing follow the Sustrans route 46 cycleway along the railway trackbed through Garnfiffaith and Varteg to

174

Ride 15 Looping over the southern mountain ridge towards the Avon Lwyd valley

Blaenafon Ironworks as _per south- east_   Access route.

Blaenafon cycleway alongside Garn lakes near the Whistle ▼

Riding along Byrgwm looking towards the Severn ▼

Riding the ridge above Six Bells ▼

Riding along the bridleway over Gwastad ridge ▼

Ride 16: Crossing the Glyn Valley to the forested slopes above Abercarn

The Ride

A ride through some of the most extraordinary diverse landscape in southern Gwent crossing over the Glyn valley to the upper slopes of Mynydd Llwyd and descending either a tarmac mountain road or alternatively an off-road track through the spectacular wooded slopes of the Nant Gwyddon valley to Abercarn. An easy return ride along Sustrans cycleway following the canal towpath and railway trackbed to Blaenafon Ironworks.

Route Information	
Start and Finish	**How easy is the Ride**
Blaenafin Ironworks	Moderate: Lots of flat and descending mountain routes; a short steep bike wheel up the side of the Coity; a short steep low gear climb before Tirpentwys; a steep low gear climb first half mile up Llwyd mountain; 24 miles of flat towpath and railway track;
Distance/ Ride Time	
Distance: 40 miles	
Ride Time: 5 hours.	
Energy Level	**What sort of terrain**
***	Off-road sections are grass or hard dirt stone tracks over mountains and through forests; canal towpaths and railway track-beds are tarmac; on-road sections are mostly single track tarmac lanes and mountain roads
Off-road Grade	
G1/G2	

The first part of the ride from the Ironworks follows the Ride 15 route south-east along the bridleway over the Coity ridge high above the Avon Lwyd and Ebbw valleys joining the Llanilleth mountain road just above St Iltyds.

The route soon switches from the mountain road to another bridleway that descends the Cefn Crib to a cattle-grid almost 250m above the village of Crumlin.

From here there is a fast descent down the slopes of the narrow Cwm Llwynau to the village of Hafodyryns at the bottom of the Glyn valley where the route joins a tarmac lane that ascends Llwyd mountain on the other side of the valley. The energy-gains of the Cwm Llwynau descent are soon put to good use on this climb. Once over the high point however there is a long flat stretch of mountain-top road through a wide open grass Common overlooking the Ebbw valley and beyond.

The mountain lane weaves its way towards an extensive forested area on the eastern side (Coed Sara) of the road from where you can choose two alternative routes down to Abercarn village at the bottom of the Ebbw valley.

The off-road route is an exhilarating descent along a forestry track down through wooded slopes of Craig-y-Trwyn along the west side of the Nant Gwyddon brook all the way to Abercarn.

Top of the Nant Gwyddon valley about 3 mile north of Abercarn ▼

The on-road route is another superb ride along the tarmac lane which steeply descends the mountain slopes to Abercarn just west of Coed Sara.

From Abercarn there is an easy stretch of riding along a fairly quiet B road through Cwmcarn to the start of the canal towpath section at Pontywaun.

Ride 16 Crossing the Glyn Valley to the forested slopes above Abercarn

From Pontywain bridge there is nothing but lazy summertime cycling along 24 miles of canal towpaths and railway tracks all the way back to Blaenafon including an exciting ride down through a spectacular series of 14 locks just near Rogerstone.

Along canal towpath Crosskeys ▼

Near the Nant Gwyddon brook close to location of Craig Furnace

Heritage Interest Along Route

Pontypool and Newport: see Town & Canal section

Mon & Brecon Canal: see Town & Canal section

Craig Furnace: Remains of mid 18C water powered ironworking furnace about 2 miles north of Abercarn on the mountain slopes east of the Nant Gwyddon; (**Note**: I was not successful in locating the remains of this furnace during a short detour I made north of the Nant Gwyddon bridge reference Segment 6A of ride; however J Newman's Guide to "Buildings in Monmouthshire" indicates remains of the site do indeed exist.)

Abercarn Furnace: recently discovered (1993) site and few remains of 18C water powered charcoal furnace on private premises in Abercarn; it is near the location of Mon & Brecon canal (dismantled) and not far from Nant Gwyddon brook which provided the water power to drive the furnace bellows.

Benjamin Hall of Abercarn: Big Ben named after Benjamin Hall who was Lord of Abercarn Manor; he resided at Abercarn House; Hall provided the finance to build St Lukes (on hillside above the Gwyddon valley) for conduct of services in Welsh; he later moved to Llanover.

Griffithstown Railway Museum: history of the Monmouthshire railway with lots of memorabilia; located just off the Sustrans route 46 cycleway (railway track-bed)

Pontypool Blaenafon high level railway; at the Pontypool end the high level line joined the low level line at Trevethin junction ; from here the Mon Railway & Canal company extended the line in 1876 to Talywaun which was later extended to Blaenafon by the LNWR (London & North West railway company); the line crosses the massive Ffrwd valley viaduct at Talywaun; it is now a superb tarmac cycleway (Sustrans route 46);

British Ironworks: located through Big Arch near the route 46 cycleway (old railway) road crossing Pentwyn; Ironworks started 1826: all that remains are the quadrangle of 19C office buildings/workshops and the 19C Beam Pumping Engine-House that served the Ironworks Colliery.

The Route

Segment 1 (1 ½ miles): From Blaenafon Ironworks follow the west access route around Garn lakes to the Whistle Inn as per *Access route A* (see section Bike Access Routes).

Segment 2 (1 ¼ miles): From the Whistle Inn follow the route to the bridleway junction at the top of Coity mountain as described in *Ride 15 segment 2*

.

Segment 3 (just under 4 miles): From the Coity bridleway junction follow the bridleway eastwards up to the intersection with the Talywain-St Illtyd mountain road as described in *Ride 15 Segment 3.*

Segment 4 (2 miles): From the intersection of the bridleway with the Talywaun-St Illtyd mountain road continue south for just under a mile and then turn left over a cattle grid on to a single track tarmac road just opposite a radio mast. Follow this around for about a mile and then make a steep climb. Just at the brow of the hill near a stone wall watch out for an unsigned bridleway grass track on the right heading south over the mountain (Cefn Crib).

Segment 5 (5 3/4 miles): Follow this track over

the mountain (rideable) and after about half a mile it becomes a hard dirt track leading to a cattle grid and then a single track tarmac lane. Descend the lane down Cwm-LLwynau as far as a tee-junction on the outskirts of Hafodyryns. Turn left and continue to the junction of the main road near the Hafodyryns Inn. Cross over and take the minor road directly ahead.

Be prepared for a steep to moderate low gear climb up to a Y-fork. Turn left at this fork and continue to climb up Llwyd mountain. It is an easy to moderate low gear one mile climb up the tarmac lane. Pass by Pen-y-Caeau farm and cross over a cattle grid leading to wide open grassland Common. Superb views over the Ebbw valley.

Bike through the Common and watch out for the start of the large area of woodland (Coed Sara) on the left.

At the beginning of Sara Wood there is a small pull-in on the right and about one hundred yards below this on the left is the start of a forest track via an access gate.

From this point there are two alternative descents down to Abercarn. Choose either the off-road Segment 6A forest route or the on-road Segment 6B route

Segment 6A Option (just under 2 ¾ miles): At the gate entrance to Sara wood bear left on to the wide well compacted forest track and

181

descend a short way towards a two- way track split. Bear right and continue the descent down Craig-y-Trwyn.

About halfway down there is clearing where another track veers off to the left down to the bridge over the Nant Gwyddon brook. Stay on the track straight ahead (south) and follow it down through the Nant Gwyddon valley until it emerges on to the B road at Abercarn. Continue at Segment 7.

Segment 6B Option (2 miles): From the gate entrance to Sara wood continue straight ahead along the tarmac lane. There follows a steep descent down to the village of Abercarn at the bottom of the Ebbw valley.

As the outskirts of Abercarn are approached towards the bottom follow the road down and keep to the left. From Twyn road continue to Coed Moelfa road and along Gwyddon road to the junction of the B4591 road near the Commercial Inn. You can't really go wrong.

Segment 7 (1 ½ miles): From the Commercial Inn Abercarn follow the B road (very light traffic) through to Cwmcarn passing the New Inn, Old Swan Inn, Emmanual Church, row of 19C terraced houses, and the imposing Cwmcarn Inn in the centre of Cwmcarn village. Continue through the village passing Cwmcarn Primary school bearing left at the next tee-junction which is the start of Pontywaun district.

Just at this point near the Pontywaun signpost is the start of the cycleway route 47 on the other side of the road. Unfortunately the 1 ½ miles to the canal bridge was not open at the time of writing. If this section is closed simply continue on the B road along Twyncarn road passing the Castle and Philanthropic Inns as far as the canal bridge. Turn left on to Halls road terrace and this leads directly to the canal towpath which is Sustrans cycleway route 47.

Segment 8 (just over 24 miles): From the Pontywaun canal bridge simply follow Sustrans cycleway all the way back to Blaenafon Ironworks as described in _Ride 14._

The canal bridge at Pontywaun is the entry point for start of the canal towpath ride along the Crumlin arm of the Mon & Brecon canal which extends to Newport.

It passes through Crosskeys, Risca, Pontymister and Rogerstone before descending through the spectacular series of 14 locks and along the bottom of Allt-yryn to Newport.

From Newport the ride follows Sustrans cycleway route 46 along the canal towpath through Malpas and Cwmbran as far as Sebastapol. It then crosses on to the old railway track joining up with the purpose built cycleway through Pontypool and on to Blaenafon.

At the bridge in Nant Gwyddon valley ▼

Canal towpath cycleway through Cwmbran ▼

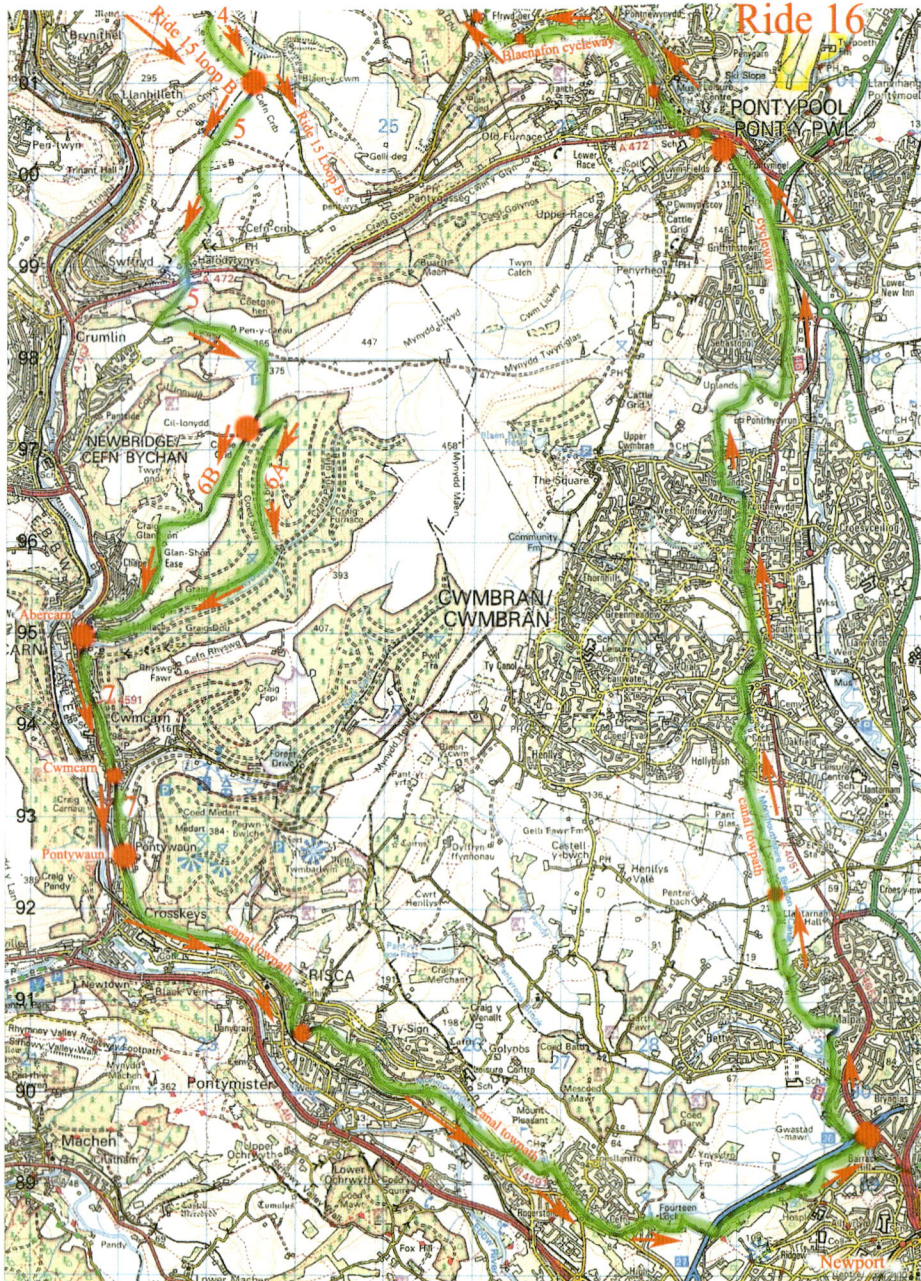

Ride 17: Cwmtillery Reservoir valley and Bailey's Round House

The Ride

A fairly short ride over Coity mountain to Cwmtillery reservoir, looping back around the Ebbw valley to Bailey's Roundhouse – a poignant reminder of the turbulent ironworking days.

Route Information	
Start and Finish	**How easy is the Ride**
Blaenafon Ironworks	Reasonably easy short ride over flat and gentle inclines with just a couple of very short climbs; a wheel up the side of the Coity at the start of ride; route is completely rideable with exception of a few ruts here and there
Distance/ Ride Time	
Distance: 17 miles	
Ride Time: 3 hours	**What sort of terrain**
Energy Level	Mix of on-road and off-road including - minor tarmac lanes, grass/stony mountain tracks and bridle-ways, stony tracks over disused railway beds; challenging descent down stone track to join road near reservoir
**	
Off-road Grade	
Largely G1/G2 with one G3 section	

From Blaenafon Ironworks the ride begins along the south west access route crossing over Coity mountain and descending a rather challenging stony track to join a tarmac lane on the Cwmtillery side.

185

There follows a fast easy descent along a tarmac lane down through the attractive reservoir valley of Cwmtillery to the East Bank district about a mile below.

Descending the mountain track towards Cwmtillery Reservoir ▼

There is a short steep climb from the East Bank to the top of the West Bank where there are excellent views down the lower Tillery valley towards the town of Abertillery. The route then loops around to the west descending an off-road dirt track along the wooded slopes of Coed Castellau to the bottom of the Ebbw valley.

From here there is a surprisingly scenic and off-the-beaten-track cycleway ride following the Ebbw fach river through Duffryn Park to Blaina and then a climb up to Cwmcellyn lake which is superbly located high up on the hill overlooking the Ebbw valley completely surrounded by hills and long undulating distant ridges.

The ride continues a short way along a minor road before crossing a footbridge to reach Baileys Roundhouse Tower that looms menacingly on the hillside just above the site of old Nantyglo Ironworks that once dominated this part of the valley. The Roundhouse fortress was built by the 19C Ironmaster to protect his family against the possibility of worker unrest.

The route to Brynmawr is along a cycleway that skirts around the perimeter of yet another attractive lake near the site of the old Brynmawr Rubber factory (dismantled) that was at one time regarded as an architectural tour-de-force of the post war period.

The return leg is along a tarmac section of the old Brynmawr Abergavenny railway trackbed to

Lower Cwm Nant-gam and then along the west access route through Waunafon to Blaenafon Ironworks.

Heritage Interest Along Route

Cwmtillery Reservoir: two million gallon early 20C reservoir is the termination of the water pipeline that is laid 22 miles from the Grwyne Fawr reservoir in the Black mountains; the pipeline goes through a tunnel under Coity mountain; see Ride 2 for information on the Grwyne Fawr.

Ty Mawr Nantyglo: foundation remains of house owned by Bailey the Ironmaster; tunnel from Ty Mawr to Roundhouse was escape route for Bailey and family in case of worker unrest.

Nantyglo Roundhouse Tower: defensive tower structure designed to protect the Ironmaster and his family from worker uprising; there were originally two towers.

Site of Nantyglo Ironworks: location is just opposite Market road not far from the footbridge that crosses the busy A 467 road; important 19C ironworks that dominated this area; (nothing to see only imagine); Brynmawr town grew as a result of Nantyglo Ironworks; Coal Brook Vale Ironworks as well as Blaina & Cwm Cellyn Ironworks were located a stones throw away just down the valley below Nantyglo Ironworks

Brynmawr Rubber factory complex: Major architectural post-war industrial building; the Boiler house (inverted parabolic concrete roof) is all that remains; can be seen across the lake from the cycle/walkway path.

Welfare Park Brynmawr: built from Miners welfare funds during the 1920/30's; used to be site of Heathcock pond - one of a chain of ponds associated with 19C Nantyglo Ironworks; *Waun Pond* (now attractive lake) also part of the pond complex that fed Nantyglo Ironworks

Abergavenny Merthyr Railway: section of spectacular railway line through Clydach Gorge; Brynmawr Abergavenny section opened in 1862 by LNWR; other sections soon followed; closed 1958.

Brynmawr- Blaenafon railway: section of LNWR branch line that opened in 1868 closed entirely in 1954; *Waunafon Halt* at 1400 feet was the second highest on standard guage in Great Britain.

The Route

Inns Along Route

Whistle Inn   Garn-yr-erw
Racehorse   Waunafon
Royal Exchange Inn   Blaina

See section "Bike Access Routes" for description and maps of access routes from and to Blaenafon, reference the route segments at beginning and end of ride.

Segment 1 (1 ½ miles): Follow the west access route from Blaenafon Ironworks around Garn lakes to the Whistle as per *Access route A*

Segment 2 (1 mile): Continue south from the Whistle to the top of the Coity as described in *Ride 15 Segment 2*

Segment 3 (1 ½ miles): From the bridleway crossing on the Coity just above Blaentillery farm, take the track south down towards the wall (reservoir ahead) that connects with the bridleway heading south east. Follow this track (hard dirt-grass-stone) around joining another descending track heading south towards another wall.

This track become a little steep and stony but eventually descends on to a tarmac lane just above the reservoir.

Descend this lane for about a mile along the side of the reservoir, through the very attractive Tillery valley, over a cattle grid as far as the tee -junction in the East Bank area of Cwmtillery.

Segment 4 (2 miles): Turn right and just after the road swings back around towards Abertillery take the right hand turn and make a short steep low gear climb up through the West Bank area. Continue on this road for a little more than a mile and then look out for a public access footway sign (near houses) on the right.

Follow the lane between the houses, go through the open gate and just by the bungalow the tarmac lane changes to good dirt track. Follow this track around for about half a mile until it joins an open clearing. The track continues at the end of clearing and descends down to a road near a children's playground on top of a housing estate.

Follow the road down through the estate for about half a mile and then just near some garages take the path with railings on the right and descend a short distance to the main (Rose Heyworth) road with Rose Heyworth primary school directly opposite.

From this junction cross over the road, descend the long series of steps (easy) opposite and take the cycle track on the left. Follow this track around up to the point where it emerges on to the A467 road. Cross over this road with care and descend the steps directly opposite (easy). At the bottom turn left, go through the Rugby field a short distance to join the cycle track (unsigned) near the Ebbw Fach river.

Segment 5 (just under 2 ½ miles): Follow the cycleway and the Ebbw Fach river westwards through the very attractive parkland up to the point where it emerges on to Old Blaina Road. Look out for an unsigned cycleway access gate on the opposite side of the road on the left.

Go through the access gate, follow the cycleway (was at one time a real traffic road) near the river, pass through Duffryn Park and just after a mile the cycleway terminates at an access to a road tunnel which leads into Blaina High Street near the Blaina Institute and just opposite the United Reformed church.

Continue up High street, go past Salem Baptist chapel turn right by the Royal Exchange Inn. Steepish climb up The Laurels and Cwm-Celyn road leading to the attractive Cwm-Celyn lake (near the Infants School).

Segment 6 (2 ¼ miles): From Cwm-Celyn lake head north-west on Surgery road which joins Queen St on the Blaina-Nantyglo border (look out for stone border monument). Continue along this road a short way, turn left down a hill (brown CC sign) near St Annes Church.

At the bottom of the hill take the footbridge over the A 467 and then turn left on the footway path

that winds its way through the houses emerging on a lane near the Nantyglo Roundhouse tower. Turn left down the lane past the row of 19C terrace houses to the remains (foundations) of Ty Mawr.   Return back up the lane to the

Roundhouse Tower that can be viewed from the lane leading to Waun Fawr road.

Segment 7 (1 ¼ miles): From the Roundhouse Tower join Waun Fawr road and continue as far as the junction with Pond road turning right then left through the new Lakeside housing estate adjacent to the lake (just opposite Nantyglo Comprehensive school).

Follow the road through joining the cycleway near the lake (Waun Pond).

Continue up to the junction of another new cycleway along the old railway line near Warrick road.   (From this point you can optionally make a small detour to another reservoir lake a half a mile west).

Continue down the cycleway a short way (towards Brynmawr) joining Warwick road just in front of the Welfare Park gates.

At the junction of Warwick road and Lake road cross over and wheel the bike through the short access which leads to Market Square and the War Memorial in the centre of Brynmawr.

Segment 8 (under ½ mile): From Market square continue north down Alma street to the start of cycleway above the Heads of Valley roundabout as per *Route through Brynmawr*

Segment 9 (just over ½ mile): From the cycleway start-point above the Heads of Valley roundabout Brynmawr follow the tarmac track along the old railway route as far as the gate access at Lower Cwm Nant-Gam as per *AccessRoute E*

Segment 10 (1 ½ miles): From Lower Cwm Nant-gam follow the route through Llanmarch to the gate at the old railway crossing Waunafon (near cattle grid) as per *Access Route D*

Segment 11: (1 mile): From the Waunafon gate follow the west access route along the old railway track bed to the junction of the cycleway near the Whistle Inn as per *Access route B*

Segment 1 (just over 1 ½ miles): From the cycleway junction near the Whistle Inn follow the west access route via Garn lakes back to the Blaenafon Ironworks car park as per *Access route A*

Cwmcellen Lake ▼

190

Roundhouse Tower Nantyglo ▼

Lake-like pond near the cyclepath just above Brynmawr Welfare park ▼

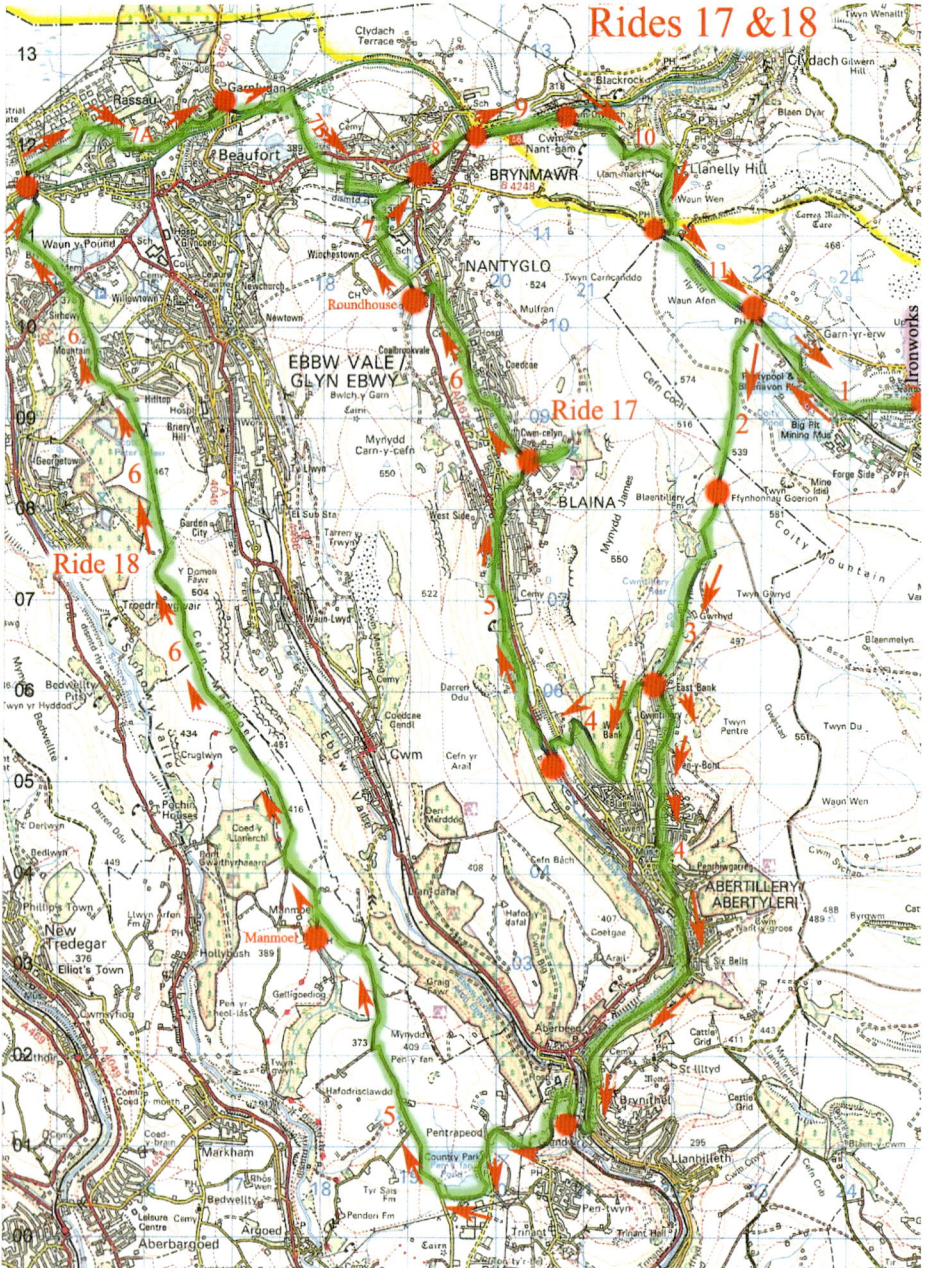

Ride 18: Through Manmoel and over the Sirhowy Ridge to Tredegar

The Ride

A mountain ride through the scenic Cwmtillary valley to the attractive country park around Manmoel village. The bike route crosses the remote Sirhowy ridge to the Aneuron Bevan memorial stones near the Iron town of Tredegar.

Route Information

Start and Finish

Blaenafon Ironworks

Distance/ Ride Time

Distance: 28 ¼ miles

Ride Time: 4 ¼ hours

Energy Level
   ***

Off-road Grade

G1/G2 one short G3 section

How easy is the Ride

Moderate: A ride of just under 30 miles with plenty of flat and descending sections; wheel-up side of Coity from Whistle; three-quarter mile climb towards Pen-y-fal country park steep at the bottom only; short steep climb into Garnlydyn; route is completely rideable.

What sort of terrain

Mix of on-road off-road including minor tarmac lanes, grass/stony mountain tracks and bridle-ways, stony tracks over disused railway bed

---

The ride from Blaenafon Ironworks begins along the south-west access route crossing over Coity mountain and descending a tarmac lane down through the verdant and lake-like valley of Cwmtillery as per Ride 17. The route winds itself around the top of Abertillery and along the traffic-light B-road down the Ebbw valley to Aberbeeg.

It crosses over a footbridge that spans both the river and A-road emerging on a lane just near Christ Church whose dominating presence commands the entire hillside just above the two Ebbws.

There follows a steep to moderate climb along the minor road through Cwm-nant-gwynt and then around the attractively landscaped lake within Pen-y-fan Country Park.

From here it is an easy relaxing ride through the open meadows and tree lined lanes along the top of Pen-y-fan mountain to the small village of Manmoel that sits about 350 metres high above the Sirhowy and Ebbw valleys.

The route then continues west over the wide open grass Common on top of Sirhowy ridge following the path of an old stone road (old railroad) with superb views over the Sirhowy valley towards Markam and Tredegar.

Along the Sirowy Ridge mountain road from Manmoel ▼

The stone track bends around just above Garden-City Ebbw Vale, descending through Mountain Air to the four massive stones that mark the Aneuron Bevan Memorial not far from the site of the old Sirhowy Ironworks (see Ride 22).

The ride then heads north through a fairly traffic free area of Rassau and Garnlydan, joining an old cart road just below a large reservoir and crossing an open grass Common just above Beaufort to link up with a cycleway into Brynmawr.

The return leg is along a tarmac section of the old Brynmawr Abergavenny railway trackbed to Lower Cwm Nant-gam following the west access route through Waunafon to Blaenafon

194

Ironworks.

Heritage Interest Along Route

Cwmtillery Reservoir: two million gallon early 20C reservoir; is the termination of the water pipeline that is laid 22 miles from the Grwyne Fawr reservoir in the Black mountains; the pipeline goes through a tunnel under Coity mountain; see Ride 2 for information on the Grwyne Fawr.

Christ Church Aberbeeg: early 20C stone church whose tower is a landmark for miles around above the Ebbw valley

Parran Calvanistic Methodist church Manmoel: built in 1828 by David Wyn biographer of Howyl Harris.

Aneiron Bevan Memorial near Tredegar: three massive self standing stones around a centre stone representing Tredegar, Ebbw Vale and Rhymney; marking the spot where Bevan spoke to the people of his constituency.

Sirrowy Ironworks: not far from the Bevan Memorial stones see Ride 22

Tredegar: see Town & Canal section

Welfare Park Brynmawr: built from Miners welfare funds during the 1920/30's; used to be site of Heathcock pond - one of a chain of ponds associated with 19C Nantyglo Ironworks;

Abergavenny Merthyr Railway: section of spectacular railway line through Clydach Gorge; Brynmawr Abergavenny section opened in 1862 by LNWR; other sections soon followed; closed 1958.

Brynmawr- Blaenafon railway: section of LNWR branch line that opened in 1868 closed entirely in 1954; *Waunafon Halt* at 1400 feet was the second highest on standard guage line in Great Britain.

The Route

Inns Along Route

Whistle Inn	Garn-yr-erw
Racehorse	Waunafon
Manmoel Inn	Manmoel
Six Bells Hotel	SixBells
Castle Inn	Nant-y-Croft
Farmers Arms	Beaufort Road

See section "Bike Access Routes" for description and maps of access routes from and to Blaenafon, reference the route segments at beginning and end of ride.

Segment 1 (1 ½ miles): Follow the west access route from Blaenafon Ironworks around Garn lakes to the Whistle as per *Access route A*

Segment 2 (1 mile): Continue south from the Whistle to the top of the Coity as described in *Ride 15 Segment 2*

Segment 3 (1 ¾ miles): Descend the south side of the ridge to Cwmtillsry reservoir continuing the descent along the tarmac lane to the Church Lane junction in the East Bank district of Cwmtillery as per *Ride 17 segment 3.*

Segment 4 (4 miles): At this junction turn left heading south east along the top of Tillery road passing Blaentillery primary school and the Mynydd Lodge guest house.

Keeping to the left continue down Tillery road for almost a mile passing Abertillery comprehensive school as far as the junction with High street. Turn left, go up the hill a short distance and take third on right leading into Princess Street and then straight through to Richmond road.

Follow Richmond road up to a tee-junction. Turn right and then continue a short distance down to junction with Bridge street (main road) This is the village of Six Bells.

Turn left and go around the elbow bend near Six Bells Hotel.

Follow this main road (traffic very light) for a little more than a mile; it soon joins with the B 4471 that emerges from the right near Aberbeeg. From here continue on the B-road (Commercial Road) for just under half a mile and take next turning on right (watch for it!).

Go down the hill, cross over railway, pass Glandwr Baptist church on left and then take the footbridge that crosses the Ebbw river and the busy A 467 road to join a tarmac lane on the other side.

Segment 5 (4 ½ miles): From the footbridge turn right and follow a short distance up to a junction of Pantddu road; Christ church is just opposite.

Turn left and make a steep low gear climb for about quarter mile followed by a moderate mid gear climb for further half a mile as far as a turn-off on the right (watch for it) sign-posted to Pen-y-fan pond country park.

Turn right and follow the track around the attractive Lake; on the west side of the Lake look out for a short section of footpath leading to the Manmoel road (tarmac lane).

Keep on this road passing by the Travellers Rest on left; a relaxing ride through the rural green countryside on top of Pen-y-fan; after two miles you arrive at Manmoel village.

Segment 6 (6 miles): From the Manmoel Inn follow the lane in the direction west for about half a mile as far as a cattle grid which is the start of Manmoel Common. A tarmac lane winds its way on top of Manmoel ridge changing into an old stone road after about a mile.

Superb views overlooking the Sirhowy valley towards the southwest.

Follow the old stone Manmoel road along the mountain top for another two miles past the radio mast and descend down to a junction with Tredegar road.

Cross over this road keeping straight ahead

continue on Manmoel road (which is now a tarmac road) for just over a mile up to the junction with A 4047. Cross over this road and head for the Aneiron Bevan Memorial centre which is just on the right.

[*From here it is possible to make a short detour to the site of the Sirhowy Ironwork (see Ride 22): from the Memorial follow the wide dirt track towards the west a short distance and then take the footpath heading south towards Dukestown. Follow this around past Sirhowy Infants school crossing over Chartist Way leading to the Ironworks site*].

From the Bevan Memorial centre follow the wide dirt track a short distance to the west and then take the footpath on the left (west) which heads up over a tump.

Once over the rise the path joins a wide track and descends the hill towards the west connecting with Bryn Serth road just at the bridge crossing the Heads of the Valley road near Nant-y-Croft. Cross over the bridge and turn right on to a track which connects with the Rassau Industrial estate road just above the Nant y croft roundabout and near a north-west road junction..

Segment 7A Nant-y-croft-Garnlydon (2 miles): From this point just above the roundabout turn right (north) and follow this road (quiet) around for about half a mile as far as the Yuasu Battery factory on the left. Look out for a dirt track on the right opposite the factory. Follow this track which winds itself around a short distance crossing Rassau brook and joining Stonebridge road in Rassau (Housing) Estate.

Turn left then right on to Honeyfield road, go straight ahead at the first roundabout (near Rassau Stores) descending the road to another

197

roundabout at the bottom of the hill.

Turn left making a short steep climb up Reservoir road leading to Prince Philip road in Garnlydan (Housing) Estate; follow the road around until it meets the Llangynidr mountain road. Turn right and just near the point where this road joins with the Heads of the valley road look out for a wide dirt track with a gated access on the left hand side.

Segment 7B Garmlydon-Brynmawr (2 miles): Continue on this cart-road track (leads to reservoir) a short distance, go through tunnel under the A465; this leads to a wide open grass Common. Follow track a short way, turn right (north east) on to another track towards a Substation keeping straight ahead at a track crossways.

There are small reservoirs on right and ponds on left. Follow track to the gate which leads to Big Lane and the junction of King Street (A4047) between Beaufort and Brynmawr. Farmers Arms is just up the road.

Cross over King Street go straight ahead on a lane that leads to a tarmac walkway/cycleway (Twyncynhordy). Continue a short distance on this cycleway which joins Windsor road.

Go down Windsor road, take second right on to Henderson road which descends on to Warwick road. Look out for the cycleway which is just a short distance away with the very attractive lake-like pond behind it to the south.

Follow the cycleway down towards Brynmawr town rejoining Warwick road near the Park gates (Welfare Park). At the junction with Lake road cross over and walk bike through the access leading to Market Square and the War Memorial in the centre of Brynmawr .

Segment 8 (under ½ mile): From Market square continue north down Alma street to the start of cycleway above the Heads of Valley roundabout as per *Route through Brynmawr*

Segment 9 (just over ½ mile): From the cycleway start-point just above the Heads of Valley roundabout Brynmawr, follow the tarmac track along the old railway route as far as the railway road crossing at Lower Cwm Nant-Gam as per *AccessRoute E*

Segment 10 (1 ½ miles): From Lower Cwm Nant-Gam crossing follow the route through Upper Gellifellen and Llanmarch to the old railway crossing Waunafon (near cattle grid) as per *Access Route D*

Segment 11 (1 mile): From the Waunafon follow the west access route along the old railway track bed to the junction of the cycleway near the Whistle Inn as per *Access route B*

Segment 1 (just over 1 ½ miles): From the cycleway junction near the Whistle Inn follow the west access route via Garn lakes back to the Blaenafon Ironworks car park as per *Access route A*

Bevan Memorial Stones near Bryn Serth Hill Tredegar ▼

Lake-like pond adjacent to cycleway near Warwick road Brynmawr ▼

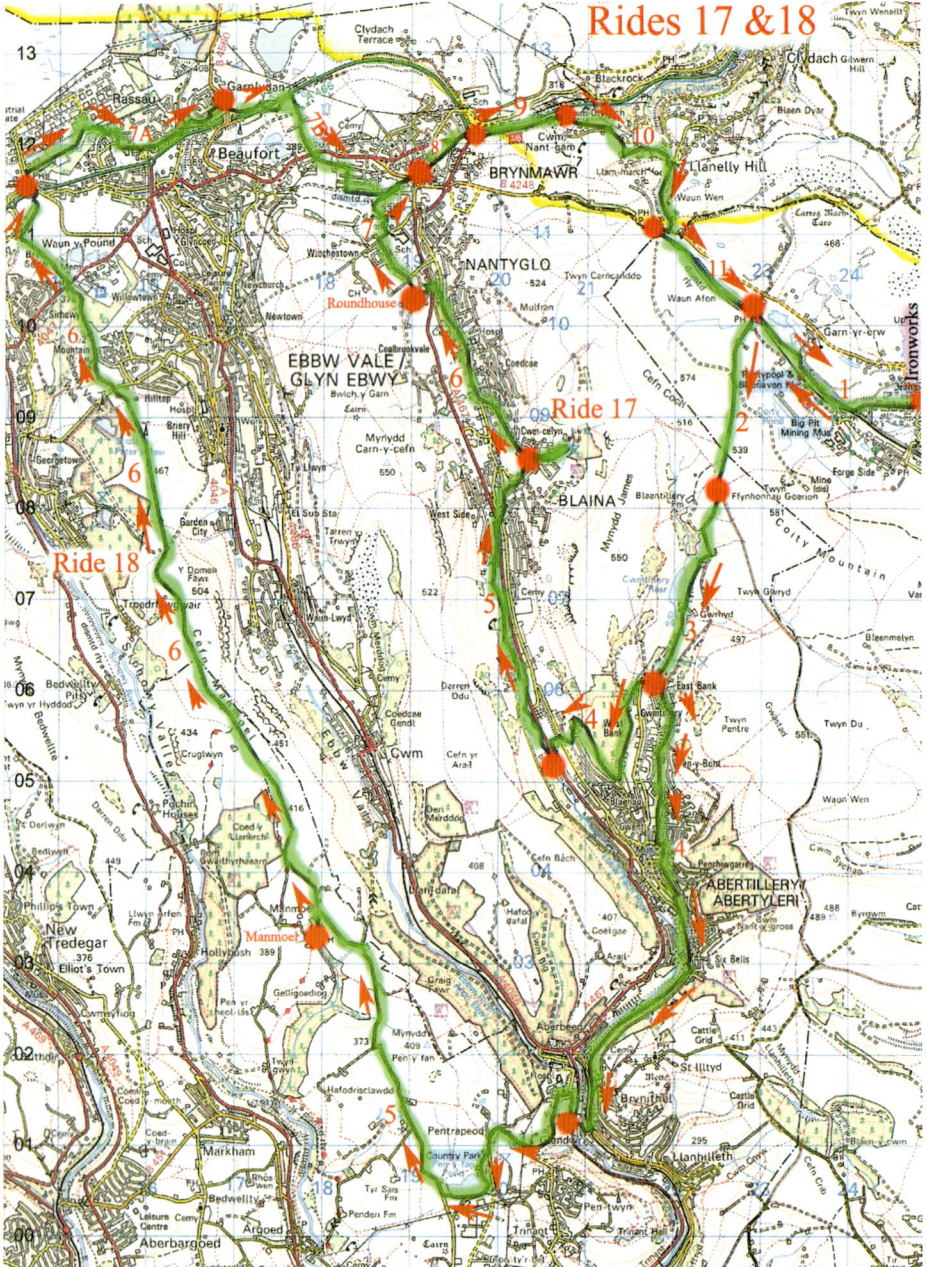

Ride 19: Reservoir Valley Loops around Talybont and Llangynydr

The Ride

From the moorlands of Trefil to the spectacular lake-like district of the Taf Fechan and Caerfannel valleys. This circular ride provides an opportunity to choose one of four highly scenic routes descending the mountain slopes and valleys to the Mon & Brecon canal. Try out each loop on a different day.

Route Information

Start and Finish

Blaenafon Ironworks

Distance/ Ride Time

Ride via Loop 1 -   Distance: 33   miles:
Ride Time: 5 hours

Ride via Loop 2 - Distance: 42 ¼ miles
Ride Time: 6 hours

Ride via Loop 3 -   Distance: 45 ¼ miles:
Ride Time: 6 ½ hours

Ride via Loop 4 -   Distance   47 ¾ miles:
Ride Time: 7 hours

Energy Level

Loops 1/2   **

Loops 3/4   ***

How easy the Ride

Loops1/2 moderate: Loops3/4: moderate plus.
All rides are fairly long but most of route is flat or descending; energy needs are governed by distance and off-road tracks not by hills; only one short steep climb to Torpantau (Loops 1/2); some short climbs on final return section via Llanmarch   to Waunafon.

What sort of terrain

All loops involve off-road mountain track sections; some are challenging but you can choose to wheel bike; other off-road tracks include canal towpath and railway track bed (hardcore gravel-dirt-grass-stone) – all easy.
.

Off-road Grade

G1/2/3

The ride begins at Blaenafon Ironworks along the west access route to Brynmawr where it links up with a cycleway close to the path of the old Brynmawr-Merthyr railway just above the site of the old Nantyglo Ironworks further down in the valley.

The route then crosses over the grassland Common above Beaufort, winding its way past a large mountainside reservoir and emerging at Garnlyden not far from the Heads of Valley road; it then continues through the Rassau linking up with the old Trefil railroad (bridleway) at Nant-y-Croft.

From here it is an easy ride along the mountain bridleway through the quarrying village of Trefil and along the path of the historic Brynore Tramroad (metalled road) to the Bevan Heritage Trail Stone at the top of the Duffryn Crawnon valley

The Bevan landmark is in the midst of wide open and lonely moorlands that stretch for miles around. This is the starting point of the Loop1 ride

The Loop 1 Llangynydr ride begins with a challenging descent down a dirt stone track that weaves its way down through the narrow wooded Pergad Cwm to join a tarmac lane near the head of the Duffryn Crawnon valley.

Loop1: descending top of Pergad Cwm above the Duffryn Crawnon ▼

From here it is an easy relaxing 5 mile ride following the river down the valley through fields and woodland; the Duffryn Crawnon is a pastoral green valley bounded by hills and grassland and way off the beaten track. Llangynydr village is at the bottom of the valley close to the Mon & Brecon canal and Usk river.

The other alternative routes begin a little further west of the Bevan Heritage Stone. Loop 2 and 3 rides start from the top of a mountain pass (Pen Bwlch Glasgwm) high up above the south end of Talybont reservoir. Loop 4 ride begins at the end of the Trefil road just beyond the Apache looking canyons and old quarry area.

The Loop 2 Talybont-reservoir ride is a gradual but spectacular long descent down the side of the mountain above the large expanse of shimmering water at the bottom of the Caerfannel valley.

Loop 2: track skirts alongside Talybont Reservoir ▼

It is a fairly easy off-road ride along a wide dirt track with superb views over the reservoir towards the distant Black mountains on the northern side. The route which traverses some sections of the Brynore tramroad eventually emerges along Taffs Trail (Sustrans Route 8) around the perimeter of the reservoir and from here it follows a woodland trail (Brynore tramroad) into Talybont wharf on the Mon & Brecon canal.

Loop 3 Dolygaer ride begins along a mountain bridleway track south west of Pen Bwlch Glasgwm, eventually merging with a stone road that descends through a heavily forested area of Cwm Callan to the valley below. This can be a bone shaker ride in parts but it soon changes to a tarmac lane that drops down into at Dolygaer on the banks of the Pontsticill and Pentwyn reservoirs. Dolygaer is one of the stops on the Brecon Mountain Railway which is a key tourist attraction in the area.

Loop3: end of Cwm Callan descent at Pentwyn Lake Dolygaer ▼

The ride continues along Taffs Trail around Pentwyn reservoir making a long loop through the Taf Fechan forest rejoining the minor road on the high mountain pass of Torpantau - a one-time lonely railway stop on the Merthyr & Brecon line. The descent to the Usk valley is yet another spectacular (not-too-be-missed) ride down the seven mile Bank of the old railway line east of Talybont reservoir finally emerging at the canal near the White Hart Inn Talybont.

Loop 4 starts just beyond the Trefil quarries and follows a two mile bridleway track over the moorlands between Merthyr and Trefil, connecting with yet another bridleway high up above the southern dam-end of Pontsticill reservoir. The views can only be described as dramatic and stunning; forested hillsides rise up on either side of the lake and the mighty Beacons dominate the western skyline. It is a steep but not difficult descent down the grass mountain track that drops right down to the minor road near the Waterworks building on the southern edge of the reservoir.

From here the route follows Taffs Trail (Sustrans Route 8) crossing over the dam on the south side and skirting around a large forested section before rejoining the minor road near Dolygaer.

The ride to Talybont then takes the same route as Loop 3 above, crossing the Torpantau mountain pass and swooping down the valley past Talybont reservoir into the village of Talybont.

Loop 4: riding along the Cefn-yr-Ystrad bridleway above Pontsticill Reservoir ▲

The next section of the ride is along the Mon & Brecon canal towpath. From either Talybont or Llangynydr it is an easy relaxing ride through Llangattoc to Gilwern Wharf along some of the most picturesque and scenic parts of the canal.

From Gilwern Wharf the route departs from the towpath following the old tramroad along the river Cydach and linking up with the trackbed of the Abergavenny Merthyr railway just above Clydach Ironworks. The return leg is through Llanmarch and Waunafon to Blaenafon.

Loop4: Descending bridleway towards Pontsticill ▼

Heritage Interest Along Route

Trefil Railroad: joins the Brynore tramroad at Trefil; existing bridleway grass track between Trefil and Wells farm Nant-y-croft; former mineral line in the Ironworks period

Brynoer Tram road: opened in 1815 extends from Trefil to Talybont Wharf (8 miles) on Brecon & Mon canal; at Trefil village it linked with the tramroads from Tredegar Ironworks and Rhymney Ironworks; the tramroad is 12 miles long between Brynoer Colliery Rhymney and Talybont Wharf; it enabled iron products and limestone to be transported to the canal at Talybont.

Trefil Quarries: provided limestone for Ironworks and Limekilns nearby

Merthyr & Brecon Railway: opened between Brecon and Pant in 1863 with Stops at Tal-y-lyn, Talybont, Pant-y-rhiw, Torpantau, Dolygaer, Pontsticil and Pant. The railway junction at Dowlais Top linked service to Merthyr and through Bargoed and Bedwas to Newport; passenger train was stuck for several days in Torpantau tunnel in severe winter of 1947; disused railway track now part of Taffs Trail.

Taffs Trail: 55 mile trail extending from Cardiff via Merthyr to Brecon; utilises disused railways, tramroads and towpaths; Ride 19 utilises northern section of Taffs Trail (Sustrans route 8) between Pontsticill and Talybont and is over parts of disused M & B railway track and Brynore tramroad .

Pentwyn reservoir: built 1863 to supply Merthyr and Dowlais.

Pontsticill reservoir: built in 1927 to augment Pentwyn reservoir which leaked water due to geological fault; both reservoirs hold up to 3,400 million gallons of water.

Talybont Reservoir: built to supply Newport and district; the first phase was construction of a Weir and pipeline completed in 1927 but was thwart with problems; replaced by present reservoir opened in 1939; the flooding of the Glyn Colwyn valley resulted in the loss of about a dozen farmhouses with three underwater; the reservoir is 2 miles long by two thirds of a mile wide and has a capacity of 2,500 million gallons; the 33 mile pipeline is through the Usk and Avon Lwyd valleys to Llantarnum service reservoir and then to Malpas

Brecon Mountain Railway: scenic tourist line running on the east side of the reservoirs between Pant and Torpantau; along the path of the old Brecon Merthyr railway.

Dolygar: was a busy Victorian railway station in the 1860s bringing passengers to the annual boating regatta held at Pentwyn reservoir.

Cwm Calun stone track: shown as a Roman road on earlier ordinance survey maps

Clydach Ironworks, Llanelli Forge, Abergavenny-Merthyr railway: see Ride 22 West Heritage ride

Mon & Brecon canal: see Towns & Canal section

The Route

There are four alternative rides (loops) to choose from. Try them all out on different days

See section "Bike Access Routes" for description and maps of access routes from and to Blaenafon, reference the route segments at beginning and end of ride.

Segment 1 (1 ½ miles): Follow the west access route from Blaenafon Ironworks around Garn lakes to the Whistle as per *Access route A*

Segment 2 (just over ¾ miles): Continue the West access route from the Whistle along the old railway track bed to Waunafon as per *Access route B.*

Segment 3 (just over 2 ½ miles) : Continue along the West access route from Waunafon descending hill to Brynmawr market square as per *Access route C.*

Segment 4 (2 miles): From the market square Brynmawr cut through the short one way link (Grasshoppers Inn) to the junction with Lake road. Cross over to Warwick Road opposite, pass by the Welfare Park entrance gates and after a short distance turn left on to a cycleway/walkway.

Continue along the cycleway, pass by another attractive Lake); proceed up to a point roughly in line with the top of lake and then cross a short path plus Warwick road to join Henderson road just opposite. Ascend Henderson road, turn left on to Windsor road, cut through Twyncynghordy cycle access-way at the top, proceed to the junction of the A4047 near the Farmers Arms.

Cross over King Street (A4047) to join Big Lane opposite. After a short distance Big Lane connects with an old Cart Road at a gate access leading to the large area of grassland Common between Beaufort and the Heads of Valley road (A465).

Follow the cartroad track along the Common keeping straight ahead (towards west) at the crossroad of tracks (near Sub station) and bearing left just near the A465. Descend the cart road along the Common (cart road follows the near-by A465) pass through the A465 road tunnel, go through gate access (large reservoir near by) and continue down to the exit gate just near the A465 road junction at Garnlydan

Segment 5 (2 miles): From the gate access Garnlydyn (near A465) turn right and right again on to Llangynydr road, and then left into Garnlydan housing estate. Continue down through the estate along the main road (Prince Philip road) descending a hill to a roundabout. Cross over and ascend Honeyfield road to another roundabout in Rassau Housing estate. Keep straight ahead follow the road around until it almost reaches the top then turn left on to Stonebridge road.

After a couple of hundred yards watch out for a small path on the right close to the iron fence over the Rassau brook (near bus stop). Follow the dirt track around until it joins the main road in Rassau Induustrial estate opposite the Yuasa battery building. Turn left and continue along this road (very little traffic) for about half a mile up to a junction, turn left and go down the hill to the Nant-y-Croft roundabout. Go around the roundabout and exit on to a lane on the west side near New House farm.

Segment 6 (2 miles): From New House farm Nant-y-Croft pass through two gates near Wells farm and continue on the bridle-way track past the Radio mast.

Go through another two gates (all will open) and follow the easily rideable stone track (was the old Trefil Railroad) that winds over open desolate moorlands passing Shon-Sheffreys Reservoir on the left.

After two miles the old railroad track joins the minor road in Trefil village. A Brynore Heritage plaque with information on the tramroads is just opposite the Quarrymans Inn (Tafarn-y-Uchaf). The Trefil road is the path of the old Brynore tramroad.

Segment 7 (just over 1 ½ miles): From the Quarrymans Arms continue on the Trefil road through the wide open moorlands along the lower slopes of Llangynydr mountain with the two mighty Beacons directly ahead.

After about a mile and a half, the Aneiron Bevan heritage trail plaque on a large stone can be seen on the right. (The Chartist caves are just behind GarnFawr ridge towards the north.)

Loop 1 through Duffryn Crawnon starts from the Bevan Heritage Stone. For any of the other three optional loops continue at segment 8 below.

Loop 1 - Duffryn Crawnon to Llangynydr (just over 5 ½ miles)

From the Bevan Heritage Stone take the dirt track on the right heading roughly north-west. After a short distance the track bends around to the left and begins to descend the narrow wooded Pergad valley.

Descend the wide stone track (challenging) through a gate and continue down for under a mile (it is rideable but can be rutted and stoney in parts) until it merges with a single track tarmac lane near a farm.

This is almost the top of the Duffryn Crawnon which is a lush green pastoral valley wedged between two wooded slopes rising up on either side.

Follow lane down through the gently descending valley close to the Crawnon river and passing the 19C Soar Independent Chapel. After almost five miles the lane routes through Llangynydr village near St Cynidr & St Marys church merging with the minor Llangynydr-Talybont road just below the Red Lyon Inn.

Cross over the road and follow the lane directly opposite for half a mile joining the canal at bridge 129 (need to haul bike over stone style to access towpath). [alternatively follow the B4588 a short distance west and access the canal at Bridge 131]. Continue the ride along the canal towpath as per Segment 10 from Llangynydr.

Segment 8 (1 ¾ miles): From the Bevan Heritage Stone on the Trefil moorlands continue west on the metalled road around the head of the Duffryn Crawnon valley and through the dramatic Trefil quarries on either side of the road.

The old quarry buildings on top of the cliff ahead look like something out of the Greek Odyssey.

After almost three-quarters of a mile from the large canyons on either side of the road watch out for a bridleway track on the right (signpost to Pen Bwlch Glasgwm just off road) that crosses over the moorland to the north west.

Loop 4 ride continues from this junction (see Loop 4 below). The other two loops (2 and 3) start about a mile north west of this junction. To choose Loops 2 or 3 go to Segment 9 below.

Segment 9 (1 mile): At the junction of the Bridleway with Trefil road turn right on to the Bridleway towards Pen Bwlch Glasgwm and follow it around the mountain approximately north west with the Duffryn Crawnon valley

now on the eastern side and the Black mountains directly ahead.

The grass track is a bit rutted at the start but improves later. After about a mile the track joins up with another track from Dolygaer (underlined: unsigned bridle-way post at junction).

Both Loop 2 and Loop 3 routes start from this location. Choose one of these routes.

Loop 2 - Pen Bwlch Glasgwm to Talybont (8 miles)

Continuing from Segment 9. At the track junction take the track heading west towards Talybont; descend the stone road and pass through the gate; the track begins to descend the mountain above the Caerfannel valley. Talybont reservoir soon comes into sight. Absolutely stunning and dramatic views.

After about a mile the stone dirt road joins the path of the Brynore tramroad near a stone heritage plaque and three-way signpost (to Trefil, Dolygaer, Talybont).

Continue the descent on a wide hard gravel-dirt road go over a cattle grid and descend through a wooded area with occasional glimpses of the reservoir through the trees. At the bottom the road joins Taffs Trail near the reservoir and continues towards Talybont.

At the northern tip of the reservoir continue along the track on the right signed Taffs Trail and Brynore tramway and follow these signs to Talybont. The track emerges on the canal in front of the White Hart Inn Talybont. Continue the ride along the canal as per Segment 10.

Loop 3 – Through Doly-Gaer to Talybont (11 miles):

Pen Bwlch Glasgwm to Dolygaer (2 ¾ miles): Continuing from Segment 9. At the track junction take the track heading roughly south west to Dolgaer. Follow the track for just over a mile around the mountain (Bryniau Gleision) as far as the gate access through the forest.

The mountain track is deeply rutted in parts but can be easily bypassed.

Go through the gate and descend the stone track

(Roman road?) down Cwm Callan through the forest.

It is a bone shaker ride in some parts but improves towards the bottom. Go straight ahead at the clearing and continue the descent passing through two gates at the bottom.

Pass by the Dolygaer outdoor education centre go under the railway tunnel and descend the metalled road to the lake. Follow the road over the lake up to the junction of minor road to Talybont. At this point the ride joins Loop 4.for the remaining 8 miles to Talybont.

Dolygaer to Talybont (8 ¼ miles): From the Dolygaer turn-off follow the minor road past Pentwyn reservoir as far as the Taffs trail turn-off on the left.

Take the Taffs trail route up through the Taf-Fechan forrest following the river for some of the way. The trail emerges back on the minor road not too far from the mouth (south) of the old Brecon & Merthyr railway tunnel and not far from the old Torpantau station.

It is a short steep climb up over the Torpantau mountain pass; watch out for the   the turn-off on the right along Taffs trail. Turn right and enjoy the spectacular 7 mile descent along the path of the old railway down to Talybont lake. Stunning views going down towards lake.

The ride joins Loop 2 route halfway down the length of the reservoir. At the northern end of the reservoir bear right and follow Taffs trail (and Brynore Tramway) for just over a mile to the canal bridge opposite the White Hart Inn Talybont. From here continue the ride at Segment 10.

Loop 4 - Around Pontsticill (14 ¾ miles):

Trefil to Pontsticill (3 miles): Continuing from Segment 8. Stay on the Trefil quarry road (heading west); the road winds its way up towards a clearing at the top. From here the bridleway track to Pontsticill can be seen on the right gently descending the mountain towards the west.

Follow this track through the moorlands for about two and half miles to a point just above the Pontsticill reservoir in the Taf Fechan valley; superb views of the Beacons. The middle part of the ride will need to be walked in parts because the track is heavily rutted; however wide spaces means lots of by-pass opportunities.

When you are roughly in line with the southern end of the Reservoir look out for a distinctive stone walled and slate roofed British Waterways building just above the conical roof of the Reservoir valve house.

At this point and just below a rise in the track watch out for an unsigned bridleway track (easily missed) that branches off to the right from the main track, descending the steep slope to the valley below. Turn on to this bridleway

descending down to a gate, providing access through the stone wall.

Pass through the gate, continue the descent down along the fenceline and under the railway tunnel (Brecon Mountain Railway); the bridleway track soon exits on to the road just in front of the lower Pontsticill Waterworks Building near the reservoir.

Pontsticill to Dolygaer(just under 3 ½ miles): From the junction of the minor road with the bridleway follow the road around over the Reservoir dam through the outskirts of Pontsticill village in the direction to Talybont.

After a short distance the signed track Taffs Trail will be seen on the left. Turn left on to Taffs trail and follow it around through the wood until it emerges back on the minor road just near the turn-off to Doly Gaer. [Alernatively simply follow the minor road to the same point]

Dolygaer to Talybont (8 ¼ miles): From the Dolygaer turn-off follow the route as per Loop 3, through Torpantau dropping down to Talybont village past the reservoir.minor road. Continue at Segment 10 below.

Canal Towpath

Segment 10 (11 ½ miles): From the White Hart Inn Talybont there is an easy 12 mile ride along the flat canal towpath through Llangynydr and

Llangattoc to Gilwern Wharf. One of the most picturesque sections of canal. Only deviation from towpath is the Ashford tunnel just outside Talybont where there is a short section of road riding. Watch for the path on right hand side of road just at the rise of the hill. This leads down to the towpath on the Llangynydr side of the Ashford tunnel.. The main sections of the towpath ride are as follows:

Towpath Talybont – Llangynydr: good smooth compact grit towpath track - easy riding; fine views of Buckland Hill.

Towpath Llangynydr-Llangattock: smooth grit towpath for a short distance changing to a grass path but easily rideable.
Fine views of Crug Howel, Pen Cerrig-calch towards north, Gliffaes on north side of river Usk, and spire of the 14C St Edmonds church Crickhowell

Towpath Llangattock – Gilwern *(Access route I)* grass path for about half distance and good hard dirt path for the remainder; easy riding all the way to Gilwern Wharf bridge 104.

Segment 11 (1 ¼ miles): At Gilwern Wharf near bridge 104 turn on to the tramroad and continue to Clydach Ironworks as per *Access route M.*

Segment 12 (½ mile): From Clydach Ironworks take either of the alternative routes to Clydach Halt or Llanelli Sidings on the disused

Abergavenny-Merthyr railway track as per *Access route L*

Segment 13 (2 miles): From Clydach Station (or Llanelly Quarry) follow the disused railway track bed through Gellifelon to the road crossing near Crossing Cottage at Lower Cwm Nant-gam as per Access *Route K*

Segment 14 (1 ½ miles): From Lower Cwm Nant-Gam railway-road crossing follow the route through Llanmarch to the gate at the old railway crossing Waunafon (near cattle grid) as per *Access Route D).*

Segment 15 (1 mile): From Waunafon follow the west access route along the old railway track bed to the junction of the cycleway near the Whistle Inn as per *Access route B*

Segment 16 (just over 1 ½ miles): From the cycleway junction near the Whistle Inn follow the west access route via Garn lakes back to the Blaenafon Ironworks car park as per Access routeA

Loop 2 Brynore Milage Stone ▼

Canal towpath Llangynydr Lock ▼

Loop 4: riding along Cefn-yr-Ystrad bridleway from Trefil towards Pontsticill ▲

Loop 3: riding along minor road (Taffs Trail) leaving Dolygaer ▲

213

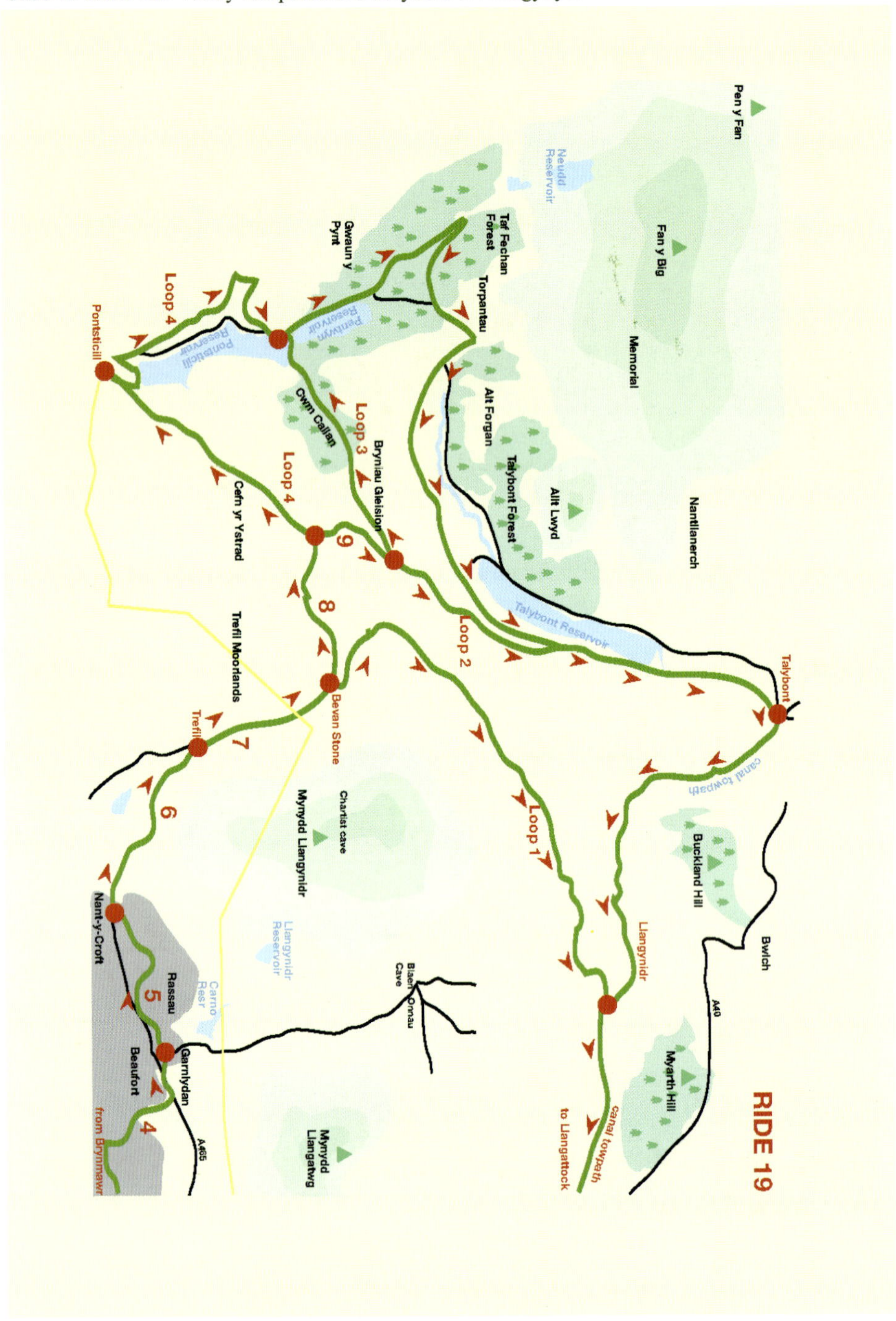
RIDE 19
Pen y Fan
Neuadd Reservoir
Fan y Big
Memorial
Taf Fechan Forest
Torpantau
Gwaun y Pynt
Pentwyn Reservoir
Pontsticill Reservoir
Pontsticill
Loop 4
Loop 3
Loop 2
Loop 1
Cwm Callan
Alt Forgan
Talybont Forest
Allt Lwyd
Nantllanerch
Bryniau Gleision
Cefn yr Ystrad
Talybont Reservoir
Talybont
canal towpath
Buckland Hill
Bwlch
A40
Trefil Moorlands
Bevan Stone
Trefil
Chartist cave
Mynydd Llangynidr
Llangynidr Reservoir
Llangynidr
Blaen Onnau Cave
Myarth Hill
canal towpath
to Llangattock
Nant-y-Croft
Rassau
Carno Resr
Beaufort
Garnlydan
A465
from Brynmawr
Mynydd Llangatwg
4
5
6
7
8
9

Ride 20: Through the borders of the Black Mountains to Llangorse Lake

The Ride

A highly scenic and fairly easy ride around the hills and valleys that border the eastern fringe of the Black mountains near Llangorse. The lake is in the bowl of the Llynfi valley surrounded by rising hills and spectacular high ridges. It will appeal to those who enjoy biking around lakes and mountains. There is also an opportunity to visit the medieval court of Tretower as well as try out the much shorter Roman road loop around Bwlch.

Route Information

Start and Finish

Blaenafon Ironworks

Distance/ Ride Time

Llangorse Ride: 49 miles: Ride Time: 5 ½ hours (½ mile difference between Segment 8A and 8B)

Ride via Roman Road Loop: 35 miles: Ride Time: 4 ½ hours

Energy Level

***

How easy is the Ride

Moderate: most of ride is over long flat and downhill sections; some mid and low gear climbs through mountain sections but none are overly strenuous; short hill sections on the return route through the Gorge

What sort of terrain

Lots of on-road tarmac lanes; off-road sections are mountain tracks, canal towpaths and disused railway beds; a short section of the Roman road loop and the last half mile of the off-road section of 8B is a bike wheel

Off-road Grade

G1/G2

The first ten miles of the ride from Blaenafon Ironworks is virtually all flat and downhill. It follows the west access route around Llangattock escarpment, descending a steep single track lane to the Mon & Brecon canal just near Crickhowell in the Usk valley below.

215

The route then follows a tarmac lane around the lower slopes of Pen Cerrig-calch overlooking Glanusk Park and the river Usk just in front of Myarth hill. An off-road dirt track descends the hillside leading to the medieval Court and Norman castle of Tretower in the Rhiangol valley.

Another good off-road dirt track links Tretower with Cwmdu, from where there are two alternative routes leading to the top of Cocket Hill between Llangorse and Troed mountains. You will need to choose one of these alternative routes.

The segment 8A route is for the most part along a tarmac lane on the eastern side above the Rhiangol valley joining another single track lane that gently ascends the remote Sorgwm valley (Cwm Sorgwm) to the top of Cocket Hill.

The segment 8B route begins along a tarmac lane on the western side of the Rhiangol and Sorgwm valleys and finishes over an off-road mountain track that leads to the top of Cocket Hill.

At the top of the hill there are wide open panoramic views over Llangorse lake towards the Brecon Beacons. The surrounding landscape is a patchwork of green and gold meadows that rise up to rugged black mountain tops and ridges.

Start of descent from top of Cocket Hill to Llangorse lake ▼

From here there is an exhilarating descent down through Llangorse village to the edge of the lake which is usually busy with sightseers as well as outdoor enthusiasts who come to enjoy walking sailing and kayaking in completely natural and unspoilt surroundings.

The ride continues around the west side of the lake through the old railway station village of Tal-y-lyn to the secluded hamlet of Llangasty whose ancient church stands right on the edge of the lake in a designated wildlife reserve.

From Llangasty the tarmac lane winds its way through the medieval settlement of Castell Blaenllynfi and then into Bwlch crossing the narrow stone arched bridge over the Usk at Llangynydr where the route joins up with the Mon & Brecon canal.

The next eight miles is an easy scenic ride along the canal towpath to Gilwern and then along the old railway trackbed above the Clydach Gorge through Llanmarch to Waunafon finally linking up with the Garn Lakes cycleway that leads back to the Ironworks.

There is also an opportunity to try out on another day the much shorter but nevertheless quite spectacular Roman road ride that makes a complete circular loop starting from and returning to Bwlch which is easily accessed from the canal towpath at Llangynydr.

Roman road loop: descending tarmac lane along lower slopes of Cefn Moel towards Cwmdu ▼

The Roman road ride skirts around the slopes of Cefn Moel where there are stunning views over the Rhiangol and Usk valleys dropping down to Felndre and looping back around to Pen-y-gaer the site of an ancient Roman fort where the route joins up with the path of the old Roman road (grass track) to Bwlch..

217

Heritage Interest Along Route

Llangattock mountain road: path of old tramroad route from Brynmawr to Llangattock quarries and Llangattock canal wharf

Early limestone quarry workings Llangattock Daren Cilau quarries

Llangattoc canal wharf: old Lime Kilns and termination of tramroad

Crickhowell and Mon & Brecon canal: see Town & Canal section

Tretower Court & Castle: the Norman castle is Motte and Bailey style and dates from the 12C; remains of Great Tower, mound and part of Bailey wall; adjacent Court is a medieval residence dating from 14C; responsibility of CADW and open to public.

Llangorse Lake: largest natural Lake in South Wales; evidence of very early habitation on island; wildlife habitat; sailing, canoeing and kayaking

Talylyn Station: used to be a junction station (passenger stop) on the old Brecon to Merthyr (Newport) railway line as well as the Brecon to Hay-on-Wye/Hereford/Builth line; Talybont station was the next stop from Talylyn on the Merthyr line.

Castell Blaenllynfi: site on private grounds – difficult to see any remains of site of Norman castle

Pen-y-gaer and Roman Road: Pen-y-gaer is the site of a Roman fort; it is one of the three forts located between Abergavenny and Brecon;. a Roman road ran between the three forts; path of Roman road is identified near Pen-y-gaer and west of Bwlch.

Llangynydr Bridge: classic 16C very narrow stone-arched bridge over the Usk.

Clydach Ironworks, Llanelli Forge Abergavenny-Merthyr railway route: see West Heritage ride

The Route

See section "Bike Access Routes" for description and maps of access routes from and to Blaenafon, reference the route segments at beginning and end of ride.

Inns Along Route

Whistle Inn	Garn-yr-erw
Racehorse	Waunafon
Horshoe Inn	Llangattoc
Vine Tree Inn, Bridge Inn,	
White Hart Inn	Crickhowell
Farmers Arms	Cwmdu
Castle Inn, Red Lyon Inn	Llangorse
Black Cock Inn Llanvihangel Tal-y-Llyn	
New Inn	Bwlch
The Coach & Horses	Llangynydr
Navigation, Bridge, Lyon Inns	Gilwern
Cambrian Inn	Clydach

Segment 1 (1 ½ miles): Follow the west access route from Blaenafon Ironworks around Garn lakes to the Whistle as per *Access route A..*

Segment 2 (1 mile): From the Whistle continue along the old railway track bed to Waunafon as per *Access route B.*

Segment 3 (1 ¾ miles): From Waunafon descend hill to Brynmawr market square as per *Access route C..*

Segment 4 (¾ mile): From Brynmawr Market Square proceed via Bailey and Intermediate road to junction of Black Rock road and Llangattoc mountain road just in front of the EMS building as per *Route through Brynmawr*

Segment 5 (5 ½ miles): From the junction near the Brynmawr EMS factory continue along the west   access   route   around   Llangattock escarpment descending to canal bridge (no 114) just above Llangattock village as per *Access*

routeF-G.

Segment 6 (4 miles): From the canal bridge (no 114) at Llangattock descend through the village passing the church and Horsehoe Inn as far as the   bridge at Crickhowell. Cross over the bridge and ascend the hill as far as car park on left.

Go through the carpark towards Crickhowell High school, follow path around to the road through small group of houses and continue to junction of A40. Turn left on to A40 (be careful with traffic) pass the White Hart Inn and continue for about quarter mile past the Manor Hotel (up on the right) and the left turn-off to Gallop & Rivers (Architectural Salvage).

[There is an alternative route which bypasses the busy A 40 road between Crickhowell and the junction of the Gallop & Rivers turn-off from the A40.

At Crickhowell bridge follow the footpath along the river for about half a mile as far as the first stile. A house can be seen up on right not far from road . Turn right on to path leading up to gate. Continue along edge of cornfield through Gallop & Rivers to the junction of the A40.]

From the Gallop & Rivers lane junction with the A 40 continue a very short way west and then take the unsigned turning on right (watch for it) ascending the single track tarmac lane. It is a slow low gear climb (not strenuous) for about half a mile with superb views over the Usk river, Glan Usk park and Myarth Hill.

219

Continue on this lane, cross over Cwm Gu brook as far as the Y-junction near Llandegeman. Take the right fork and continue a short way as far as the gate access; turn left on to the stone grass dirt track and descend to the A 479 road just opposite the medieval Court and Norman Castle at Tretower (open to visitors) not far from St Johns Church.

Segment 7 (1 ¾ miles): From Tretower Court proceed a very short distance north along the A479 road and watch out for a dirt track on the right near two gates. The track you want is towards the left of the second gate.

Follow this dirt stone track and after almost a mile it joins a tarmac lane just above a caravan site. Continue on the tarmac lane, pass by Efail Isaf house and descend hill to the Farmers Arms Inn just opposite St Michaels church in Cwmdu village in the Rhiangoll valley..

From here there are two superb alternative routes between Cwmdu and Llangorse mountain. Choose either Segment 8A or Segment 8B; try the other route on a different day.

Segment 8A Option (3 ¾ miles)

From the Farmers Arms Cwmdu, head north past the church along a tarmac lane that winds itself up around the hill on the lower slopes of Pen Allt-mawr above the A 479. Continue on the tarmac lane for just over a mile crossing Nantgarreg brook, passing by the sign to Neuaddfach farm; watch out for a wide dirt track on the left just opposite a gate to some farm buildings.

Descend the track, cross a stream at the bottom and follow through to a tarmac lane. Cross over the lane and continue along the track opposite. After a short distance it joins the A465 at Pont Waun-fach bridge. Cross over bridge and bear immediate left passing Waun-fach Forge on left.

A tarmac lane gently ascends the remote Cwm Sorgwm valley wedged between Pen Tir and Troad mountains. After about a mile pass through a gate, ascend the easy low gear hill which begins to get a little steep towards the top.

At the top of Cocket's Hill there is a small car pull-in where there are stunning panoramic views over Llangorse lake to the Beacons. Continue the ride at Segment 9.

Segment 8B Option (just over 3 ¼ miles)

From the Farmers Arms Cwmdu follow the A 479 a short distance up to Cwmdu village car park (and Village Hall) on the left. Turn into the

220

car park, cross over the Rhiangol bridge and ascend the tarmac lane. It is a slow low gear climb (not strenuous) along the lower slopes of Pen Tir above the Rhiangol valley.

There is a fairly flat mid gear section past Lower/Upper Pentrebach farms and Pencaeau farms. After the second gate the partially metalled road bears off to the right. Continue on the wide grass track straight ahead keeping to the left where the track splits in two.

The track is rideable at the beginning but unfortunately becomes quite rutted further on and the final mile will need to be walked. The track finally emerges at a small car pull-in on top of Cockets Hill above Llangorse lake and the Llynfi valley as per segment 8A above. Continue the ride at Segment 9.

Segment 9 (2 ¾ miles): From the top of Cockets Hill descend the tarmac lane on the other side to the junction of the B 4560 in Llangorse village. Turn right on the B 4560, pass by the Castle Inn, Red Lyon Inn and Church, turn left and left again at the Lake signpost and follow lane down to the Lakeside front.

Segment 10 (5 ½ miles): From the Lake return to the junction of the minor road, turn left (sign-posted to Brecon) and continue for about a mile to the village of Llanvihangel Tal-y-lyn. Pass the Black Cock Inn and turn left (signposted to Tal-y-lyn) on to a minor road.

Continue on this lane around the back of the lake to Tal-y-lyn.

The old Tal-y-lyn railway station used to be located just near the lane that branches off the road by the post box. Continue on the road to Penorth village, pass over the Railway bridge adjacent to the Tabernacle Reform Church (was Congregational meeting house).

Follow the road through to the turn-off to Llangasty.

Make a short half mile detour down to Llangasty church located right on edge of Lake

221

in a designated nature reserve.

Segment 11 (just under 5 miles): From the lakeside Llangasty, return back to the minor road and continue to the junction of the B 4560 at Castell Blaenllynfi just on the ouskirts of Bwlch.

Follow this road to Bwlch, turn left on to the A40, pass the New Inn, turn right on to Old road just opposite the Star Bunk House and continue back down to junction of A40; proceed a short distance on A 40 to the Llangynydr road turn-off. Turn right, follow the minor road to the old stone-arched bridge at Llangynydr, and ascend the hill to canal bridge 131.

Canal Towpath Section

Segment 12 (just under 8 miles): From Llangyndyr Bridge (131) continue along the canal towpath through .Llangattock to Gilwern Wharf canal bridge 104 (as per *Access route I*

Clydach Gorge to Blaenafon Section

Segment 13 (1 ½ miles): At Gilwern Wharf turn on to the tramroad and continue to Clydach

Ironworks as per *Access route M.*

Segment 14 (½ mile): From Clydach Ironworks take either of the alternative routes to Clydach Halt or Llanelli Sidings on the disused Abergavenny-Merthyr railway track as per *Access route L.*

Segment 15 (just under 2 miles): From Clydach Station (or Llanelly Quarry) follow the disused railway track bed through Gellifelon to the road crossing near Crossing Cottage at Lower Cwm Nant-gam as per Access *Route K.*

Segment 16 (1 ½ miles): From Lower Cwm Nant-Gam railway-road crossing follow the route through Llanmarch to the gate at the old railway crossing Waunafon (near cattle grid) as per *Access Route D*

Segment 17 (1 mile): From Waunafon follow the west access route along the old railway track bed to the junction of the cycleway near the Whistle Inn as per *Access route B.*

Segment 18 (just over 1 ½ miles): From the cycleway junction near the Whistle Inn follow the west access route via Garn lakes back to the Blaenafon Ironworks car park as per *Access route A*

Optional Roman Road Ride

This is a circular loop around Bwlch which can be easily reached from the canal towpath at Llangynydr.

Ironworks to Llangynydr (just under 15 miles): The 10 mile ride from Blaenafon Ironworks to Llangattock follows the same route (segments 1- 5) as that above. Between Llangattock and Llangynydr it is an easy 4 mile ride along the canal towpath.

The Roman Loop (5 ½ miles): From Llangynydr canal bridge descend the minor road (north), cross over the stone arched road bridge, and proceed to junction of A 40 road on the outskirts of Bwlch. Turn left and follow A 40 for about half a mile going around the bend and turning right on to a lane near Wells Cottage (white) – watch for it.

From here it is a low gear climb for about quarter mile (not too bad) gradually flattening out on top. There are sensational views down the valley to east and south.

Continue on the tarmac lane making a long swooping descent down the mountain towards Felindre and nearby Cwmdu.

Turn right at the first junction and left at the next junction if you want to visit Cwmdu. To continue along the return part of loop turn right at this junction and follow tarmac lane for about a mile into Pen-y-gaer (site of Roman Fort) as far as second junction.

Take the right fork and proceed along the Roman road (now tarmac lane) as far as Ty Mawr house.

Go through gate and take right (upper) track through another gate. The Roman road now becomes a grass track and is a little over grown in parts.

The bike(s) will need to be wheeled for about quarter mile as far as the gate access to the A40 (just below bend) at Bwlch.
From here descend the A40 a short distance to the Llangynydr turn-off and return to Llangynydr canal bridge as per the start of the loop.

Final Part of Ride (just under 15 miles): To complete the ride back to Blaenafon Ironworks simply follow the canal towpath to Llangattock canal bridge (114) and then continue along the same route as above (segments 12-18).

Tretower Court ▼

Llangorse Lake ▼

Segment 8B ride: ascending off-road track on Cockets Hill looking towards Troad ▼

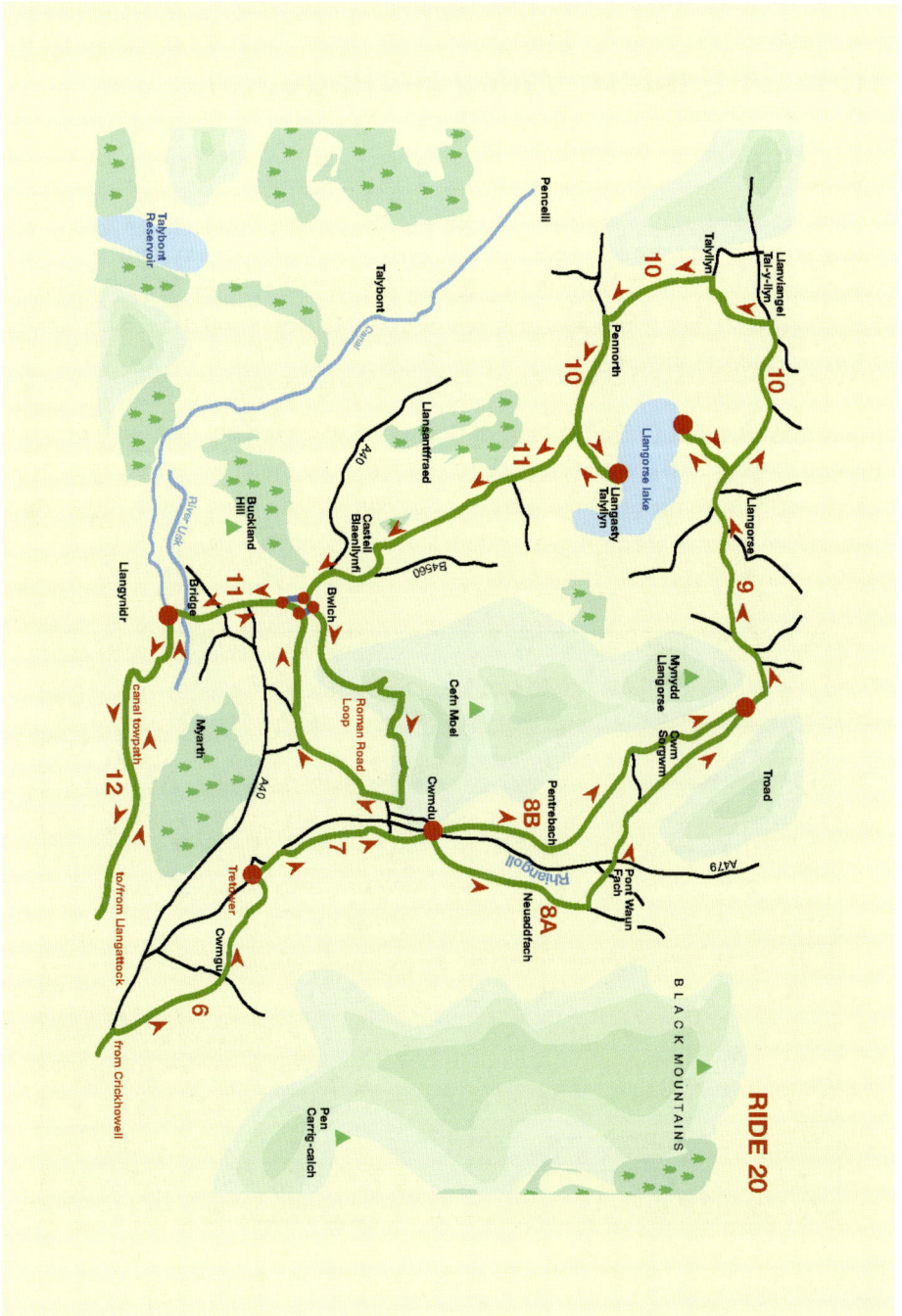

Ride 21 Eastern Valley Heritage Ride

The Ride

A fascinating ride around some of the early iron and coal working sites that dominated the eastern valley during the early 19C. Most of the sites can still be accessed over old tramways and railroads that once served as the primary transport links to the sites.

The Ironworks and Collieries east of Blaenafon were largely located along the craggy hollows and dingles that shape and puncture the hillside above the Afon Lwyd. Some remains of the early works can still be seen but unfortunately many have disappeared. A lively ride full of twists, turns, ups and down.

Route Information

Start and Finish

Blaenafon Ironworks

Distance/ Ride Time

Distance: 33 ½ miles
Ride Time: 4 ¾ hours

Energy Level

***

Off-road Grade

G1/G2

How easy is the Ride

Moderate: mix of flat descending and ascending inclines; not a difficult ride given there are lots of stopovers; route is completely rideable with exception of a few ruts here and there

What sort of terrain

Mostly off-road with some on-road sections; off-road includes mountain tracks (grass-stony-dirt) disused railroads and some designated public access footpaths; on-road include tarmac lanes and minor roads.

226

From Blaenafon Ironworks the ride follows the Blaenafon-Pontypool cycleway (old Railway track) passing under an old cable operated railroad near Varteg Station and climbing up Snail Creep to the former site of Varteg Ironworks. From here it follows an old Colliery track around the mountain to the site of Viponds Varteg Hill Pit almost at the top of the Frwd valley. There are superb views overlooking Varteg, Garndiffaith and the British.

Riding along Redash Colliery (Viponds) track above Garndiffaith and Viaduct ▲

From Viponds there is a great off-road ride down a mountain track above the Balance, crossing over the Frwd brook, descending an old railroad track down the Frwd valley towards the site of the former Golynos Ironworks and nearby mining shaft.

A stones throw away is the site of the important British Ironworks with a few scattered remains and nearby British village built to house the Iron workers. Just below the British is the site of yet another Ironworks at Pentwyn and just above the British is the remarkable site of the early 19C Cwmbergwm Water Balance pit where a few fragmentary remains are still strewn around the site.

An off road track from Cwmbergwm links up with the old Colliery road in the Nant-du valley (Cwm Nant-du) leading to the sites of Llanerch and Blaensychan Collieries both now dismantled.

The blackened remains of the coal mining era have now largely disappeared and the superb off-road ride above the picturesque valley gives few clues to its previous existence. However the memorial plaque at the site of Llanerch colliery commemorating the lives of 176 miners killed in a major pit disaster is a swift reminder of the past.

The ride turns around at Blaensychan Colliery at the head of the Cwm Nant-du valley and descends the road along the same route to the gate access at the bottom. It then winds its way along a narrow lane through the secluded Frwdoer valley (Cwmfrwdoer) to the site of Tirpentwys Colliery that at one time employed around 1400 men underground; it was closed for coal working in 1969 and later demolished. The valley extending above Tirpentwys Colliery has now been greened and attractively landscaped and is well worth the ride.

From here the ride heads back down the valley joining the Blaenafon-Pontypool cycleway at Plas-y-Coed and ascending Blaendare road at Pontypool to the Upper Race on the south side of the Glyn valley. An old railway track weaves its way around the mountainside to the site of Glyn Pits which still retains its 19C engine house and even more remarkably the remains of an almost unique in-situ 19C steam winding engine and beam engine pump. It is earmarked as a heritage site.

The return route links with the cycleway at Pontypool and continues along this tarmac track to Blaenafon Ironworks

Riding along Redash Colliery (Viponds) track looking towards the British ▼

The Heritage Route

Inns Along Route

Plas-y-coed Inn   Plas-y-coed
Little Crown Inn Pontnewenydd

Segment 1 (3 miles): Follow the south east access route from Blaenafon Ironworks along the cycleway (old Blaenafon-Pontypool railway) as far as the first topless bridge just before Varteg station.

- This bridge was part of the old cable operated railroad-Incline that carried coal from the Varteg Hill top pit (see below) to the Lower Level railway at Cwmavon below. Incline started 1861.

Continue on cycleway under next bridge (Shop road) to old Varteg station.

- Shop road links Varteg with Cwmavon and was named after the Company shop that was associated with Varteg Ironworks. (the Forge at Cwmavon is also known as Varteg Forge)

- Varteg station was the first stop on the Upper Level railway from Blaenafon to Pontypool; platform still recognisable; now adorned with wooden sculptures of early luggage cases.

Segment 2 (2 ½ miles): A little further down from Varteg Station is the Snail Creep bridge. Leave the cycleway and walk bike up Snail Creep. It is a little steep and narrow but only a short climb.

- Snail Creep is a winding dirt stone track linking Varteg with Cwmavon (Westlake Inn) and is part of the old Parish Road Varteg-Cwmavon-Llanover.

At the Coach House it changes to a tarmac lane. Continue up the lane to the Varteg Wesleyan Methodist chapel (now Community Centre) and nearby Welsh school.

- Former Varteg Wesleyan Methodist Chapel started in 1868 and replaced an earlier chapel known as Varteg Iron Works Weslyan Chapel that stood nearby.

- In the space roughly between the Chapel and the Crown Inn once stood rows of houses that were the heart of Varteg village including Post office Row, Incline Row, The Square, Slate Row.

Follow lane to junction of Blaenavon road. Turn left and after after a hundred yards or so turn right on to a lane sign-posted to Community Wood. Continue a short distance. The site of Varteg Ironworks is roughly the grass area behind the grey shed off Blaenafon road more or less opposite Gladstone Terrace.

- Varteg Ironworks: started operation in 1803 with a single furnace and by 1826 had expanded to four furnaces; it ceased operations around the 1860's; a tramroad incline linked the Ironworks with the tramroad at Cwmavon below, and then to the canal head at Pontnewenydd; no remains;

Return to the road junction, turn left towards Blaenafon, after a short distance turn left up Salisbury terrace as far as the start of the dirt road. Follow the dirt road up a short incline, turn left and continue along the ashlar road that winds its way around the mountain.

Superb views down the valley towards the Garndiffaith Viaduct and Pontypool. After about one and quarter miles the road terminates at the site of Varteg Hill Red Ash Colliery (Viponds Top Pit) at the top of the Ffrwd valley.

■ Varteg Hill Colliery is now demolished. One 19C stone building (engine house?) as well as red brick building is all that remains. As indicated above the pit was linked to Cwmavon railway station via a steam engine operated Incline.

Segment 3 (2 ½ miles): From Varteg Hill Colliery site follow the same road back and after about half a mile watch out for a dirt stone track on the right heading towards the Ffrwd valley (south).

Descend this track and after about quarter mile take the track heading towards left (near a lonely tree). After a short descent this track joins a crossroad of tracks. Turn right still heading south towards the Ffrwd brook.

The track joins an open space near some old partially grassed tips and in the distance to the right is a bridge (embankment) over the Ffrwd brook.

Cross over the Ffrwd and follow track through a wooded area to join up with another wider track (old railroad). After a short distance an attractive terraced row of two or three white 19C cottages can be seen towards the north (left) not far from the Ffrwd brook in the general area of the Balance.

■ In 1890 the numerous coffins for those who were killed in the major Llanerch Pit disaster (see below) were made at these premises

Continue descending the track passing through two gate accesses (haul bike over low level gates) until it joins a tarmac lane near the Talywaun Golf Club. The lane passes by Talywaun Rugby field and joins the Blaenafon-Talywaun road just above the Globe Inn.

■ Watch out for an access on left just before the track joins the tarmac lane at Talywaun Golf Club. From this access there is a footpath leading to the remains of an 1899 stone faced colliery level with two trams standing at the entrance.

■ Golynos Ironworks: site location is near the Talywaun rugby field close to the Ffrwd brook; started in 1837 had three blast furnaces; no remains

Segment 4 (2 miles): At the junction with Blaenafon Talywaun road (Thickpenny corner) turn right and continue a short way and then turn right just opposite the Globe Inn. This leads on to Farm road and a large open area with black tip mounds. Down below on the left is the site of the British Ironworks (can't see it from here).

Continue past the turn-off on right to Castle Woods and proceed as far as the next turn-off on the right. This is the start of the mountain road to Llanillith St Iltyds.

At this junction make a short detour for about quarter mile along the Llanillith road as far as the site of the old Lower Navigation Colliery.

- Engine Hall is on side of road (fenced off in private property) - red bricked Edwardian building of steam coal era; tall segment-headed windows.

Return to tee junction and turn right in direction towards British Cottages (East View). After a short distance the British Welfare Hall (now Jehova's Witnesses hall) will be seen on left side. Just before the hall is a track leading down to the site of the British Ironworks.

Follow track down bearing right and then bend around to left; this leads to the site. It is a large open site with cluster of 19C office buildings and Engine House. The Big Arch just below enabled access to the site under the railway line

- British Ironworks started 1826: all that remains are the quadrangle of 19C office buildings and workshops and the 19C Beam Pumping Engine-House that served the Ironworks Colliery. Ironworks had six furnaces, refineries, puddling train, intermediate train for mill bars, three rolling mill trains, and Colliery. It was designed by

London architect Decimus Burton. Tram road (Manor road) connected Ironworks with Avon Lwyd valley tramway and canal head at Pontnewenydd.

Return to the tarmac lane near Jehova's Witness Hall. Follow road through to the only row of remaining British houses (East View) and continue along the back of houses as far as the gate and the heritage sign leading to footpath..

- British Village: Built for the Iron workers and originally comprised a number of terraced rows of worker houses; only one remains.

- Pentwyn Ironworks: Not far from the British Ironworks; look east (from East Row) towards Pentwyn school. Site of Ironworks is just below school; started 1825 and had three furnaces; nothing remains.

From the gate near British East View follow the footpath straight ahead (not left) and this leads to Cwmbergwm Water Balance pit and the nearby Chymney Stack.

- Cwmbergwm Water Balance Pit: early 19C; supplied coal to British Ironworks; coal raised from pit by balancing tram against water filled iron basin; strewn around site are the wheel, parts of the cast iron frame and iron drum. Sole survivor of this kind of pit in South Wales.

- A model of Cwmbergwm Water Balance pit can be viewed at Blaenafon Ironworks Museum. At Big Pit Museum Blaenafon you can see a fairly complete Water Balance pit headgear and wheel; it is installed just outside the old Baths.

Segment 5 (3 ½ miles): Return on the same track to the gate near East view of British. Follow the track towards the east and after about quarter mile it crosses a gate (locked) and stile. Continue on this footpath for approximately half a mile passing through four gates (all open). At a fifth gate the path joins a bridleway. Turn left descend down through gate (opens) and join another wide dirt track.

Turn right on this track towards south east and follow it around until it joins a tarmac lane via a gate. Cross over gate turn right on to lane which immediately joins another gate. This is the start of the Blaensychan and Llanerch old Colliery road.

Cross over gate and follow the old colliery road up the Cwm Nant-du valley. After almost half a mile a footpath sign will be seen on right and there is a fenced path ascending the mountainside leading to the site of the Llanerch Colliery.

- Llanerch Colliery: sunk 1858; major disaster occurred on 6 Feb 1890 killing 176 miners; at the site there is a Memorial Plaque (by Torfaen Council) on stone pillar

commemorating the 176 men and boys who died in the underground explosion.

Return to the road and follow it all the way to the top of the Cwm Nant-du valley. The road bends around at the top. Blaensychan Colliery was located just in this area.

- Blaensychan (Blaenserchan) Colliery: first shaft sunk in 1890; originally had fine set of 19/20C buildings including two head-frames; last working pit in the eastern valley closed in 1985; completely demolished.

Segment 6 (4 miles): From Blaensychan Colliery return back down the road to the access gate at the bottom of the valley. From this gate access follow the tarmac lane to the junction of Pentwyn road. Turn right and continue down this road as far the railway bridge (over the cycleway). Just before the bridge at Pentrepiod turn right on to Gypsy lane.

Follow this minor road along the Ffrwdoer valley for about 1 ¼ miles crossing over the Ffrwdoer brook and two dismantled railways continuing as far as the junction with the Pantygasseg road.

Turn right, ascend the hill for just under half a mile and turn right on to a lane just near a council sign. This leads into a large open grassed area. This is approximately the site of Tirpentwys Colliery.

Pass by the Race Labour & Social club and the Methodist church (green zinc building) as far as the point where the Blaendare road turns around sharply right leading to the A road at the bottom of the Glyn valley. Don't bear right but continue straight ahead at this point and then bear right up the hill (Blaendare Farm road) for a short distance.

Just at the top on the right there is a locked gate which is the access to the Glyn Pits railway now a dirt track. Follow the old railway track (rideable) around the mountain for just under a mile as far as the location of the old Glyn Pits Colliery on the left.

- Tirpentwys Colliery: two shafts sunk in 1878; originally had fine 19C buildings including vertical engine house and fan house and unusual headframe designed to work with large vertical steam engine. Closed in 1969 but shafts and winders retained for pumping and ventilation for continued operation with Hafodyryns; now completely dismantled

Take a short detour for about ¾ mile up the through a very pleasant valley alongside the Ffrwdoer brook (flat) passing some old Limekilns where it is hard to see any trace of the past industry.

- Glyn Pits: sunk around 1840-45 by Capel Hanbury Leigh to supply fuel for his Pontypool Iron and Tinplates work; site is now fenced off but three buildings can be viewed (externally);

- engine house that contains an 1840 vertical steam winding engine made by the Neath Abbey works – one of the earliest surviving in Britain; a pumping house that contains a Neath Abbey beam pump and flywheel gear. These extraordinary remains of early 19C mine workings are earmarked for restoration as a heritage site by Torfaen Council.

- The Upper Race was a site used for early coal (and ironstone) mining in which stored water was released and allowed to race over and scour shallow measures exposing the coal (or ironstone) beneath. Ponds were used to store the water.

Segment 7 (5 ½ miles): From the junction with the Pantygasseg minor road turn left descend the hill passing the Plas Coed Inn on the right continuing as far as the bridge over the old Railway (Blaenafon cycleway). Cross over bridge and turn into small car park immediately on the right for access to the cycleway.

Follow the cycleway (Sustrans signs) for just under two miles through Pontypool as far as the Blaendare road - West Mon Comprehensive School junction (West Mon is a large impressive red brick early 20C Grammar school building). Turn off the cycleway and make a steepish climb up Blaendare road passing the Further Education College to the Upper Race.

Segment 10 (10 ½ miles): Follow the same route back to join the cycleway near West Mon School. The return route is along the Sustrans cycleway to Blaenafon Ironworks.

Plaque commemorating 1890 Pit disaster at site of Llanerch Colliery▼

Scattered remains around site of 19C Cwmbergwm Water Balance Pit ▼

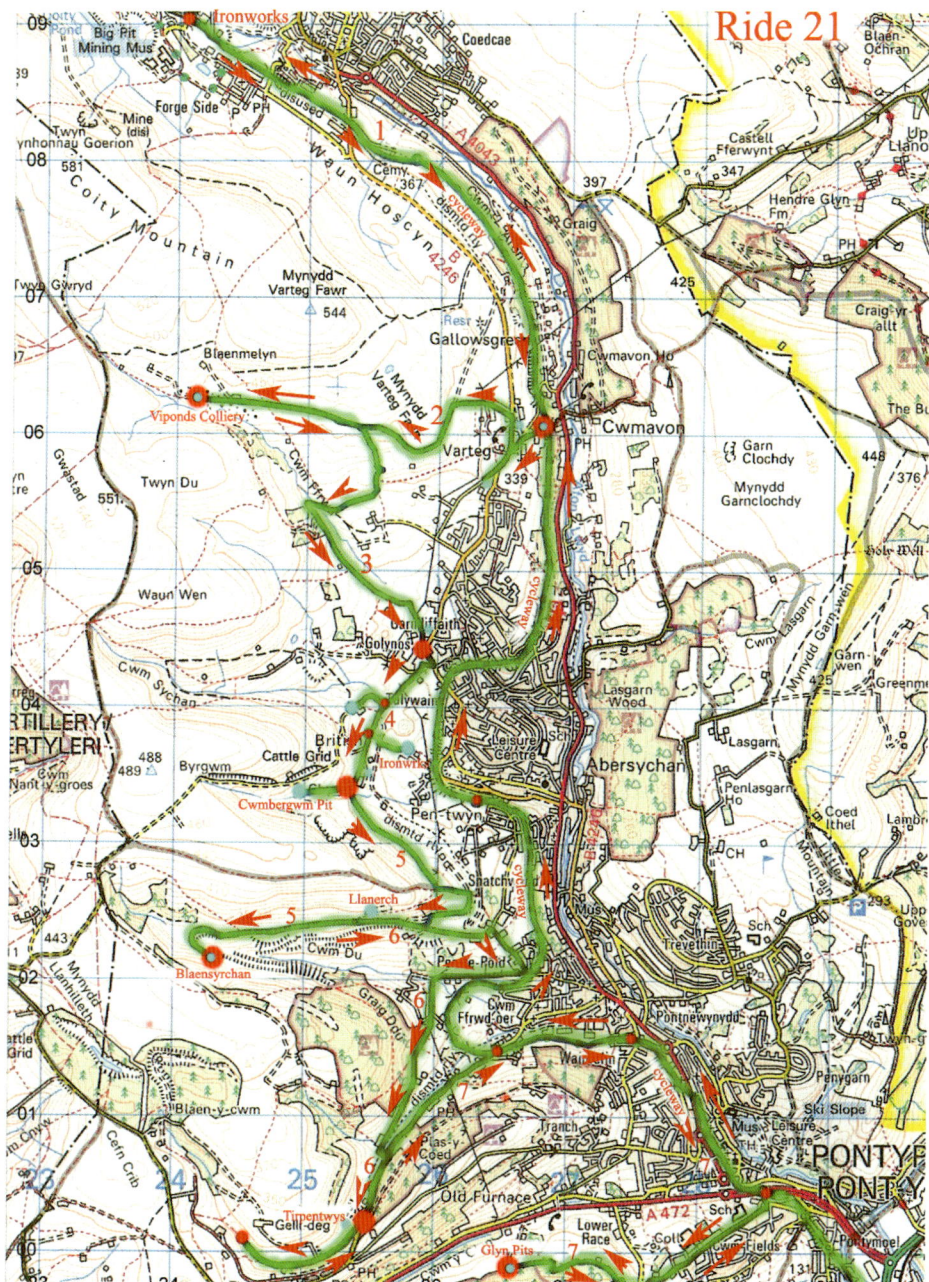

Ride 22 Western Valley Heritage Ride

The Ride

Another fascinating ride around some of the early iron and coal working sites that dominated the valleys west of Blaenafon during the early part of the 19C. Virtually all the major Ironworks at this time were located along the Heads of the valleys between Nantyglo and Merthyr. This relatively short ride to Clydach and Sirhowy Ironworks follows the paths of old railways and tramways that were once the main transport arteries of the industrial valleys.

Although some of these sites have already been identified in previous Rides this particular Ride provides an opportunity to spend more heritage time at the sites.

Route Information

Start and Finish

Blaenafon Ironworks

Distance/ Ride Time

Distance: 30 miles

Ride Time: just under 5 hours

Energy Level
***

Off-road Grade
G1/G2

How easy is the Ride

Moderate: plenty of flat and down hill sections; a two mile climb up Blackrock road but not difficult; route is completely rideable

What sort of terrain

Mix of off-road and on-road routes; off-road are rideable tracks (grass-stony-dirt) and include disused railroads and common land cart roads; on-road include tarmac lanes and minor roads.

The beginning of the ride from Blaenafon Ironworks along the Garn lakes cycleway offers no clue whatsoever to the immense black landscape that once engulfed this entire area. A complex of coal mining buildings serving Kay Slope and Garn Drift Collieries used to extend over the land now occupied by the cycleway, meadows and lake. The new green look has come about through a massive land reclamation programme.

Former site of drift mines and workings near the Whistle ▼

From the Whistle, the route over the old Blaenafon-Brynmawr railway trackbed leads to Waunafon Halt not far from the site of Milfraen Colliery that closed down in 1930. From here the route bends around through Llanmarch joining the Abergavenny-Brynmawr railway trackbed on top of the Clydach Gorge. It is an easy ride down the gently descending track through the dramatic railway landscape of the Gorge arriving at old Clydach Halt just near an eight arch stone railway viaduct.

A short steep descent to the bottom of the valley near the river Clydach leads to the impressive remains of Clydach Ironworks that employed more than a thousand men in first half of 19C. Not far away are the few remains of Llanelly charcoal Furnace and Forge established by John Hanbury of Pontypool in 1684.

It is a twisty ride along the path of the old Llanmarch tramroad down through the Gorge to Clydach Wharf on the Mon & Brecon canal at Gilwern. From the canal there is a longish but not difficult climb up Blackrock road partly along the path of the 1794 Clydach railway (now tarmac road) to Brynmawr at the top of the Gorge.

The area at the head of the Ebbw Fach valley just below Brynmawr was dominated by Nantyglo Ironworks at the beginning of the 19C, and the remains of the Ironmaster's house and nearby Roundhouse Tower can be seen not far from the site of the old Ironworks. Two other Ironworks were also located just below Nantyglo Ironworks at Coalbrookvale and Blaina.

The route through Brynmawr passes several attractive lakes that originally served as feeder ponds for the Ironworks and connects with an off-road cart track through a large grass Common area just above Beaufort. From here the route continues on a minor road west of the Heads of Valley road to Nant-y-Croft just outside Tredegar.

An old railroad track around the perimeter of Bryn Serth hill leads to the remains of the once important coke fired Sirhowy Ironworks located on the east bank of the Sirhowy river. Both the Sirhowy Ironworks and nearby Tredegar Ironworks were the dominant features of the industrial landscape at the head of the Sirhowy valley during the early 19C and without them there would be no Tredegar.

Remains of Sirhowy Ironworks ▼

The return route back to Blaenafon Ironworks retraces the same path to Brynmawr descends the railway trackbed for about half a mile before rejoining the original route through Llanmarch and Waunavon.

Remains of Clydach Ironworks ▲

The Heritage Route

See section "Bike Access Routes" for description and maps of access routes from and to Blaenafon, reference the route segments at beginning and end of ride.

Inns Along Route	
Whistle Inn	Garn-yr-erw
Racehorse	Waunafon
Cambrian Inn	Clydach
Lyon Hotel	Gilwern
Rock & Fountain	Black Rock
Drum & Monkey	Black Rock
Castle inn	Nant-y-Croft

Segment 1 (2 ¼ mile): From Blaenafon Ironworks follow the west access route as per *access route A-B* past Garn lakes to the Whistle and along the railway track bed to Waunavon:

- Kays Slope and Garn Drift Collieries were located near the Whistle extending to the area now occupied by the lake; the Colliery employed more than 500 men underground in 1958 and closed down in 1966; colliery and workings completely dismantled - site greened and landscaped.

- Milfraen Colliery was located on the moorland about quarter mile south along the track (on the left) from the gate access at old Waunafon Halt; nine men killed in accident 1929; closed in 1930; completely dismantled.

- Brynmawr- Blaenafon railway: section of LNWR branch line that opened in 1868 and closed entirely in 1954; Waunafon Halt at 1400 feet was the second highest on standard guage in Great Britain.

Segment 2 (3 ½ miles): From Waunafon Halt follow the west access route as *per access route D-K* through Llanmarch joining the Clydach

239

railway track bed at Lower Cwm Nant-gam continuing along the track through Gellifelon Halt crossing over the road just near Nazurath Baptist Chapel to Clydach Halt.

- Abergavenny-Merthyr Railway through Clydach Gorge started 1865 closed 1958. Considered to be superb feat of Victorian railway engineering. The railway line followed approximately the path of Bailey's original tramroad that connected Nantyglo Ironworks with Govilon Wharf.

- Llanelly quarries supplied limestone for Clydach Ironworks and agricultural use.

- Clydach Limeworks: supplied lime for building railway viaducts and tunnels

- The Llanmarch 1795 railroad between Clydach Ironworks and Llanmarch ran mostly along the tarmac road that crosses the old railway path at Llanelly quarries and continues down the hill to a junction near the new Clydach Community Centre.

- Clydach Halt is on the south side of the impressive Clydach Railway Viaduct near Nazureth Baptist Chapel

- Series of inclines from Clydach Ironworks to Llanelly Hill built around 1811 to supplement Llanmarch railroad

- Blaenafon stone road starts at Llanelly Hill (continue on tarmac road east past Jolly Colliers Inn). It connects with the tarmac lane at Blaen Dyar just below Pwlldu

- Between 1799 and 1812 Clydach Ironworks used the route through Blaenafon to transport its goods onwards down the Afon Lwyd valley to Newport (using packhorses before canal). The route was along the 1795 Llanmarch railroad (horse drawn) that ran along the south (east) side of the Gorge to Llanmarch connecting with the Blaenafon Stone road at Llanelly Hill. After 1812 Clydach Ironworks used the canal at Gilwern.

Segment 3 (½ mile): From Clydach Halt continue on the west access route to Clydach Ironworks as per *access route L*. Alternatively descend the steep hill from Nazureth Baptist Chapel turning on to cycleway/footway path at Bath Row just after the bend near the telephone kiosk. The track is signed to Clydach Ironworks. Follow path down crossing over road near Clydach Community centre descending the track (old incline) to Clydach Ironworks.

- Impressive remains of the Clydach Ironworks at bottom of the Gorge near the river; started operation early 1790's; it had four coke furnaces and employed 1250 men in 1841. Initial blast was provided by bellows powered by large wheel that was driven by water carried by a cleat from higher up in Gorge; later

240

changed to steam power.

- Iron Bridge carried trams over the river Clydach along the Llanmarch tram road to the canal at Clydach wharf Gilwern.

Optional: Make a short detour to see some of the dramatic scenery of the Clydach river and waterfalls at the bottom of the Gorge. From the Ironworks return to the road near Clydach Community Centre and continue into Danycoed estate. Look for the old tramroad track at the beginning (also at end) of the estate river side and follow it through the beechwoods along the gorge above the river. Return to Clydach Ironworks.

Segment 4 (1 ¼ miles): From Clydach Iron works follow the west access route to Gilwern Wharf as per *access route J*. From the Ironworks cross over the Iron Bridge and follow the tramroad up to the junction of road not far from the road-bridge. Go through the gate access on left; pass under the Heads of Valley road tunnel to connect with Black Rock road.

Turn right descend the hill turning left on to a lane at the bottom of hill just before the Heads of the Valley road junction. After a short distance the lane bends around to the left just below the imposing 17C Clydach House and another lane continues straight ahead.

- Charcoal burning Llanelly Furnace and Forge was established around 1684 by

John Hanbury of Pontypool.

- Llanelli Furnace: the original site is near Clydach house but there are few remains; go along the path just opposite house and you will see some of the stone structure just behind the shell of a garage at back of one of the houses.

- Clydach House (private) is impressive 17C mansion built to house the Clerk of Llanelli furnace Francis Lewis.

Just below Clydach House continue straight ahead passing Forge Row up to the gate entrance of Forge House (private). Go through the Forge House gate along the public footpath (follow the footway sign).

- Site of Llanelli Forge was near Forge House. Look out for another footpath on the left just opposite Forge House. Go along here a short way where the stone remains of the old Forge can still be seen.

Continue along the Llanmarch tramroad (footpath) near the river Clydach.

It passes by a British Waterways pump station near a river bridge, continues through a very wooded section of the Gorge arriving at the tramroad tunnel under the canal. Ascend the steps to the canal opposite Castle Narrow Boats and the nearby Bridge 104.

- Llanmarch tramroad connected Clydach Ironworks with Clydach Wharf on the canal at Gilwern. Most of the path of tramroad still remains. It follows river down the Gorge to the Clydach Wharf. The 1794 Clydach railroad from west side of Gorge also emerges at Gilwern wharf.

241

- At Gilwern the canal is carried over a Dadford's massive earth embankment which bridges the mouth of the Gorge.

Segment 5 (just over 4 mile): From canal bridge 104 Gilwern turn up the hill and then immediate left following *access route J* through Mysgwartha along the road that was once the path of the 1794 Clydach Railroad. Follow the road past Bethlehem Church up to the junction of Black Rock road at Cheltenham village.

From here there is a two mile mid-gear climb (easy to moderate) up Blackrock road which is almost traffic free. The only bits that are slightly strenuous (low mid gear) are short sections at the beginning and just past the Rock & Fountain Inn.

At the top you will see the EMS building just on the outskirts of Brynmawr.

- 1794 Clydach Railroad (horse drawn) used as early transport link running on west side of Gorge connecting Gellifelon Colliery and Beaufort Ironworks with Glangrwyne Forge via the tramway tunnel under the canal at Gilwern. Between Brynmawr and Cheltenham village it followed a path just beneath Blackrock road; from Cheltenham to the canal it followed the minor tarmac road through Mysgwartha bearing right on to a track at Machine House.

- Machine House (private house) dates from 1810 and used to weigh the iron and coal for assessing the appropriate tolls for carriage on the railroad and canal.

- Blackrock road was the old Govilon-Merthyr turnpike road of 1812; tolls were charged for its use

- Blackrock Limeworks: limekilns can be seen on side of Blackrock road; branch line to the Kilns from Clydach railroad

- Heads of Valley road through the Gorge just below Blackrock road; built in early sixties.

Segment 6 (½ mile): From the junction of Black Rock and Llangatoc roads near the EMS building in Brynmawr pass over bridge crossing the Head of Valley road, continue along Intermediate road to the junction of the A4047.

Cross over this road near the Bush Inn and continue down Bailey street to Market Square in the centre of Brynmawr.

- Brynmawr Heritage Museum on Alma street houses memorabilia on the history of the Brynmawr area.

Segment 7 (2 ½ mile): From Market Square Brynmawr pass through the one way access near the Grasshoppers Inn to Lake road. Cross over to Warwick road on opposite side (near the bus station just opposite the Fire Station). Continue along Warwick road a short distance turning on to the cycleway just opposite the gate access to the Welfare Park.

From here there is a short detour to the Round House tower that is also included in Ride 17.

Continue a short distance along the cycleway turning left towards the lake known as Waun Pond that was probably part of the original feeder pond complex used for Nantyglo Ironworks.

Near the lake turn right through the new Lakeside Housing estate and follow to the junction of Pond road just near Nantyglo Comprehensive school. Turn right and then left on to Waun Fawr road. Continue along this road as far as the Round House tower that will be seen on the right near a farm.

- Nantyglo Roundhouse Tower: defensive tower structure designed to protect Bailey the Ironmaster from worker uprising.

- Ty Mawr Nantyglo: remains of house foundations owned by Bailey the Ironmaster. Tunnel from Ty Mawr to Roundhouse was escape route for

Bailey and family in case of worker unrest.

- Site of the important 19C Nantyglo Ironworks is just opposite Market road not far from the footbridge that crosses the busy A 467 road just below Roundhouse (nothing to see).

- Coal Brook Vale Ironworks as well as Blaina & Cwm Cellyn Ironworks were located a stones throw away just down the valley below Nantyglo Ironworks.

Follow the same route back to the Brynmawr Welfare Park entrance gates Brynmawr.

- Brynmawr Rubber factory complex: building was an extraordinary piece of architecture that captured the "new Jerusalem" spirit of Britain during the post war period; the Boiler house (inverted parabolic concrete roof) is all that remains; can be seen across the lake from the cycle/walkway path.

- Welfare Park Brynmawr: built from Miners welfare funds during the 1920/30's;

- Park used to be site of Heathcock pond - one of a chain of ponds associated with 19C Nantyglo Ironworks; Park used to have swimming pool but dismantled some time ago.

Segment 8 (2 miles): From the Brynmawr Welfare Park gates, go along Warwick road a short distance and then turn left on to another cycleway/walkway. Continue along the cycleway, pass by another attractive Lake; proceed up to a point roughly in line with the top of lake and then cross a short path plus Warwick road to join Henderson road just opposite.

Ascend Henderson road, turn left on to Windsor road, cut through Twyncynghordy access-way at the top, proceed to the junction of the A4047 near the Farmers Arms.

Cross over King Street (A4047) to join Big Lane opposite. After a short distance Big Lane connects with an old Cart Road at a gate access, leading to the large area of grassland Common between Beaufort and the Heads of Valley road (A465).

Follow the cartroad track along the Common keeping straight ahead (towards west) at the crossroad of tracks (near Sub station) and bearing left just near the A465.

Descend the cart road along the Common (cart road follows the near-by A465) pass through the A465 road tunnel go through gate access (large reservoir near by) and continue down to the exit gate just near the A465 road junction at Garnlydan

Segment 9 (2 miles): From the gate access Garnlydyn (near A465) turn right and right again on to Llangynydr road, and then left into Garnlydan housing estate.   Continue down

through the estate along the main road (Prince Philip road) descending a hill to a roundabout. Cross over and ascend Honeyfield road to another roundabout in Rassau Housing estate. Keep straight ahead follow the road around until it almost reaches the top then turn left on to Stonebridge road.

After a couple of hundred yards watch out for a small path on the right close to the iron fence over the Rassau brook (near bus stop). Follow the dirt track around until it joins the main road in Rassau Induustrial estate opposite the Yuasa battery building. Turn left and continue along this road (very little traffic) for about half a mile up to a junction, just above the Nant-y-Croft roundabout.

Segment 10 (1 mile):   From the junction just above the Nant-y-Croft roundabout turn left and immediately   on   the   left   is   a   short cycleway/walkway track descending to a bridge over the A465 near the Castle Inn (or simply descend road to the roundabout turning left on to the Bryn Serth road that crosses the A465).

Pass over the bridge and immediately turn right crossing over the Bryn Serth road to connect with a dirt track opposite on a grass Common.. Take the dirt track on the right that parallels the HOV road southwest for short distance (the southeast track on the left that goes up over the hill can also be used to access Sirhowy Ironworks but the southwest track is an old Railroad and a better route to take).

Follow the old railroad for just under half a mile as far as track crossroads.   Continue ahead towards left crossing over some wooden planks above a culvert. Follow this track around (crossing another culvert) until it emerges near a housing estate.   The track continues a short distance before joining a road (Chartist Way).

Descend the hill turning left at the bottom. Go past Astral garage and then turn left down a lane opposite Butleigh Terrace through an access gate that leads to the Ironworks. The site is opened up to visitors during normal hours but is otherwise locked.

- Sirhowy Ironworks started in 1778. Coke fired furnaces with limestone from Trefil quarries. The works were bought by Abraham Derby in 1844 when five furnaces were in operation. Later another huge cylindrical furnace with hydraulic water lift was added. Associated for time with nearby Tredegar Ironworks.

- Sirhowy tramroad connected with Forge at Ebbw Vale Ironworks (through tunnel) and then to Newport docks.

- Site of Tredegar Ironworks is not that far away but there are no remains.

- Nearby Carmel Baptist church was built in 1833 and in use during Sirhowy Ironworks period

Return Segment to Brynmawr (5 miles): From Sirhowy Ironworks return on the same route (segments 10-9-8) to Brynmawr market square.

Segment 11 (just under ½ mile): From Brynmawr Market square continue north down Alma street to the start of cycleway above the Heads of Valley roundabout as per *Route through Brynmawr*

Segment 12 (just over ½ mile) From the cycleway start-point above the Heads of Valley

roundabout Brynmawr follow the tarmac track along the old railway route as far as the railway road crossing at Lower Cwm Nant-Gam as per *AccessRoute E.*

Segments 2 and 1 (4 miles): The final part of the ride is over the same route as the first two segments of the ride.

From Lower Cwm Nant-gam follow the route through Upper Gellifellen and Llanmarch to the old railway crossing Waunafon (near cattle grid) as per *Access Route D.*

From the Waunafon continue along the old railway track bed to the junction of the cycleway near the Whistle Inn as per *Access route B.*

From the cycleway junction near the Whistle Inn follow the route around Garn lakes back to the Blaenafon Ironworks car park as per *Access route A.*

Tourist train leaving the Whistle ▼

On the tramroad just above river at bottom of Gorge not far from Clydach Ironworks ▼

Earmarked cycleway over the Viaduct at Clydach Station ▼

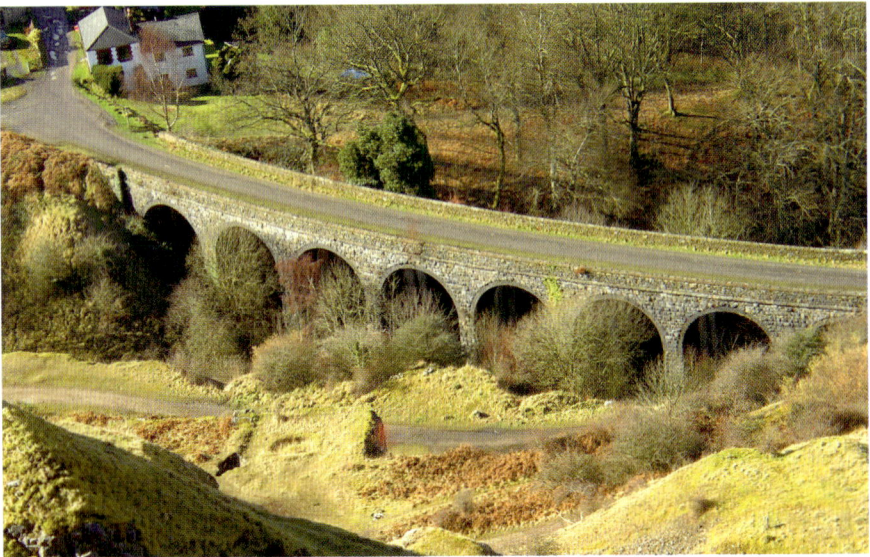

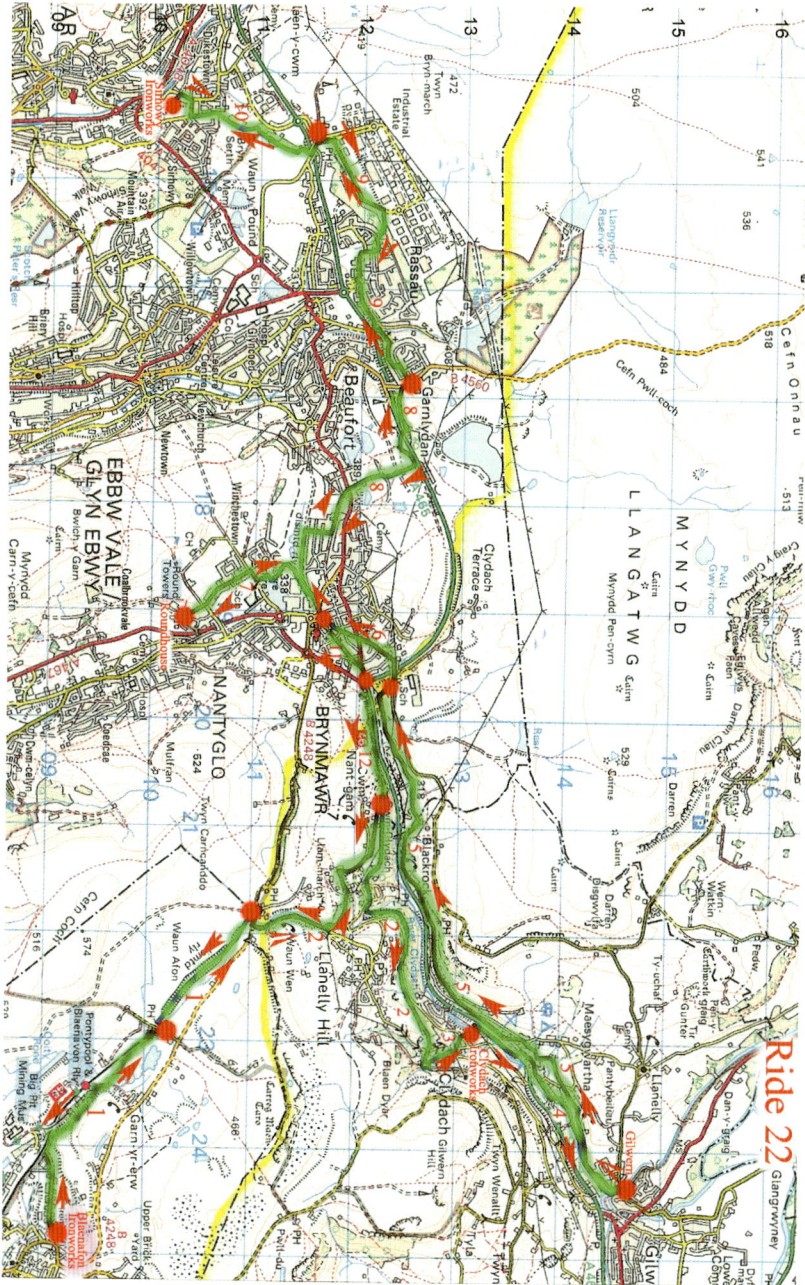

Town Rides

Many circular rides described in this book are along routes that either pass through or circle close to towns in the Gwent and border area but the length of the ride may not allow adequate time to take a leisurely look around. Why not therefore take the opportunity of making a dedicated bike ride from Blaenafon Ironworks to any of these towns over traffic free routes and spend an hour or so visiting the town's heritage. Refer to the route maps in the section Bike Access Routes and/or the appropriate Ride map.

Newport/Pontypool

Ride
This is an easy ride along Sustrans Route 46 cycleway over the old railway track to Pontypool joining the Mon & Brecon canal at Griffithstown and continuing along the towpath to Newport.

Energy Level **
Terrain: casy tarmac off-road tracks
Off-Road Grade: G1
Round Trip Distance 38 miles (Newport) 18 miles (Pontypool)
Round Trip Ride Time: 5 hours
Heritage Sites: See Towns & Canal section

Route
From Blaenafon Ironworks follow the Sustrans route 46 cycleway to Pontypool as per south-east Bike Access Route. To visit Pontypool exit the cycleway at Crane street Bridge (with the mosaic mural) not far from Tescos. Continue the ride to Newport from the same point along route 46 to Griffithtown joining the canal towpath all the way to the canal junction under the M4 bridge at Newport. From here follow the Route 47 signs along the cycleway to Newport castle. This is good central point to visit places of interest. The route from the Castle to Newport Transporter bridge continues along the riverside cycleway signed Sustrans route 47. Return to Blaenafon along the same route. Rides 9, 14 and 17 include the Newport-Pontypool-Blaenafon section.

Monmouth:

Ride
The ride follows the Ride 8 Loop1 route to Llanarth and then the minor road through Dingestow to Monmouth.

Energy Level ****
Terrain: virtually all tarmac lanes and minor roads
Off-Road Grade: No off-road sections:
Round Trip Distance: 57 miles
Ride Time: 5 ½ -6 ½ hours. Allow a full day or 8 hours for trip. Long ride best tried in summer.
Heritage Sites: See Towns & Canal section

Route
From Blaenafon Ironworks follow the Ride 8 Loop 1 route up to the minor road junction with Great Oak just below the entrance to Llanarth Court. From here follow the lane through Great Oak and Bryngwyn as far as the crossroads near Tregare as per Ride 9 segment 7 (but in opposite direction). From this crossroads follow the minor road for almost 7 miles through Tregare, Dingestow, Wonastow to Monmouth. The route between Dingestow and Monmouth has been designated as Cycleway 30 and is relatively up and down;

climbs are not long but do involve low gear work. Return along the same route to Blaenafon Ironworks or alternatively join the canal near Goitre and return along the towpath to Griffithtown and the old railway track to Blaenafon (note this is a longer return route but avoids the Gilwern Hill ascent)

Merthyr

Ride:
The ride follows Ride 19 Loop 4 route to Pontsticill and then along Taff's trail into Merthyr.

Energy Level **
Terrain: includes both on and off road routes; on-road sections are minor roads and tarmac lanes.
Off-Road Grade: largely G1 with some mountain G2 /G3 sections.
Round Trip Distance 58 miles
Ride Time: 6-7 hours: allow a full day for the ride plus town visit; a long ride best tried in summer
Heritage Sites: See Towns & Canal section

Route

From Blaenafon Ironworks follow _Ride 19 Loop 4_ as far as the point where the bridleway track joins the minor road near Pontsticill Waterworks building. From here take the minor road south for about quarter mile turning right at the Taffs Trail signpost. Simply follow the Taffs Trail signposts all the way into the centre of Merthyr. It crosses over Pontysarn Viaduct, the Heads of Valley road, the massive Cefn coed Viaduct and passes through the site of the old Cyfarthfa Ironworks. Go as far as the Merthyr Technical College to visit the major heritage sites. Return along Taff's trail to Pontsticill and then follow the route of Ride 19 Loop 4 through Talybont to Blaenafon Ironworks. (Alternatively from Pontsticill return along the same route Trefil-Garnlyyden to Blaenafon.)

Brecon/Crickhowell

Ride

This is an easy ride along the Llangatoc escarpment Ride 2 route to the canal bridge at Llangatoc and from here either descend into Crickhowell or continue along the towpath/minor road to Brecon.

Energy Level **(***)
Terrain: includes both on and off road routes; on-road sections are minor roads and tarmac lanes; off-road canal towpath and disused railway track.
Off-Road Grade: G1
Round Trip Distance 53 miles (Brecon) 25 miles (Crickhowell)
Ride Time: hours: allow a full day for the Brecon ride plus town visit.
Heritage Sites: See Towns & Canal section

Route

From Blaenafon Ironworks follow the Ride 2 route through Brynmawr along Llangatoc escarpment to the canal bridge at Llangatoc as per west access access route segments A-B-C-F-G. Continue through Llanggattoc village into Crickhowell. For those choosing to go to Brecon simply follow the towpath through Llangynydr to Talybont. At Talybont there is an option to follow the towpath through Pencelli, Llanfranach, Brynich to Brecon Wharf or alternatively follow the B4558 between Talybont and Brynich to the canal towpath at Brynich Lock and then the towpath to Brecon. To return follow the towpath route to Gilwern and then follow Ride 20 segments 13-18 through Clydach, Llanmarch and Waunafon to Blaenafon.

Abergavenny

Ride
A fairly short and easy descent to Abergavenny and a moderate return climb around Gilwern hill to Blaenafon

Energy Level **
Terrain: depending on route option, terrain can either be on-road all the way or partly off-road mountain tracks; on-road sections are minor roads and tarmac lanes.
Off-Road Grade: G1
Round Trip Distance   16-17 miles
Ride Time: hours: allow a half day for the ride plus town visit.
Heritage Sites: See Towns & Canal section

Route
From the Ironworks there are three optional descents to Abergavenny.   Option 1 is down through Llanover into Llanfoist as per north access route segments X-Y-Z. Option 2 is down through Llanellen along north access route segments A-O-S-T-U-V. Option 3 is down the west side of Gilwern Hill to Llanfoist as per north route segments A-O-Q-R. (yet another option is along the Tyla).   From Llanfoist follow the cycleway path along the meadows adjacent to the river Usk as far as Abergavenny castle. The return route is moderate ascent (not difficult) around Gilwern Hill through Pwlldu to the Ironworks as per north access route segments R-Q-S-W.

Usk

Ride
An easy ride through Llanover and Goitre to Usk returning to Blaenafon along the canal towpath and cycleway

Energy Level **
Terrain: Tarmac lanes, canal towpath and tarmac cycleway along railway track
Off-Road Grade: G1
Round Trip Distance   33 miles
Ride Time: allow a half day for the ride plus town visit.
Heritage Sites: See Towns & Canal section

Route
Follow the route of <u>Ride 8 Segments 1-4</u> into Usk. Return back along Segment 4 through Chainbridge and Goitre as far as the canal bridge. Continue on towpath to Pontypool and Griffaithstown and then along the Sustrans route 47 cycleway to Blaenafon (see Bike Access Route south-east).

Tredegar

Ride
Easy-moderate ride following parts of <u>Ride 22</u> route to Sirhowy and from here it is about a mile to the town of Tredegar

Energy Level **
Terrain: mix of on-road and off-road; minor road/B road/tarmac lanes; very short section of A road entering Tredegar; remainder disused railway tracks and cycleway.
Off-Road Grade: G1/G2
Round Trip Distance 22 ½ miles
Ride Time: allow half a day for the ride plus town visit.
Heritage Sites: See Towns & Canal section

Route
From Blaenafon Ironworks follow <u>access route segments A-B-C</u> to Brynmawr and then continue through Garnlyydan to Sirhowy Ironworks a per <u>Ride 22 segments 8-9-10</u>. From here descend to the A4048 continue a short way east turning up the hill towards Tredegar town (can be busy traffic section). Return to Brynmawr along the same route and then follow access route segments E-D-B-A to Blaeanafon.

Abertillary

Ride
This is effectively <u>Ride 17</u> plus a detour from the East Bank district of Cwmtillery down to Abertillary town.

Energy Level **
Terrain: mix of on-road and off-road; over mountain bridleway tracks and minor tarmac lanes/roads.
Off-Road Grade: G2/G3
Round Trip Distance 19 miles
Ride Time: allow a little more than half a day for the ride plus town visit.
Heritage Sites: See Towns & Canal section

Route
From Blaenafon Ironworks follow the <u>Ride 17 segments 1-2-3</u> over the Coity mountain to the tee-junction at East Bank Cwmtillery. From here descend Tillery road to the town of Abertillery. Return to the East Bank Cwmtillery and follow Ride 17 back to Blaenafon (or alternatively return along the same over-mountain track to the Whistle).

Reference Information

Some of the following books were used as a reference source in collating the sections relating to Heritage Information along Bike Ride Routes as well as the sections on "Blaenafon World Heritage Site" and "Towns & Canal".

1.   Exploring Blaenavon Industrial Landscape World Heritage Sites: Chris Barber: Blorenge Books

2.   Portraits of the Past: Chris Barber & Michael Blackmore: Blorenge Books

3.   Eastern Valley The Story of Torfaen: Chris Barber: Blorenge Books

4.   Exploring Gwent: Chris Barber: Regional Publications (Bristol)

5.   The Clydach Gorge: John van Laun: Published by Brecon Beacons National Park and Gwent County Council: 2nd edition 1980

6.   Under Blorenge Mountain - Blaenavon Industrial Landscape World Heritage Site: Chris Morris: Tanner's Yard Press

7.   Rebuilding a Valley: Philip Riden: Alan Sutton Publishing ltd

8.   Blaenavon Through the Years in Photographs: Three Volumes: Malcom Thomas & John Lewis: Old Bakehouse Publications

9.   Blaenavon Ironworks: CADW Welsh Historic Monuments:

10.   Blaenafon Ironworks – A Guide to its History and Technology: Torfaen Museum Trust

11.   Old Abergavenny in Photographs: Albert Lyons: Published by Stewart Williams Barry

12.   Abergavenny A History & Celebration Richard Davies Publisher Francis Frith Collection

13.   Abergavenny The Urban Archaelogy Frank Olding Abergavenny Local History Society

14.   Govilon Heritage - The Village of Govilon in Living Memory: Govilon Village History Group: Published by Govilon Heritage 2005

15.   The Forgotten Treasures of Varteg Village: Richard Roynan & Tom Roberts: Published by Authors

16.   Book of Remembrance Eastern Valley Mining Fatalities 1829-1899 and 1900-1947: Disasters in the Eastern Valley Coalfield: Three books by Brian Foster (Garndiffaith History Group)

17.   A Scrapbook of Abersychan, Talywaun, Garndiffaith, Varteg and Cwmavon: Three Volumes: Marguerite Shaw

18.   Collieries of South Wales Vol 1 & 2; John Cornwall: Landmark Collectors Series: 2002

19.   Stone & Steam in the Black Mountains (History of the Grwyne Fawr Reservoir): D Tipper: Published by Blorenge books

20. The Talybont Saga (History of Talybont Reservoir): D.Tipper: publisher Welsh Water

21. County Railway Routes Abergavenny to Merthyr: David Edge: Middleton Press

22. Monmouthshire Eastern Valleys (Newport Pontypool Blaenavon Brynmawr) Middleton Press

23. The Merthyr Tredegar & Abergavenny Railway and Branches: W.W.Tasker: Oxford Publishing

24. The Brecon & Abergavenny Canal: John Norris: Publisher J Norris

25. Brecknock Abergavenny and Monmouthshire Canals: R. A. Stevens: Goose & Son Publishers

26. The Newport Pictorial 1906: a reprint of the original publication: Published by Cedric Chivers Bristol for Newport County Borough Council: 1998

27. The Buildings of Wales - Gwent/Monmouthshire: J Newman: Published by Yale University Press: 2002

28. Around Crickhowell: D Edge & N Seabourne; Tempus publishing: 2005

29. Journeys into Brecon's Past: Georgan & Victorian Brecon: W.S.K. Thomas: Published by Gomer Press

30. The Taff Trail: Jeff Vinter: Published by Alan Sutton Publishing Ltd.

The Author

Alwyn Thomas lives locally near Abergavenny just within the border of the Blaenafon World Heritage Site. An enthusiastic mountain bike rider who originally hails from Blaenafon and who knows the area well. Inspired by the stunning landscape around the Gwent and border region he set about producing a Guide that features some really amazing rides linked to many of the well known and not so well known heritage sites.